ADOLESCENT GIRLS IN SLUM PROBLEMS AND PROSPECTS

ADOLESCENT GIRLS IN SLUM

Problems and Prospects

By

ANUPAM SINGH

ANMOL PUBLICATIONS PVT. LTD.

NEW DELHI-110 002 (INDIA)

ANMOL PUBLICATIONS PVT. LTD.
4374/4B, Ansari Road, Daryaganj
New Delhi-110 002

Adolescent Girls in Slum: Problems and Prospects

First Edition 1997

ISBN 81-7488-590-0

PRINTED IN INDIA

Published by J. L. Kumar for Anmol Publications Pvt. Ltd., New Delhi-110 002 and Printed at Mehra Offset Press, Delhi.

Contents

	Foreword	*vii*
	Preface	*ix*
	List of Tables	*xii*
I.	Analysis of Urbanisation	1
II.	Programmes and Services for Urban Poor with Particular Reference to Slums	19
III.	Research Design and Methodology	33
IV.	Profile of Adolescent Girls.	47
V.	Housing Needs and Problesm of Slum Dwellers	75
VI.	Family and Marital Problems of Adolescent Girls in Slums	103
VII.	Educational Problems of Adolescent Girls in Slums	141
VIII.	Employment Problems of Adolescent Girls in Slums	179
IX.	Attitudes and Beliefs of Adolescent Girls in Slums	207
X.	Conclusions and Suggestions	237
	Appendix	259
	Bibliography	297

Foreword

Slum pervades throughout the world, there is no escape from it. The term slum came into vogue since the 18th century. It was used to describe squalid housing in densely populated districts of industrial cities.

Like a disease, slum seems to grow and multiply. Several factors seem to add to growth of slums in urban areas. The first and foremost is the rapid pace of rural - urban migration in recent decades.

Today nearly 20 per cent of India's urban population lives in slums. By the year 2001 AD 78 million people will be living in dilapidated structures under unhygienic conditions in slums. About three - fourth of the slum population is devoid of necessary basic facilities.

The Indian slum are more than the aggregate of the physical surroundings: they are also a way of life. Highly disease proneness and high rate of infant and childhood mortality are prevalent characteristics of slum dwellers. Juvenile delinquency and other social malaises are also born in slum and squatter housing areas. Illiteracy is exceptionally high and there is a general lack of social and cultural heritage among the slum dwellers.

In the present study the author has focussed her attention on a number of problems and challenges associated with adolescent girls in slum areas. The book will prove useful and informative to the planners and politicians, policy makers and research scholars in India and throughout the world. I am sure, this work will be valuable addition to the literature in field.

Dr. Sunit Gupta
Director
Institute for Environmental Development Studies
Lucknow.

Preface

With hardly any hope for survival in the villages, the rural poor turn to other avenues. The city with its promise of employment attracts a vast majority of these rural migrants. In the city the opportunities for work are more varied and these are greater possibilities of earning something at least by doing odd jobs. Decreased caste barriers permit them to take up any or every job that will help their survival. Gradually, these rural migrants are assimilated into the urban system, which, however, does not offer them economic security. Although the urban system accepts these rural migrants, it does so as unequals in every respect. This system treats them with inferiority in regard to various facilities like schools, hospitals and housing.

Slums, therefore, are a natural outgrowth of an unequal unjust social system. The poor are hustled to and fro, living a life of misery. But, whatever the urban or in the rural areas, vested interests are against them and deny them opportunities for development. Consequently, the plight of slum dwellers is one of untold misery. They have been rejected by villages, which offered them no employment. Struggling to make both ends meet, they succumed to the lure of potential employment in the city as causing a menace to the welfare of public.

Hence, a developmental approach for work in slums would have to be taken up to make the slum dwellers aware of the root causes of their problem situation and help them to release their potential to organise themselves and to communicate what they feel is rightly due to them.

The present study has been undertaken in order to

highlight the housing, family, marital, educational and employment problems of adolescent girls of slum areas because these girls will be responsible for running future families.

The study has been exploratory in character. Three hundred adolescent girls residing into two selected slum areas of Lucknow city have been covered. The study has been divided into ten chapters. Chapter I analyses the phenomenon of urbanisation. Programmes and Services for urban poor have been described in Chapter II. Research design and methodology have been presented in Chapter - III. Profile of adolescent girls has been discussed in chapter IV. Chapter V consists of housing needs and problems followed by Chapter VI which deals with family and marital problems. Chapter VII incorporates educational problems of adolescent girls. Chapter VIII presents analysis of employment problems followed by Chapter IX which highlights the attitudes and beliefs of respondent adolescent girls. Conclusions and suggestions have been given in the last chapter.

I am deeply beholden to my supervisor, Dr. R.B.S. Verma, Reader in the Department of Social Work, University of Lucknow without whose able guidance and erudite suggestions the present study could not have seen the light of the day.

I am highly grateful to Professor Surendra Singh, Head of the Department and Professor S.P. Srivastava of Social Work Department, University of Lucknow for not only permitting me to work on the subject but also for their constant encouragements and persistent enquiries from time to time regarding the progress of the work.

I also thank my teachers in the Department of Social Work who always made frequent enquiries about the completion of my work and who helped me at different stages.

I owe a lot to the learned authors whose work I have referred to this study. I am also grateful to the respondents, who extended their cooperation by way of providing their valuable time and furnishing required information and data.

I am grateful to my parents specially my mother Mrs. Sarojini Singh, who always encouraged me to pursue higher education and to both of my brothers and *bhabhi* for allowing and helping me to continue my research work.

I am extremely thankful to my husband Mr. Satyendra Singh, Computer Engineer and my in-laws who, I am sure, will appreciate, in due course of time, my desire and efforts to complete my research work and achieve my goal with thier help and encouragement.

My thanks are due to my dynamic friends and colleagues for the encouragement in my task. I am also grateful to staff of the Department of Social Work, Tagore Library, University of Lucknow, Giri Institute for Developmental Studies, NIPCCD Library and State Information and Broadcasting Department for untiring cooperation regarding availability of the relevant material and useful publications to me.

My sincere thanks are also for Dr. Sunit Gupta, Director, Institute for Environmental Development Studies, Lucknow, who provided all possible help and material required during the research work from his resource centre in the Institute and also for writing Foreword to this book.

I am grateful to Mr. Ashok Rastogi, for meticulously typing the manuscript.

Last but not the least I am grateful to Anmol Publications Pvt. Ltd., New Delhi for undertaking the publication and bringing out this book.

Anupam Singh

List of Tables

1.1	Trends of urbanisation in India	10
1.2	Contribution of diferent states in the growth of India's urban population	12
1.3	Indicators of urbanisation of selected states	14
1.4	Trends of urbanisation in Uttar Pradesh	15
1.5	Slum population in some major cities (1991)	17
2.1	Datails of various financial and physical progress implemented by state urban development agency	29
4.1	Age of the respondents	48
4.2	Marital status of the respondents	49
4.3	Religion and caste of the respondents	49
4.4	Background of the respondents	50
4.5	Educational status of the respondents	51
4.6	Occupation of the respondents	52
4.7	Total monthly income of the respondents	53
4.8	Type of family of the respondents	55
4.9	Total number of family members & type of family	56
4.10	Sex structure of the the family members	57
4.11	Age and sex of the family members	58
4.12	Marital status of the family members	59
4.13	Educational status of the family members	60
4.14	Main occupation of the family	61
4.15	Main occupation of the family members	62
4.16	Highest level of education in the family	63
4.17	Total monthly income of the family	64

4.18	Total number of earning members	65
4.19	Total number of school going children	66
4.20	Number of non-school going children	67
4.21	Duration of stay of family in the city and present locality (slum area)	69
4.22	Prior living status coming to this city	70
4.23	Prior living status coming to this city	71
4.24	Monthly expenditure of respondent's family on the following items	72
5.1	Nature of house of respondents	93
5.2	Facilities available in the house	94
5.3	Space available in the house	95
5.4	Information about locality	97
5.5	Availability of facilities and its distance	98
5.6	Availability of fair-price-shop facility in respondent's locality	101
5.7	Opinion about lacking of facilities in the locality	101
6.1	Problems faced by the family in case of marriage of girls	122
6.2	Role of natives in the marriage of girls	123
6.3	Table showing system of marriage prevalent in alum locality	124
6.4	Opportunity of expressing views about marriage	125
6.5	Reasons for not giving opportunity to express views regarding marriage	125
6.6	Ways of expressing view regarding marriage	127
6.7	Normal age of marriage of boys and girls	128
6.8	Age of marriage of respondents	129
6.9	Problems faced in case of child marriage at the time of marriage	130

6.10	Problems faced after marriage in case of a child marriage	130
6.11	Expected age of marriage in case of unmarried respondents	132
6.12	Confidence about surety of marriage in case of unmarried respondents	133
6.13	Hindrance in way of marriage	134
6.14	Problem of dowry faced by family	134
6.15	Nature of problem regarding dowry	135
6.16	Initiation of dowry problem	136
6.17	Results of the dowry problem faced	137
6.18	Existence of custom of child marriage in the family	137
6.19	Reasons for the existence of custom of child marriage	138
6.20	Prevalence of system of gauna after marriage	139
6.21	Period after which the gauna usually took place	139
7.1	Incidence of going to school	160
7.2	Age of joining the school	160
7.3	Class of joining school	161
7.4	Reason for not joining the school	162
7.5	Reasons for leaving the school	163
7.6	Difficulties faced in going to school	164
7.7	Desire to go to school	165
7.8	Reasons for not having esire to go to achool	165
7.9	Condition of performance of the respondents in respect to their study	166
7.10	Reasons for bad performance in studies	167
7.11	The presence of desire to study but could not study	168
7.12	Reasons for failure to study irrespective of desire to study	168
7.13	Encouragement by family members for getting education	169

7.14 Methods used by parents for encouraging respondents to get education 170

7.15 Reasons for not encouraging for education 171

7.16 Existence of feeling on the part of respondents that boys are preferred as compared to girls for providing education 172

7.17 Reasons for preference 172

7.18 Reasons responsible for blocking education of respondents 173

7.19 Preference for girls coming forward in the matter of education 174

7.20 Reasons for the preference 175

7.21 Facilities needed in the matter of education 176

7.22 Availability of separate space for study 176

7.23 In which manner respondents manage the problem of lack of space for study 177

8.1 Incidence of involvement of respondents in work outside family 191

8.2 Nature of work done by respondents 192

8.3 Age at which started working 193

8.4 Persons for whom adolescents girl work 194

8.5 Persons motivating adolescent girls to work 195

8.6 Reasons for working 195

8.7 Average duration of engagement in work in a year 197

8.8 Per day hours of work in case of working outside 197

8.9 Behaviour of employer 198

8.10 persons supervising work of adolescent girls who work outside family 199

8.11 Sex of supervisors of respondents who work outside family 200

8.12 Methods of supervision of work 200

8.13	Steps taken for getting maximum work	201
8.14	Wages earned in case of working outside family	202
8.15	Feeling of satisfaction with nature of work, behaviour of employer, supervision of work, facilities available at work place, status compared to other working people	203
8.16	Activities performed at home in case of non-working respondents	204
8.17	Problems faced by adolescent girls regarding work and employment	206
9.1	Opinion regarding slum dwellers	217
9.2	Opinion regarding fulfilment and sufficiency of different needs	219
9.3	Opinion towards taking up work in place of study	220
9.4	Opinion towards education of children	221
9.5	Opinion regarding dowry	222
9.6	Opinion regarding social tensions	223
9.7	Feeling that one can not develop as long as one lives in slum	224
9.8	Approval of discrimination between boys and girls	225
9.9	Reasons for the approval of discrimination between boys and girls	225
9.10	Reasons for the disapproval of the discrimination between boys and girls	227
9.11	Opinion regarding abolition of slum	227
9.12	Reasons for giving opinion in favour of abolition of slum	228
9.13	Reasons for giving opinion against the abolition of slum	229
9.14	Possibilities of improving your working/living conditions	230
9.15	Reasons for the possibilities of improving the living and working conditions .	231
9.16	Reasons for lack of possibilities of improving the living and working conditions	232
9.17	Improvements suggested by respondents for improving the life and living of slum dwellers	233

Chapter I

Analysis of Urbanisation

Urbanisation is either directly or indirectly linked with the level and process of development. In other words, urbanisation may be defined as the process of re-organisation of space through spatial distribution of population among hierarchical system of settlement in response to vertical shifts in population within the workforce.

The causative factors behind urbanisation have varied from time to time and accordingly have led to several urbanisation processes. In recent times, urbanisation has been associated with industrialisation and economic development. In this sense, therefore, urbanisation is essentially an economic process. To understand the dynamics of urbanisation, it is essential to view the urban process in the historical context since each historical period generates its own social, economic and political forces. These processes tend to change with changes in the socio-economic and political setting.

The Indian sub-continent, along with Mesopotamia and the Nile valley, shares a long history of urbanisation. In fact, the first phase of the urbanisation dates back to the Harappan civilisation in the Indus valley in 2350 B.C. The cities which developed during this period flourished for around 600 years upto 1700 B.C. This was followed by a period of 1000 years during which have no evidence of urban development. From around 600 B.C. we again come across towns and cities associated with the Aryan civilisation in the North and the Dravidian civilisation in the South. Since then India has a more or less continuous period of urbanisation. However, it is seen that within the overall period of continuous urbanisation there have been periods which have witnessed some phases of decline as well. When the Britishers came to India, we were perhaps the most urbanised nation in the world. The early British rule witnessed a decline in the level of urbanisation. However, during the latter half of their rule the cities gained some of their lost importance and several new towns and cities were also developed. The post-Independence period has witnessed urbanisation on a scale never before achieved.

Since Independence the processes of urbanisation have given rise to distinctly new and vigorous phases of urbanisation. It is essential to understand the processes of urbanisation along with the system of urban settlements since it is these processes which shape the form, nature and character of urban settlements. For instance, during pre-industrial India administration, defence, trade and commerce, and religion were the key factors in the urbanisation process. During the colonial period transport factor, especially railways, became an important urbanising element and stimulated the growth of many mandi towns. The spread of canal irrigation and growth of rail network combined to give rise to a number of towns in the canal irrigated areas of the country.

However, the foundation of the process of urbanisation in India has been very weak since beginning of its independency because of the anaemic and disarticulated nature of production sectors of economy such as agriculgture and industry. Therefore, the urban centres continued and have service sector as its base rather than productive sector. As a consequence of poor performance and weaknesses of secondary sector economy and bloated tertiary sector a majority of towns are floundering in the quick sands of the bazar economy.

Besides this, a significant change in the political set up of the country since Independence, such as the abolition of princely states, emergence of linguistic states, democratisation of political system and adoption of federal constitution, have strengthened the urbanising tendencies in India and have induced a new dimension in the process of urban development.

There are various processes of urbanisation at work at any given point of time. They are independent as well as interrelated. However, they are varied as far as their causes and their impact is concerned. The history of urbanisation in India reveals, broadly four processes at work throughout the historical period. These may be briefly summed up as follows:

(a) The emergence of new social relationship among people in the cities and between people in the cities and those in the villages through a process of social change;

(b) The rise and fall of cities as a result of changes in the political order;

(c) The growth of cities based on new productive processes, which alter the economic base of the city; and

(d) The physical spread of cities as a result of the inflow of migrants, who come in search of a means of livelihood as well as a new way of life.

Accordingly a study carried out by Prakasa Rao (1983) has identified distinct three distinct processes of urbanisation:

1. Centralisation-Polarisation;
2. Decentralisation or decentralised concentration, commercialisation; and
3. Urbanisation of the countrywide.

However, a study of S. Manzoor Alam and G.R. Reddy (1984) identified the following four underlying process which are stimulating urbanisation and growth of towns in India:

1. Politico-administrative processes of urbanisation.
2. Agro-based urbanisation.
3. Polarised industry and mining oriented urbanisation.
4. Multi-functional metropolitan oriented urbanisation.

The chief determinants of urbanisation and concentration of population in urban areas are factors such as the trend of development and structure of agricultural sectors, pattern of growth and sectoral pattern of urbanisation, decision of location for the distribution of manufacturing and service sectors, economic activities among the cities and finally, the pattern and level of transport and communication network.

It has been experienced that most developing countries showed no interest in spatial matter in the 1960's but the rapid growth of population and the tendency of population to concentrate in big cities have generated considerable concern for the pattern of human settlements. As a result of unprecedented concentration of population in large cities several kinds of problems such as congestion, pollution deteriorating amenities and social tension is being faced by these countries. It has also to be noted that the rate of urbanisation in developing countries is revealed at much faster rate as compared to the developed countries. Therefore, the problems related to urban development planning has been of great interest and urgent need for former groups of countries than the latter ones.

MIGRATION AND URBANISATION

Unprecedently increasing volume of population in urban

settlements has been an important challenge to urban planners as to how to effetively manage future urban growth. This fast increase in population has been recognised both by increasing trend of rural-urban migration on one hand and the increase of natural growth which have created the problem of over pressure on different infrastructural facilities, congregation, adverse effects on urban economic development and general environment on the other. However, the studies undertaken during past revealed the fact that urban growth is mainly the result of urban in-migration. It is noted that rural-urban migration occurs due to urban pulls as well as rural push factors that are mainly economic in nature. Thus, the urbanisation signifies the strength of the urban pulls leading to economic growth and positive changes in the occupational pattern.

Rural Urban Integration

An economic development and particularly industrialisation proceeds, population is redistributed between rural and urban areas and the population tends to get concentrated in and around major urban centres. Once economic activity gets concentrated over a small area, the country reaps the so-called "urbanisation economics of agglomeration" that creates an inverse relationship between production costs per unit of output and population size for many economic activities.

In the process of rural-urban continuum the development of the metropolitan region is the basic objective of the planning exercise. The process is believed to be based on the Growth Pole theory. It is expected that such a process would help in promoting a healthy rural-urban interaction, human migration, extension of urban services in rural areas, generation of additional employment opportunities both in the rural as well as urban areas and increase the standard of living. Thus, human settlements development policies seek to forge an alliance between rural and urban settlements by adopting a comprehensive regional approach to settlement planning which will achieve a continuum of functionally related communities for sustained urban and regional development.

It has been accepted that migration of population from rural to urban areas is a key factor contributing towards rural-urban linkages. However, the tendency to migrate into large metropolitan cities over the smaller size of towns is more commonly pronounced in the Indian situation. This kind of migration process has resulted in a much larger growth of Class I cities which is causing several kinds of problems in human settlements in this category of towns. Therefore, it has been proposed to have a policy aimed at decentralisation of economic activities and decentralisation of population to small towns/rural towns in the metro region. As the metroregion is inclusive of both rural and urban settlements, a special policy measure to develop in between important segments like areas where population is highly concentrated and where the small rural towns have emerged on their own. Development of infrastructure, as required, through cluster approach between rural and urban areas would be an additional approach to the planning of continuum.

Existing methodologies and mechanism of planning development of human settlements, based on compartmentalisation of rural and urban areas separately may give way to unified development planning of the urban region within the large metro region so that development proposals for both the urban areas and rural hinterland can be conceived as a single package and integrated into a single programme for developmental action. This will lead to a healthy functional rural-urban continuum enabling equitable channelisation of growth impulses over urban and rural settlements.

The need for the integration of rural-urban development so as to promote regional development is well recognised along with the need to link the process of urban with rural development. In the process of rural-urban integration the small and rural towns can play an important role. A region constitutes of at least one large and a number of small towns. These small towns support the development linkages between the large towns and the respective region. Many of such small towns function as regional or sub-regional centres and help in sustaining a dynamic economy in respect of processing, collection, distribution and several other aspects.

The Third Five Year Plan document stated that the role of urbanisation was closely associated with many problems such as migration from villages to towns and the levels of living in rural and urban areas. It also stated that the rural-urban component should be knit together for strengthening economic interdependence. In the ground of the important role played by the small towns a policy for the development of towns was launched by the Central Government and is known as *"Integrated Development of Small and Medium Towns (IDSMT)"*. In 1974, the Government set up a task force committee to examine the problems and potential of development of small and medium towns in the country.

Keeping in view the various problems, some of the suggestions to make IDSMT programme a success have been:

1. The towns should be selected on a priority basis keeping in mind the economic base of the town. The potential of the town should be exploited in such a manner so as to maximise the economic benefits in favour of the rural areas. Equally important would be to locate appropriate higher order institutions, services and other infrastructure which can positively improve the socio-economic conditions of the area surrounding the town;

2. Intensive investigation should be carried out in the town to identify those activities which have a development potential and can act as a suitable

instrument for the development of the area in question. Such an activity would prove fruitful in maximising the backward and forward linkages between the town and its hinterland; and that

3. Besides the identification of potential activities, even the social services should be brought out in the mainstream of development such that the quality of manpower in the town as well as its hinterland improves. An improved quality of manpower will enhance the levels of productivity on one hand and provide a boost to the local economy on the other resulting in higher opportunities for employment as well as earnings for the population living in the region.

Objectives

The role of small towns in the process of rural-urban continuum with the following broad objectives :

(i) To analyse the linkages of the small towns with the adjoining rural hinterland on the one hand and the larger towns and cities of the region on the other and to try and identify these linkages in terms of the flows of commodities, labour and investible resources;

(ii) To relate the degree and pattern of the linkages with the structure and development of economic activities of the town under study;

(iii) To examine the availability or otherwise of the infrastructure facilities as felicitating or constraining the development of small towns;

(iv) To try and examine the impact of linkages and infrastructure on the volume and pattern of private investment; and

(v) To try and analyse the organisational set up of the town from the point of view of its integrated development.

Trends in Urbanisation : India and Uttar Pradesh

The process of urbanisation is a part of the overall process of economic development and is characterised by various factors. Consequently, the causative factors behind urbanisation vary from time to time and between one region and another.

Here, an attempt has been made to focus the attention on how urbanisation has actually taken place in India as well as the State of Uttar Pradesh. This has been attempted by analysing the trends of urbanisation at the national as well as the state level individually and through a comparison of the two so as to find out where Uttar Pradesh stands with respect to the nation as a whole.

Urbanisation in India

A look at the data available from the different Census Reports from 1901 to 1991 reveals that India's population has increased from 238 million to 846 million. This is an increase of less than four-fold over a period of nine decades. However, over the same period the urban population has registered a much higher increase from 25.4 million in 1901 to 217.6 million in 1991 which is an increase of over eight times, but the rural population increased from 213 million to 628 million over the same period.

If we look at the difference between the urban and rural growth rates it can be noticed that the growth of the urban-population has been higher as compared to that of rural population. The only exception has been during the period 1901-1911 and 1921-1931 when the rate of growth of rural population was relatively higher than that of the urban areas. Since the growth rates of population has been rather erratic both at the urban and rural levels, so has there been an erratic trend as far as the different between urban and rural population growth rates are concerned.

Population has been growing at quite a high irate especially since 1941. This is also brought out by the change

Table 1.1
Trends of Urbanisation in India

Year	*Population '000*		*IOU*	*Decadal growth of population*	*UPGR*	*RPGR*	*UPGR-RPGR*	*Change in IOU*
	Total	*Urban*						
1901	238396	25852	10.84	-	-	-	-	-
1911	252093	25942	10.29	5.75	0.38	6.40	-6.02	-0.55
1921	251321	28086	11.18	-0.31	8.27	-1.29	6.98	0.89
1931	278977	33456	11.99	11.00	9.12	9.98	-0.86	0.81
1941	318661	44153	13.86	14.22	31.97	11.81	20.16	1.87
1951	361088	62444	17.29	13.31	41.42	8.79	32.63	3.43
1961	439235	78937	17.97	21.51	26.41	20.60	5.77	0.68
1971	548160	109114	19.91	24.79	38.23	21.86	16.37	1.94
1981	685185	159717	23.31	25.00	46.39	19.68	26.71	3.40
1991	846303	217611	25.72	23.52	36.24	19.65	16.59	2.41

IOU = Index of Urbanisation;
UPGR = Urban Population Growth Rate;
RPGR = Rural Population Growth Rate.

in the index of urbanisation. The index declined only between 1901-1911 otherwise it has shown a steady increase ever since 1911. However, there have been certain fluctuations in between which have been caused by the general erratic nature of population grow with which we have already referred to while discussing the other indicators of urbanisation (Table 1.1).

Regional Variations in Urbanisation

For the purpose of the examination of the differentials existing in the pattern of urbanisation across various states, fourteen major states have been taken into account. These states taken together account for around 92 per cent of total urban pupulation and around 96 per cent of the rural population during the Census year 1991, and thereby provide an adequate basis for studying regional variations in the pace of urbanisation. The analysis is being carried out with two basic objectives in mind namely, (i) to find out which states have been contributing relatively more towards the growth of urban population in India; and (ii) to study the pace of urbanisation in each of these fourteen states. The analysis has been carried out for 1971-1981 and 1981-1991 respectively.

It is observed that there has been only a marginal increase in the share of these states towards the total urban population between the two time periods mentioned above from 91.16 per cent to 91.77 per cent.

Table No. 1.2 depicts the different states arranged in descending order on the basis of absolute growth in urban population during the decade 1971-1981. Accordingly, out of the total states under consideration the top five namely Uttar Pradesh, Maharashtra, Andhra Pradesh, Madhya Pradesh and Karnataka together accounted for around one half of the total urban population of India between 1971-1981. During 1981-1991 their share has gone up and stands at around 52 per cent. Uttar Pradesh and Karnataka are the two states from this group which have registered a decline in the percentage contribution towards the urban population of India.

Table No. 1.2
Contribution of Different States in the Growth of India's Urban Population

States	1971-81		1981-91	
	Population '000	Percentage share	Popula tion '000	Percentage share
Uttar Pradesh	7510	14.84	7707	13.42
Maharashtra	6283	12.41	8548	14.88
Andhra Pradesh	4085	8.07	5399	9.40
Madhya Pradesh	3801	7.51	4753	8.28
Karnataka	3608	7.13	3178	5.54
Tamil Nadu	3487	6.89	3136	5.46
West Bengal	3480	6.88	4261	7.42
Gujarat	3105	6.13	3644	6.35
Bihar	3085	6.10	2634	6.33
Rajasthan	2667	5.27	2856	4.98
Punjab	1432	2.83	1345	2.35
Kerala	1275	2.52	2909	5.07
Orissa	1265	2.50	1125	1.96
Haryana	1054	2.04	1228	2.14
All states	46137	91.16	52712	91.77
India	50614	100.00	57443	100.00

The above analysis, besides bringing out the relative importance of various states by way of their contribution to India's urbanisation, also leads to the following observations:

(a) that there is a high degree of variation in the contribution of individual states to the country's urban population. So much so that half of India's urban population is accounted for by only five states;

(b) the changes which have taken place in the ranking of the states from 1971-1981 to 1981-1991 suggests that the level of urbanisation, or of development, provides partial explanation towards the inter-regional differences in the pace of urbanisation. In-depth studies are, therefore, needed to understand how urban population grows at a relatively faster rate in one region of the country as compared to another region; and

(c) in trying to associate the rate of growth of urban population with certain explanatory variables, it appears that the rate of growth in a less urbanised state is generally higher than that obtained in a relatively more urbanised one. This is empirically evident from the increase in the percentage contribution of the bottom five states and that of the top five states to India's urban population growth (Table 1.3) during 1971-1981 and 1981-1991. There is also an inverse association between the level of urbanisation and urban population growth rate.

Table No. 1.3 depicts the value of various indicators of urbanisation for different states. It is observed that the states which are relatively more urbanised had their urban population growing at a relatively lower rate and the percentage point increases in their levels of urbanisation were relatively higher as compared to the less urbanised states.

Trends in the Urbanisation of Uttar Pradesh

As has already been indicated earlier, Uttar Pradesh ranks among the urbanised staes of the country if we compare its share to the total urban population of India with

Table No. 1.3 Indicators of Urabisation of Selected States

State	Index of Urbanisation			UPGR Growth Percentage		Change in IOU	
	1971	1981	1991	1971-81	1981-91	1971-81	1981-91
Maharashtra	13.17	35.03	38.70	39.99	38.87	3.86	3.67
Tamil Nadu	30.26	32.95	34.16	27.97	19.60	2.669	1.21
Gujarat	28.08	31.10	34.49	41.42	34.39	3.02	3.39
West Bengal	24.75	26.47	27.48	31.72	29.50	1.72	1.01
Punjab	23.73	27.68	29.55	44.51	28.97	3.95	1.95
Karnataka	24.31	28.89	30.93	50.54	29.63	4.58	2.04
Andhra Pradesh	17.66	21.88	24.63	48.64	43.24	4.01	3.58
Haryana	17.66	21.88	24.63	59.47	43.36	4.22	2.75
Rajasthan	17.63	21.05	22.88	58.69	39.63	3.42	1.83
Madhya Pradesh	16.29	20.29	23.18	56.03	44.90	4.00	2.89
Kerala	16.24	18.74	26.40	37.64	60.98	1.50	7.66
Uttar Pradesh	14.02	17.95	19.85	60.62	38.73	3.93	1.90
Bihar	10.00	12.47	13.15	54.76	30.21	2.47	0.68
Assam	8.87	10.29	11.10	54.27	-	1.42	0.81
Orissa	8.41	11.79	13.38	68.54	36.18	3.38	1.59
India	19.91	23.31	25.72	46.39	36.24	3.40	2.41

UPGR - Decadal Growth Rate of Urban Population

IOU - Index of Urbanisation, Percentage of Urban Population to Total Population

Table 1.4

Trends of Urbanisation in Uttar Pradesh

Year	*Population '000*		*IOU*	*Decadal growth of population*	*UPGR*	*RPGR*	*UPGR-RPGR*	*Change in IOU*
	Total	*Urban*						
1901	48628	5391	11.09	-	-	-	-	-
1911	48155	4907	10.19	-0.97	-8.98	-0.03	-9.01	-0.90
1921	46672	4936	10.58	-3.08	0.61	-3.50	-4.1o	0.39
1931	49780	5569	11.19	6.66	12.81	5.93	6.88	0.61
1941	56535	7016	12.41	13.57	26.00	12.01	13.99	1.22
1951	63220	8626	13.65	11.82	22.93	10.25	12.68	1.24
1961	73755	9480	12.86	16.66	9.90	17.73	-7.83	-0.79
1971	88341	12389	14.03	19.78	30.68	18.17	12.51	1.17
1981	110862	19899	17.95	25.50	60.62	19.76	40.86	3.92
1991	139112	276611	19.85	25.49	38.73	22.59	16.14	1.90

IOU = Index of Urbanisation;
UPGR = Urban Population Growth Rate;
RPGR = Rural Population Growth Rate.

the other states of the unior. Between 1971-1981, Uttar Pradesh was having a share of 14.84% towards the total urban population of the country and was the top ranked state. Over the last decade (1981-91) Maharashtra has overtaken it with a share of 14.88% as against a share of 13.42% of Uttar Pradesh thereby pushing it down to the second position. However, if we look at the share of urban to total - population, the position of Uttar Pradesh is far from satisfactory as it ranks along with those states which have a relatively low share of urban to total population. In 1991, for instance, its share of urban to total population was only 19.85% whereas the national average was 25.72% and states such as Maharashtra, Tamil Nadu, Gujarat and Karnataka each had over 30% of its total population residing in urban areas. As a result of this it is observed that there has been a four-fold increase in the urban population of the state from 5.39 million in 19001 to 26.61 million in 1911. Although urban population has witnessed a much higher growth in the country as a whole yet the decadal rate of growth of urban population has always been higher in the state as compared to either the overall rate of growth of total population or that of rural population except during the decade 1901-1991.

The Phenomenon of Urbanisation: Mushroom Growth of Slums

The consequences of this 3 urban growth are changes in industrial and commercial developments bringing about changes in economic base of these cities, producing disparity in economic strata which compelled many to live in filthy conditions. Mushroom growth in all the directions of cities lead to a massive unplanned concentration of people - an 'urban sprawl' will all its attendant problems of acute congestion, functional obsolescence, ugliness, poor housing, civic and cultural stagnation, tensions, blight and decay[13] giving rise to the reality of slums, as pointed out by Desai and Pillai[14]. "The slum has come to be accepted as a living reality, an inevitable phenomenon accompanying urban growth in all capitalist countries."

Table No. 1.5
Slum Population in Some Major Cities (1991)

(Population 1,000)

Cities	*Total popul-tion*	*Slum popula-tion*	*Percentage of slum popula-tion*
Calcutta	11,022	4,861	44.10
Greater Bombay	12,572	6,066	48.25
Delhi	8,419	3,224	38.30
Madras	5,422	2,108	38.88
Bangalore	4,086	613	15.00
Hyderabad	4,280	1,070	25.00
Ahmedabad	3,298	1,078	32.70
Kanpur	2,111	971	46.00
Pune	2,484	522	21.00
Nagpur	1,661	598	36.00
Lucknow	1,642	239	49.00
Jaipur	1,514	288	19.00

Source: Census of India, 1991, Final Population Tables Vol. II.

Table No. 1.5 gives figures for slum population in some of the major cities. Population living in slum areas has been found around 38 per cent of the urban population. Slums undoubtedly house the urban poor and their level of income is much lower than that of other low income households. The culture of slum dwellers is different from that of city dwellers. This slum culture is seen by sociologists and criminologists as subculture or lower class culture. The lower class culture in slumps provides patterned solution or adaptation to such problems as broken families, chronic or seasonal unemployment, serious physical and mental illness, inadequate and crowded housing, limited education, minority group status, such value variations as serial mating, living for the day and not planning for the future, trust in fate or luck to solve problems, emphasis often in preference to family work as compared to school ties and the poor culture having aggressive or physical behaviour.

Thus, it can be concluded that slums are basically characterised by overcrowding, unsanitary conditions, absence of basic facilities and amenities of water, drainage, latrines, roads, electricity. Slums are said to be an "eyesore" and "stink" of the human race where disorganised, Second-class citizens reside. The slums are also known to be paradise of anti-social activity, where all the vices of urban areas are said to originate. But, this is also a fact that a slum has not only a distinct socio-economic and political activity of its own, but that the slum population contribute substantially to the economic activity of the city which is evident from the following :

1. The labour force for the service sector, which includes normal labourers and class IV category of workers both in public and private enterprises, is basically drawn from the slum dwellers.
2. Besides this, service sector includes those who are involved in the supply of essential needs of the city such as distribution of bread and milk, sale of vegetables, meat, eggs etc., removal of waste from the city, the collection of waste for recycling, delivery of newspapers and other jobs in the unorganised sector.
3. Slums are crucial vote banks for the political elite.

Thus, without this essentially productive force, the city's economic life would come to standstill. Yet the plight of the slum dwellers is one of untold misery. They have been rejected by the villages, which offered them no employment. Struggling to make both ends meet, they succumbed to the lure of potential employment in the city as causing a menace to the welfare of the public.

Chapter II

Programmes and Services for Urban Poor with Particular Reference to Slums

Improvement of the life and living of urban poor with particular reference to slums has been the concern of planners and policy-makers in all the Five Year Plans. These may be listed as follows.

Slum Clearance, Provision of Housing and Improvement

This scheme was introduced in 1956 as a centrally sponsored programme under which financial assistance was given to states and union territories for the clearance and improvement of slum areas and re-housing and slum-dwellers whose income does not exceed Rs. 250/- per month.

From April 1969, the scheme was transferred to state. In this scheme, the following two considerations were kept in view :-

* That these should be a minimum dislocation of dwellers and attempts should be made to rehouse them at the demolished or nearly sites, and
* That minimum standards of environmental hygiene and essential services were maintained.

Under this scheme, financial assistance is extended to local bodies and development authorities in the shape of 50 percent loan and 372 percent amount is raised by local bodies themselves. Those agencies undertake the work of construction of houses for the rehabilitation of slum dwellers and allot houses on subsidised rent.

The original slum clearance scheme was extended to cover slum improvement following the recommendation of VII Housing Ministers Conference in 1962 and was to be financed on the same pattern of loans and subsidies. Problems became so overwhelming and the resources so limited that it was decided to resort to slum improvement rather than wholesome clearance of slum.

Environmental Improvement of the Slum

The Central Scheme for Environmental Improvement in Slum Areas was launched in 1972 in ten cities of India including Lucknow and Kanpur of U.P. During 1973-74 ten more cities were covered under the scheme. The concerned State Governments were given full financial assistance for the provisions of drinking waters, sewerage and drains, community bath and latrines, street lighting, and widening and paving of existing lanes in slum areas. The scheme was transferred to the state sector from April 1, 1974 as one of the Minimum Needs Programmes. The operation of this scheme has also been extended to cover cities with population of three lakh and above or one city in each state where the scheme has not so far been extended.

Environmental Improvement of Urban Slums in VIIIth Plan (1992-97)

The scheme was made an integral part of the Minimum Needs Programme in 1974 and transferred to the state sector. The scheme is applicable to notified slums in all urban areas and aims at provision of basic amenities like water supply, services, storm water drains, community baths and latrines, widening and paving of existing lanes and pathways and street lighting. During the Seventh Plan, the scheme provided for a per capita expenditure of Rs. 300/-. Against the target of 76.91 lakhs slum dwellers, 99.78 lakhs slum dwellers were covered during the VIIIth plan. During 1990-91 the targeted number of beneficiaries was 15.40 lakhs, against which the achievement was 19.35 lakhs. The per capita expenditure was enhanced to Rs. 525/- from 1991-92. During the VIIIth plan the scope of the EIUS is being widened to ensure that the EIUS the Urban Basic Services programme, the NRY and the scheme of liberation of scavengers from a coordinated whole. Assurance of providing tenurial rights and evolving feasible cost recovery mechanism and important pre-conditions for the success of the programme in a longer term context.

Urban Basic Services for the Poor

The Urban Basic Services Scheme (UBSS) was initiated on a pilot basis in 1986, with the involvement of UNICEF and the state governments. The programme aimed at child survival and development provision of learning opportunities for women and children and community organisation for slum population. The services, meant to be delivered, included environmental sanitation, primary health care, pre-school learning, vocational training and convergence of other social services at the slum level.

The Urban Basic Services for the Poor (UBSP) is a revised scheme based on the experience of UPSS. The revised scheme includes assistance to mentally regarded and handicapped children, rehabilitation of alcoholics and drug addicts and special programmes for street children. It also enables formation of registered societies/cooperatives of slums dwellers at the community level. The scheme is to operate on the principle of convergence of programmes aimed at the urban poor and limited to those slums covered by EIUS. The central government will give Rs. 175/- per capita for provision of social services in the Ist Year of the new project. In addition, the state government will provide Rs. 525/- per capita for physical amenities. From the IInd year onwards per capita provision will be limited to the recurring component of Rs. 88/- per capita. This will be shared on matching basis between the centre and the state. The scheme will also include provisions for strengthening of urban Local Bodies, NGOs, some physical works and creation of an organisation for monitoring and evaluation and organisation of marketing assistance.

While India's population has more than doubled since 1947 to nearly 840 million in 1991, the urban population has grown almost twice as fast. Today, over 200 million people live in about 3600 cities and towns in India.

Nearly one of every three urban residents live below the poverty line and their ranks grow each year by about 15 million. About 50 million of these people live on pavements, in poorly serviced tenement houses, in unhygienic slums and illegal squatter colonies.

They work as street vendors, domestic servants, scavengers, small-time mechanics, rag-pickers and perform a host of other activities comprising the informal sector.

About 68 per cent of the urban poor are women and children. They are both vulnerable and exploited. Their large numbers and unacceptable conditions challenge both the government and the private sector to find solutions to break the cycle of deprivations.

It is accepted that the most critical point at which to begin is with the mother and child. Their survival, development and ability to secure a respectable place in society are vital.

Ensuring that they have access to the basic social services such as health care, nutritional supplementation, education, employment and income is the key to the success in overcoming urban want and exploitation.

The UNICEF expert says: "The future cities of the third world will be very different from the cities we knew. They will be different not only in size and population but also on account of their age and labour structures. They will be cities of adolescents and children. Many work before the minimum age established by law because their income are crucial for their families and for their own survival. Most will not complete primary school even though completing school is a family aspiration. Many will die young or live in poor health and will abandon their homes and live a their own one the city streets threatened by violence and the process of dehumanization. Different values and codes resulting from poverty and unemployment, combined with the massive presence of children and adolescent and of households headed by single women, will give rise to a mixture of aggressiveness and solidarity of expectations and frustrations."

The major programmes for amelioration of the conditions of the urban poor may be discussed as follows:

Nehru Rozgar Yojna: Nehru Rozgar Yojna was launched by the Government of India in October 1989 to provide various employment avenues to the urban poor mainly the urban youth. The Yojna consists of three components : (i) Scheme for setting up of micro-enterprises and providing training and infrastructure setup, (ii) Scheme for wage employment for public assets creating, and (iii) Scheme of employment through housing and shelter upgradation.

The total financial outlay for the Yojna is of the order of Rs. 650 crores out of which the institutional finance amounts to Rs. 432 crores. The subsidy element is established at Rs. 218 crores for which Rs. 150 crores and Rs. 68 crores are to be provided by the Centre and State/ U.T. Governments and Urban Local Bodies respectively. The Yojna is expected to provide direct employment opportunities to about 10 lakh persons in five years and to open additional employment avenues in newly established enterprises, services centres, public works programmes, training and shelter upgrading activities, etc. A multi-pronged programme of the Nehru Rozgar Yojna with components of Scheme for Micro-Enterprises (SUME) to encourage unemployed and underemployed to upgrade their skills and technologies, Scheme for Urban Wage Employment (SUWE) to provide employment, and Scheme for Housing and Shelter Upgradation (SHASU) to train construction labour.

Prime Minister's Rozgar Yojna for Self-Employment : The Integrated Urban Poverty Eradication Programme (IUPEP) also known as the Prime Minister's Programme on Urban Poverty, has been started by the Ministry of Urban Affairs and Employment, Government of India since March 1995 which integrates the multi-sectoral aspects of community empowerment, convergence of various sectoral programmes like healthy housing, employment, etc. through the establishment of a sustainable support system, skill upgradation of workers and employment generation, as well as extended water supply sanitation, solid waste management and environmental improvement.

Any unemployed educated person living in any part of the country, rural or urban, fulfilling the following conditions will be eligible for assistance -

- Age - Between 18 to 35 years,
- Qualification - Metric (Passed or failed) or IT passed or having undergone Government sponsored technical course for a minimum duration of 6 months.
- Residency - Permanent resident of the area for at least 3 years.
- Family income - Upto Rs. 24,000 per annum.
- Defaulter - Should not be a defaulter to any nationalised bank/financial institution/ cooperative bank.
- Reservation - Preference will be given to weaker sections including women. The scheme envisages 22.5 per cent reservation for SC/ST and 27 per cent for other backward classes (OBCs).

Shelter - Related Programme : Among the shelter related programmes, slum eradication had featured as a key approach during the first and second plans. In view of resource limitations resistance of local populations to shifting and maintenance failure and the approach was abandoned in favour of Slum Improvement and Sites and Services Schemes. About 15.3 lakhs slum improvement scheme. The Seventh Plan aimed at securing coverage of about 90 lakhs slum dwellers.

The Economically Weaker Sections (EWE) Housing Programme had succeeded in construction of 65,432 shelter units in public sector during the Sixth Plan Period. Besides, the urban poor are concentrated in bustees and chawls and whole families of 6-7 persons live in congested; one room tenement, immigration, and population growth from within. Thus even though the public policy response to the housing needs of the urban poor has improved, it cannot meet more than 10 per cent of the backlog.

Nutrition Supplement Programmes : Programmes of nutrition have been significantly expanded in the Seventh Plan. The Special Nutrition Programmes (SNP) and Mid-day Meal (MDM) are proposed to be integrated with Integrated Child Development Scheme (ICDS). The expected coverage of beneficiaries is likely to be 1.1 crore children and pregnant mothers under SNP and about 50 lakhs children under MDM by the end of 1994.

The public distribution system also aims at providing a balanced diet at reasonable prices in the endemically poverty stricken, malnourished and undernourished parts of the country. A review of the literature shows that off take from the public distribution system is greater in urban areas than in rural areas in per capita terms.

Child Development : Among the general programmes of child development, the spread of free education has certainly brought benefits nearer to the urban poor. However, owing to economic and social conditions the school drop-out rate is higher among the urban poor than the rest of the urban population. Health services have improved in pilot project areas, thanks to tensive efforts of Integrated Child Development Scheme (ICDS), Urban Basic Services (UBS) and Urban Community Development (UCD) projects, but these have still not approached national coverage.

Employment Generation and Employment Oriented Training Programmes - Recently the Government India have started a Self-Employment Programmes for the Urban Poor (SEPUP) by earmarking a sum of Rs. 200 crores to be distributed to poor urban entrepreneurs whose income does not exceed Rs. 600 per month. The maximum credit available is Rs. 5000. The list of economic activities for which loans are available contains 35 items covering activities like hawking on hand-cart, laundering, welding, cycle-rickshaw operation, shoe making, hair dressing, etc.

STEP - The Support to Training and Employment Projects (STEP) programmer aims to upgrade the skills of poor and assetless women, mobilize them and provide employment on a sustainable basis in fields such as agriculture, dairying, fisheries, sericulture, handlooms, handicrafts, etc. In addition to training and employment support, the three special features included in this programme are 'Gender Sensitization', 'Women in Development Inputs' and provision of 'Support Services'. Over two lakh women in the country have been provided assistance through forty STEP projects.

T-E-P Centres - Another major programme for economic empowerment of women is the 'Training-cum-Employment- cum-Production centres'. The programme extends financial assistance to public sector undertakings/ corporations/autonomous bodies/ voluntary organisations to train women in nontraditional sectors and provide employment. Priority is given for training in modern and upcoming trades like electronics, watch assembly, computer programming, printing and binding, garment making, fashion technology, bakeries/ confectionery, beautician courses, office management, etc. Over forty-nine thousand women belonging to weaker section have been provided training and employment under this programme.

Socio-Economic Programme : Yet another major programme which aims at economic empowerment of poor and needy women such as destitutes; widows, deserted, economically backward and the handicapped is the Socio-Economic Programme (SEP). The programme which is implemented through the Central Social Welfare Board provides 'Work and Wage' for such women. Through this programme, the Board endeavors to provide them facilities to engage themselves in full time or part-time work to earn wage to supplement the meagre income of their families. So far, 13,100 units have been sanctioned under this programme to cover 1.62 lakh needy women.

Mahila Samriddhi Yojna - Mahila Samriddhi Yojna (MSY) was launched on 2nd October 1993. Under the Mahila Samriddhi Yojna every rural adult women is encouraged to have her MSY account in the post office which has jurisdiction over her village. For an amount of Rs. 300/- in a year, the Government contributes 25 per cent as incentive. In other, for the deposit of Rs. 300 which remains in the account for a period of 12 months, the Government gives an incentive of Rs. 75/- upto May 31, 1995, around 93 lakhs MSY accounts with a deposit of Rs. 93.77 crore had been opened.

Rashtriya Mahila Kosh - Rashtriya Mahila Kosh (RMK) a National Credit Fund for women, in 1993, is yet another initiative on the part of the Department of Women and Child Development towards economic empowerment of women. The Kosh aims at reaching the poor and assetles women who are in need of credit but cannot reach the formal banking or credit service.

RMK provides credit to poor women both in rural and urban areas, in the informal sector through the intermediation of non-governmental organisation and other women's organisations like special help groups in a simple and flexible manner at reasonable rates of interest. The Kosh supports short term loans upto Rs. 2,000/- to 2,500/- and medium term loan upto Rs. 5,000/- for borrower.

So far Rashitrya Mahila Kosh has sanctioned Rs. 10.88 crore for loan through 61 NGOs to benefit seventy thousand women.

Programmes and Services for Urban Poor in Uttar Pradesh

Uttar Pradesh is going through a period of rapid urbanisation. Its urban population has almost quadrupled. Urbanisation has both the positive as well as negative aspects but it has to be recognised that the growth of urbanisation is inevitable. The policies and programmes adopted so far have not been able to respond adequately to the problems and implications of urbanisation.

Now that the State Government has started its exercises which will lead to formulation of suitable strategies to be adopted during the VIIIth Plan. It is time that the critical appraisal of the past policies and programmes was made and the issues emerging out of it were highlighted for assisting the Government in policy making. Urban poor have been by far a neglected segment of society and they have been unable to derive advantage from the ongoing programmes of development nor any programme specifically catering to them needs has been launched by the Government. What is, therefore, needed is to ensure the convergence of services on the urban poor to create a definite impact on their quality of life especially their children and women. Therefore, there is an urgent need of making a frontal and multi-pronged attack on the problem of urban poverty by launching an "Integrated Development Programme" for the Urban Poor (IDPUP) which should take care of all the development needs of the urban poor to mitigate their sufferings and deprivation. These welfare schemes should be headed by the Mayor of Municipal Council or Chairman Municipal Board and the

Table No. 2.1
Details of Various Financial and Physical Progress Implemented by State Urban Development Agency U.P., Lucknow

Sl.No.	Name of Yojna	Financial Achievement upto 31.3.95	Physical Achievement upto 31.3.95	Balance of 1.4.95	Financial Goal of the Year 95-96	Financial Achievement from 1.4.95 to 31.10.95	Physical Goal of the 95-96	Physical Achievement from 1.4.95 to 31.10.95
1.	Nehru Rojgar Yojna							
A.	S.U.M.E.	3786.39	164402	1343.59	1343.59	172.07	45322	6399
B.	S.U.M.E. (Training)	366.64	42035	410.42	409.05	37.87	34090	3590
C.	S.U.M.E.	5981.88	10238581	1120.64	1023.64	214.86	1204186	254828
D.	S.H.A.S.U.	1022.69	34516	328.11	68.45	000.82	000	1186
E.	S.H.A.S.U. (Training)	86.96	6582	98.38	104.46	42.42	6964	931
Total Nehru Rojgar Yojna		11234.56	10486116	3301.14	2965.11	468.04	1290562	266934
2.	U.B.S.P.	664.64	609512	1105.46	771.245	245.84	905825	151250
3.	L.C.S.	1117.25	40308	85.40	1156.42869*	1141.6738	*49098	4118
	Grand Total	13016.45	11135936	4492.00	4892.78369	1858.618	2245485	418994

* Yojna from the beginning.

Administrator/Executive Officer should be its Secretary. It will include representatives of all development departments and the members elected from each word. It should be effectively implemented to keep programme objective into sharp focus at all times.

Nagar Vikas Yojna - Under this scheme, financial assistance is provided to Nagar Palikas, Nagar Mahapalikas and Development authorities etc for the development of parks, construction of offices and community centers, and beautification schemes. The assistance was provided in the shape of loan up to the year 1986-87, but from the year 1987-88 grants are provided under this scheme, keeping in view the non-remunerative aspects of the scheme.

Environmental Improvement of Slums - This programme is under implementation at present in 63 towns. The thrust of the scheme is on improving the environmental conditions of slums in the urban areas. Out of this, 30 are less, 9 towns having population more than one lakh, and remaining 33 are mostly small and medium towns, selected under the scheme of "Integrated Development of Small and Medium Towns" including 3 hill towns. Financial assistance is provided to the local bodies of the selected towns, in the shape of grant, at the rate of Rs. 250 per capita.

Integrated Development of Small and Medium Towns - This is centrally sponsored scheme on the basis of 50:50 matching contribution from central and State Government being implemented in accordance with the guidelines issued by the Ministry of Works and Housing, Government of India.

Kanpur Urban Development Project - The World Bank assisted Kanpur Urban Development Project externally aided with an estimated cost of Rs. 41.35 crores is being implemented in Kanpur since April 1981. The major component of the project are - 1. sites and services, 2. slum upgrading, 3. sewerage, 4. water supply, 5. drainage, 6. solid waste management, 7. traffic and transportation, 8. maintenance and 9. technical assistance and training.

Urban Basic Services - The Government of India and the UNICEF proposed this scheme during the VIIIth Five Year Plan period although there was no allocation. The scheme aims at improving the environmental conditions of slum areas and implementing the low cost sanitation programmes in the urban areas. The programme is designed to enhance the survival and development of men and women of urban low income families and to provide them basic education of personal and environmental hygiene so as to reduce the infant mortality rate and improve environmental conditions of the area. Scheme also envisaged creation of creches, Balwaris for infants of working mothers so that they may be in the position to work whole heartedly and improve their economic conditions.

U.P. Urban Development and Water Supply Project - The state government formulated an urban development and water supply project covering 12 cities in the state for assistance of the World Bank.

The basic objectives of the project is to improve urban management finance and resources mobilisation through the strengthening of lye urban institutions in the project tours particularly management and financing of services through a programme of physical works.

Urban Transport Scheme - All major cities in the state are facing transport problems due to increase in population and expansion of limits of the urban areas. With a view to achieve maximum degree of access as per master plan of towns and within the limited resources. Under this scheme, financial assistance will be provided to the development authorities in the shape of loan for implementation of the transportation projects.

Although the outlays have been increasing from one plan to another but these are hardly related to the problems and their magnitude which are being faced by the urban centres in our state.

[illegible] [illegible] physical [illegible]

[illegible]

Chapter III

Research Design and Methodology

Indian cities, specially metropolitan areas, have witnessed a significant increase in their developmental activities in the forms of renewed urban planning and constructions, establishment of industries and trade, expansion in transport and communication systems, availability of their infra-structural facilities in post-independence era. These have opened new avenues of employment, resulting into migration of population to these cities from rural areas as well as from small towns adding to the spurt of urban population. These migrated persons get some gainful employment but face the problem of shelter because city system hardly allows them to have good shelter. Consequently, over the years, these low income migrants have settled in pockets of city known as slums which are characterised by over-crowding, faulty arrangement of design of building, narrowness or faulty arrangement of street, lack of ventilation, light or sanitation facilities, inadequacy of open spaces and community facilities or any combination of these factors and violating every norm of systematic and planned urban growth and development. These slums have come to be known differently in different cities such as Jhuggi-Jhopari in Delhi, Jhopadpatti in Munbai, Bastis in Calcutta, etc.

Government has shown its concern to the problems of slum dwellers right from Second Five Year Plan which consisted of a strategy incorporating slum clearance and rehabilitation of slum dwellers in planned areas which have the civic amenities. But, The Scheme of Slum Clearance did not make much headway due to serious constraints of funds and developed land. Consequently, the emphasis of Government policy was shifted to slum improvement which provides for larger coverage of slum population using the minimum means. As a result, the Scheme of Environmental Improvement of Urban Slums (EIUS) came into operation in 1972 having the purpose of bringing improvement in the living environment of slum dwellers by providing the basic civic facilities of water supply - one tap for 150 persons, sewer-open drains with normal outflow avoiding accumulation of water, storm water drains for draining out storm water quickly, community baths - one bath for 20 to 50 persons, community latrines - one lavatory seat for 20-50 persons, widening and paving of existing lanes and arrangement for street light - one pole for 30 metres apart. Considering the urgency of ameliorating the lot of maximum slum population within as minimum time as possible, the scheme started operating in Central Sector. However, with a view to involve the states in implementation of the scheme, it was transferred to State sector under Minimum Needs Programme during the Fifth Five Year Plan. The Government's concern for the scheme was further reiterated when the scheme was included in the 20-Point Programme of Prime Minister. Due to some factors such as absence of long term strategy of slum improvement in the states; lack of adequate administrative and technical expertise at State and Local Levels, inadequate budgetary resources of local bodies, absence of city-wise data on slums and projects, local problems in taking up slum improvement in private slums and problem of maintaining the improved slums, the expected achievement's of the scheme could not materialize even if on the basis of physical verification of improved slums in various State's, it is found that the provision of these facilities, in particular water supply and community baths and latrines have made the lives of slum dwellers, specially women and children, much more comfortable and added cleanliness to the area. But, still a wide and effective plan of action for the improvement of conditions in slum areas is needed because the remedies that we have so far found do not treat the cause but only system.[1]

Definitions and Concept of Slum

Slum is relative term. Though slums are spread all over the world from Bombay to Bermuda and from Manchester to Manila. Yet it is understood differently at difference places. This is a relative concept in terms of its geographical settings and outlay. The concept and definition of slum vary from one society to another and even from one study to another study conducted in the same society. There is no general agreement over the definition of the term which can be universally accepted and applied to slums of all over the world. The term slum has been defined differently by economists, town-planners, social workers, administrators, sociologists, etc., keeping in view their own disciplines and professional backgrounds. Moreover, various terms such as 'blight areas', 'deteriorated areas', 'marginal areas', 'transitional areas', 'sub-standard settlement', 'unplanned settlement', 'uncontrolled settlement', 'spontaneous settlement', 'provisional settlement', 'squatter settlement', 'overnight settlement', 'urban villages', etc. are very loosely used to denote slums. Important definitions of the term 'Slum' are as follows:

* "Congested urban or suburban residential district characterised by deteriorating and unsanitary housing, boarding and social disorganisation." (Encyclopaedia Britannica, 1978)
* "A slum may be described as a chaotically occupied, unsystematically developed and generally neglected area which is over populated by persons and over crowded with ill repaired and neglected structures" (Indian Conference of S.W., 1957)
* "Slum is taken to mean hutting areas with squalid surrounding. In such areas, huts are created in

a haphazard manner without proper access. Minimum basic amenities are lacking in these areas. The term 'slum' will also include such dwellings which on account of such over crowding, dilapided, lack of ventilation are detrimental to safety health and social morals". (Census of India, 1961 - Madras).

* "Any predominantly residential area where the dwellings which by reason of dilapidation over-crowding, faulty arrangement of design lack of ventilation, light or sanitary facilities or any combination of these factors are detrimental to safety, health and morals". (Slum Improvement & Clearance Act, 1950),
* "A slum is a building, a group of building, or area characterized by over crowding, deterioration, unsanitary conditions or absence of facilities or amenities which, because of these conditions or any of them, in danger the health, safety or morals of its inhabitants or the community." (UNESCO Document).
* "Slums may be characterized as areas of substandard housing conditions within a city. A slum is always an area. A single, neglected building even in the worst stage of deterioration does not make a slum". (Bergel).
* "The slum is a residential area in which the housing is so deteriorated so substandard, or so unwholesome as to be a menace to the health, safety, morality, or welfare of the occupants". This makes housing too dominant as the cause of slum conditions. (Ford).
* Slums were defined as "Areas where buildings (a) are in any respect unfit for human habitation; (b) are by reason of dilapidation, overcrowding, faulty arrangements and design of such buildings,

narrowness or faulty arrangement of streets, lack of ventilation, light or sanitation facilities, or any combination of these factors are detrimental to safety, health or morals." (Slum Clearance Improvement and Clearance, Act, 1956).

* "A slum area means any area where such dwellings predominate which by reason of dilapidation, overcrowding, faulty arrangement of street, lack of ventilation, light or sanitation facilities, inadequacy of open spaces and community facilities, or any combination of these factors, are detrimental to health, safety or morals". (The Scheme of Environment and Clearance).

* A slum is (i) an area characterised by inadequate housing facilities, overcrowding and congestion, faulty arrangements of streets, lack of ventilation, light or sanitation facilities; (ii) an area characterized by its own way of life, a subculture with a set of norms and values, and the people in slum area without being fully integrated into the urban community; (iii) an area having minimum social organisation beyond the level of family; (iv) an area consisting of people characterised by strong feeling of marginality, helplessness, sense of resignation, fatalism, wide-spread belief in superstitions, and high level of tolerance; and (v) an area consisting of people earning low wages, suffering from chronic unemployment and under-employment and incapable of saving, reducing the possibility of effective participation in the growing economic system." (Thakur and Dhadave).

Thus a slum may be defined as an overcrowded area characterised by sub-standard houses without even essential amenities like water, light, ventilation, drainage, approach roads, latrines, sewer lines, etc. which are generally inhabited by the illiterates, poors and intermediates and scheduled caste population forced by the circumstances to lead sub-human and disorganised life.

To design is to plan. Designing, in fact, is process of making decisions before the situation arises, in which decisions are to be carried out. It may be called a process of deliberate anticipation directed towards bringing a expected situation under control. Design should be methodologically prepared, so that it might be worthy of being evaluated before hand and should render the method of making research decision worthy of being evaluated. Research design is the plan structure and strategy of investigation, conceived so as to obtain answers to research questions and to control variance.[1] Research design designates the logical manner, in which individuals or other units are compared and analyzed. It is the basis for making interpretations of the data in order to ensure that comparison made, is not subject to alternative interpretations.[2] The research design is more of logical strategy in any scientific investigation in the sense that it deals with the plan developed to answer a question, describe a situation or test a hypothesis. It is a strategy of dealing with the rationale by which a specific set of procedures, which includes both data collection and analysis is expected to meet the particular requirements of a study by arranging the conditions for collection and analysis of data in a manner which aims at combining relevance to the research purpose with economy in procedure.[3]

In every research design, certain procedure is followed, which entails the highlighting of the rationale for the selection of present problem, classification of objectives, detailed specification of various aspects of problem including definitions of different concepts used in the study and the method and manner in which the information relevant for the study is to be so collected and analyzed that answers to the research question become available. In the context of the present study, various steps of design are being described in the ensuing paragraphs.

Statement of the Problem

The Indian cities have been growing at more than double the rate of villages. Urban population in the seventies increased at an annual rate of 3.87% as compared to the rural population's rate of growth of 1.87%. This was due to the large scale of migration of an impoverished rural peasantry because of agricultural sector's inability to absorb this rural manpower. Thus, these poors are huddled in slums and on pavement of urban areas.

Consequently, in urban areas, the slums are distinct example of social and economic backwardness. The slums have cremated many social, moral; and democratic problems and the situation has been further aggravated due to uncontrolled migration, unbalanced distribution of income, inadequate community facilities, lack of urban planning, absence of community participation and ineffective legal measures. The consequences of this state of affairs are social disruption and dislocation, congestion, shortage of accommodation and shelter of all types, unemployment, increase in crime of various categories, inadequacy of social services, lack of civic and social amenities causing an unbearable strain on eventual services as well as erosion of social values.

The World Population Conference held at Bucharest in 1974 clearly admitted the fact that population dimensions are integrally related to social and economic development. Five factors - health, education, economic growth, organisation and status of women - are associated with population growth. Some selected elements of developments are related to it e.g. literacy, nutrition and infant mortality. Generally small farmers and landless laborers are among the lowest income group in rural society whose productivity is often very low and they are able to live only upto the subsistence level. But, what about millions of poor who migrate to the cities and the chunk of city population who lives below the poverty line in slum.

The policy problem of uplifting this section is considerably more complex because urban socio-economic relationship by their nature are both more varied and complicated in their traditional rural situations. Slums in the city are doubling themselves in every year resulting into increase in human crowding, unbearable stress and dysfunctional family relationships. So unless the benefits are directed more equitably to the downtrodden strata of our society including slum dwellers, any amount of economic growth as such will mere move the society to limited level of progress. It is thus, an urgent need to identify a study of such section of society which assumes importance for any programme of social and economic uplift.

Thus it can be concluded that while most section of the people become victims of the urbanisation phenomenon but women and children are among the major sufferers. Female labour is ruthlessly exploited by greedy employers and women also suffer from various ailments because of congestion, inadequate food and child bearing. The adolescent girls are the worst sufferers, because they, on the one hand, are subjected to work for manual jobs mostly of maid servants where the chances of their economic as well as physical exploitation are high and on the other hand they remained uneducated and unemployed or underemployed. Keeping in view these facts, the present study has been undertaken with focus on housing, educational, marital and employment problems of adolescent girls in slums in Lucknow city which has expanded largely during the present century, particularly after 1921, since when its population has increased slightly less than seven times (1921 - 2,40,566 lakhs and 1991- 16,69,135 lakhs).

Hypothesis

Due to urbanization, every section of society has to suffer but worst suffers are adolescent girls who have to face various problems related to their housing, education, marriage and education.

Aims and Objectives

The general aim of the present investigation has been to know about the housing, educational, marital and employment problems of adolescent girls living in slums specifically the objectives of this study has been:

1. To analyze the problems of urbanization
2. To describe programmer and services for the poor.
3. To present a profile of adolescent girls living in slum areas.
4. To enumerate housing needs and problems.
5. To present an analysis of educational problems of adolescent girls living in slum areas.
6. To investigate into family and marital problem of these adolescent girls.
7. To unravel the employment problems of these girls.
8. To investigate into the attitudes and beliefs of these girls.
9. To suggest strategy for intervention in order to improve the lot of these adolescent girls.

Definitions of Key Concepts

For the purpose of this study *slum area* means an overcrowded area characterised by substandard houses without even essential amenities like water, light, ventilation, drainage, approach road, latrine, sewer lines, etc. which are generally inhabited by the illiterates, poors and intermediate and lower caste population forced by circumstances to lead sub-human and disorganised life.

Adolescent Girls : means girl between 10-16 years of age for the purpose of this investigation.

Nature and Scope

The present study is mainly exploratory in character. Its exploratory character is self evident as throughout the investigation, efforts have been made to know about the problems of adolescent girls. The width of scope is distributed in various heads of the subject matter covered in the study. These are analysis of urbanization programmes and services for urban poor, profile of adolescent girls, housing needs and problems, educational problems, family and marital problems, employment problems, attitudes and beliefs and finally a suggested strategy for intervention. The study has been conducted in two slums of the Lucknow city namely Meva Nursery Basti, below Indira Bridge and Munshi Pulia, Indira Nagar, Lucknow covering 300 adolescent girls.

METHODOLOGY

Sources

The use of both field as well as documentary sources of information has been made use of in course of the present investigation. Undoubtedly, the field sources have primarily been depended upon the use of documentary sources has been made either with a view to supplementing the material needed for proper fitting in the information collected or for corroborating the collected information with one already available so that its veracity may be verified. Adolescent girls living in slum areas have constituted the field sources of information whereas hand written, typed and printed material available in form of reports, bulletins, journals and books etc. has furnished the documentary sources, used in the present study.

Universe and Sample

The universe of the study has been constituted by all the adolescent girls living in slum areas of the city of Lucknow. The sampled universe has been constituted by adolescent girls residing in two slums namely Meva Nursery Basti, Near Nishatganj Bridge and Munshi Pulia, Indira Nagar.

The Lucknow city has 38 areas properly declared as slums. The names of these areas along with their population have been listed below:

List of Slum Areas

Sl.No.	*Name of Slum*	*Where Located*	*Population*
1.	Pratap Nagar	Near Peer Baba's Mazar	1400
2.	Kaaula	Indira Nagar	350
3.	Across Gomti River	From Nishatganj to Motimahal	700
4.	Birbal Sahni Road	New Hyderabad	350
5.	Munshi Ki Pulia	Indira Nagar	700
6.	Akbar Nagar	Nar Kukrail Bridge	6000
7.	Meva Nursery Basti	Below Indira Bridge	700
8.	Balmiki Nagar	Paper Mill Colony	525
9.	Near Jalnigam Pump	Across Railway Mall Avenue	700
10.	Irrigation Office	Cant. Road	1400
11.	Nawab Purwa	Gomti Nagar	525
12.	Bealaha	Gomti Nagar	200
13.	Gulam Hussain Purwa	Gomti Nagar	630
14.	Risaha	Gomti Nagar	245
15.	Gawari Goan	Gomti Nagar	7000
16.	Uthawan	New Berry Road	700
17.	Jai Prakash Nagar	Wazir Hazan Road	2100
18.	Mallapur	Rana Pratap Road	2000
19.	Baaloo Adda	Prag Narayan	2100

Sl.No.	Name of Slum	Where Located	Population
20.	Uzaria Goan	Gomti Nagar	7000
21.	Chamar Dhulia	Gomti Nagar	2000
22.	Martin Purwa	Gomti Nagar	3500
23.	Rais Nagar	Chowk	1400
24.	Patanala	Vegetable Market Chowk	1260
25.	Company Bagh	Behind Imam Bara	7000
26.	Husainabad	Durga Devi Road	700
27.	Mukti Ganj	Hussainabad	700
28.	Rajendra Nagar	Sohan Lal Hata	1400
29.	Rajaji Puram Colony	Rajaji Puram	2000
30.	Tehri Pulia	Alambagh	350
31.	Kailash Puri	Jail Road Alambagah	2100
32.	Jama Maszid	Chowk	3150
33.	Mirza Ka Hataa	Thakur Ganj	1050
34.	Haidar Canal	Paan Dariba to Balika Vidyalaya	7000
35.	Rain Basera	Taxi Stand Mawaiya	700
36.	Vijay Nagar	Behind Gurudwara	700
37.	Bihar Nagar	Gulnar Nagar, Aishbagh	1400
38.	Ambika Nagar	Aishbagh, Tal Katora Road	1400

Out of these 38 slums, two slums have been selected on purposive basis. Out of the residents of these slums 150 adolescent girls from each selected area have been selected by using the method of quota sampling in which following steps were taken:

Firstly a quota of 150 adolescent girls was fixed for each slum area.

Secondly, a list of adolescent girls residing in these two areas was prepared and arranged in order of numbering of houses.

Thirdly, one hundred fifty adolescent girls were selected from each area by using the random numbers making the total three hundred adolescent girls for detailed investigation.

Tools and Techniques of Data Collection

Interview schedule with attendant techniques has been used as tool of data collection. Techniques of interviewing and observation have been used for gathering the needed information. Tool of the present study was carefully prepared and was tested for their comprehensiveness mutual exclusiveness, reliability and validity. The method of pre-testing has been of much help in holding such tests.

Method of Data Collection

Field data for the present study were collected by interviewing the adolescent girls residing in slum areas. Documentary data were collected by surveying the available material on the subject.

Processing, Analysis and Interpretation of Data

The data collected from the field have been edited in order to see that the desired information has been supplied by respondents in response to the questions posed before them. After editing, responses to different questions have been noted and divided into different categories. While categorizing the responses due care and attention have been paid with regard to mutual exclusiveness, comprehensiveness and unitariness of the categories formed. According to the plan already prepared, uni-variate and multi-variate tables were drawn. Variables have been so arranged that definite inference regarding the presence or absence of actual relationship as hypothesised may be drawn. In order to arrive a different conclusions, both logical and .lh.16" statistical methods have been applied but greater reliance has been placed on statistical methods descriptive as well as inferential.

Report Writing

The analyzed and interpreted information was presented in the form of simple research report written in narrative style for use by all interested prospective consumers.

Limitations of the Study

Due to the single handed efforts on the part of researcher, the present investigation has certain limitations which are caused due to the lack of adequate time, money and resources with the present researcher. These are being briefly given as follows:

1. The present investigation has been limited to only one district and that too to two slums only.
2. Only adolescent girls have been interviewed, their family members could not be contacted due to the lack of time and resources.
3. Difficulty has been faced in interview of adolescent girls because they have been elusive to questions. For this, special efforts were made by contacting them again and again.

Chapter IV

Profile of Adolescent Girls

Personality structure of individual is an outcome of an interaction between heredity and environment in which the individual lives. Heredity shapes the individual biologically and its influence can not be reported on the overall psycho-physical makeup of personality. Environment plays an important role in providing opportunities for development of unique, correct and responsive personality structure through the process of continuous learning and experience gained from it. Any social investigation can not overlook the bio-social characteristics of an individual because they exercise the considerable influence in developing opinions attitudes and belief consequently, bio-social characteristics of the health personnel are being discussed in the ensuing paragraphs.

Personal Background

(1) *Age* - Age of a person is an important factor more so in the case of an adolescent girls who lives in the slum area, Different strategies need to be adopted for providing different types of services for adolescent girls who are of different age group.

Information pertaining to the age of respondents has been collected and tabulated in Table No. 4.1. The table clearly shows that majority of respondents (42.33%) has been found in the age of 12-14 years followed by the age group of 14-16 years (31.33%) and 10-12 years (26.33 %). The minimum age of respondents have been 10 years and maximum age 16 years. The average age of respondents has been calculated as 13.1 years.

Table 4.1
Age of the Respondents

Age (in yrs)	*No. of the respondents*	*Percentage*
10-12	79	26.33
12-14	127	42.33
14-16	94	31.33
Total	300	100
Average	13.1	

This brings out the conclusion that majority of adolescent girls in slum area belong to the 12-14 years of age group.

Marital Status of the Respondents

In the Indian context, marriage is an important institution. Through this institution, sex need of person is fulfilled and continuity of family is maintained through procreation and upbringing of children. Marriage also plays an important role in shaping and developing the personality structure of any person which ultimately decides their nature, attitudes, beliefs and behaviour patterns. It also plays a dominant role in enhancing the prestige and overall social acceptance of persons in the community, particularly in Indian social order. Keeping in view, information regarding marital status of the respondents has been collected and is being presented in tabular form in Table No. 4.2.

The table shows that more than half of the respondent girls (57.7%) have been found married followed by unmarried respondents (42.3%). This brings out that adolescent girls in the slum go for marriage relatively at an early age.

Table 4.2
Marital Status of the Respondents

Marital status	*No. of respondents*	*Percentage*
Unmarried	173	57.70
Married	127	42.30
Total	300	100

Religion/Caste

Religion is universal. It has given a particular type of environment to every human being. It has controlled persons physically, mentally and socially by assigning social obligations and controlling them through different religious ideas. Consequently it has affected individual personality as well as the milieu in which the personality operates resulting into the shaping and developing of attitudes, beliefs, morals etc. in human personality.

Caste plays an important role in Indian social setup because it divides people into different hirer child and puts restrictions in their social intercourse such as dining marriage and other kinds of social obligations. This definitely affects the growth and development of human personality resulting into the determination of their status and role in overall context. Keeping the above in view, information regarding religion and caste has been gathered and presented in Table No. 4.3.

Table 4.3
Religion and Caste of the Respondents

Religion and caste	*No. of the respondents*	*Percentage*
Hindu :		
Upper	11	10.68
Intermediate	9	8.74

(Contd.)

Religion and caste	*No. of the respondents*	*Percentage*
Lower	83	80.58
Sub-total	103	34.33
Muslim	197	65.67
Total	300	100

The table clearly maintains that more than half of the respondents have been found muslims (65.67%) followed by Hindus (34.33%) out of Hindus the dominant majority of respondents belongs to lower caste (80.58%) followed by upper caste (10.18%) and intermediate caste (8.74%).

This shows that slum areas understudy has been found dominated by muslims and lower caste Hindus.

Background of Respondents

India is predominantly rural and most of the person living in urban areas have been drawn from the villages. In this background, information has been gathered and is being presented in Table No. 4.4. However, the table already shows that more than half of the respondents (57.67%) have drawn from urban areas because respondents of this study are adolescent girls who have probably taken birth in the city 42.33 per cent respondents have drawn from rural areas.

Table 4.4
Background of the Respondents

Background	*No. of the respondents*	*Percentage*
Rural	127	42.33
Urban	173	57.67
Total	300	100.00

To conclude, it can be said that majority of adolescent girls has been from urban areas.

Educational Status

Education also plays a very important role in achieving the economic status. Higher the education, higher would be the possibilities of achieving a higher economic status. Education also plays an important role in gaining self confidence in developing capabilities to gain status in the society.

According to Census Report 1991 about 24.82 per cent female population was literate as compared to 46.89 per cent male literate population. In rural areas female literacy was 17.96 and 47.82 per cent in urban areas.

Table 4.5

Educational Status of the Respondents

Educational status	*No. of the respondents*	*Percentage*
Illiterate	179	59.67
Literate	23	7.67
Below Primary	47	15.67
Primary	29	9.67
Junior High School	15	5.00
High School	7	2.33
Total	300	100.00

The table clearly indicates that more than half of the respondents (59.67%) have been found literate followed by below primary level (15.67%), primary (9.67%), just literate (7.67%), junior high school (5.00%) and high school (2.33%).

To conclude it can be said that most of the adolescent girls of the slum areas have been found illiterate. They have very low level of education because the maximum level of educational status has been found upto high school level only.

Occupation/Employment

The history of female employment in gainful professions outside the family particularly in developing countries like India, is a recent one. Their role since the Vedic period has been traditional. The domestic side was under the guardianship of women and the work place was under the control of men, But due to social, economic, cultural and technological changes role of women is also changing. Now women have entered in different fields of employment.

Information pertaining to occupation/employment of adolescent girls understudy has been collected and is being presented in tabular form in Table No. 4.6.

Table 4.6
Occupation of the Respopndents

Occupation	*No. of the respondents*	
	Main	*Subsidiary*
Daily wager earnings	81 (27.00)	50 (16.67)
Caste occupations	34 (11.33)	10 (3.33)
House workers (Maid servant)	29 (9.67)	6 (2.00)
Non-workers	40 (13.33)	-
Unemployed	116 (38.67)	-
Nil	-	78 (26.00)

(Contd.)

Occupation	*No. of the*	*respondents*
	Main	*Subsidiary*
Not applicable	-	156 (52.00)
Total	300 (100.0)	300 (100.0)

The table makes it clear that out of 300 adolescent girls 156 (72%) girls have been found economically ineffective because they have been either non-workers (13.33%) or unemployed (38.67%). The main occupation of economically effective girls have been daily wage earnings (27%); performing caste occupations (11.33%); and working as maid servant (9.67%). Only 22 per cent respondents have been found engaged in subsidiary occupation also of which the largest single group of respondents has been going for daily wage earnings (16.67%) followed by caste occupations (3.3%) and maid servant (2%).

Monthly Income of Respondents

Adolescent girls in the slum areas are also engaged themselves in economic activity so that they may be able to contribute in fulfilling the basic needs of their family. In order to know about the monthly income of the adolescent girls understudy information was gathered from respondent and is being tabulated in Table No. 4.7.

Table 4.7
Total Monthly Income of the Respondents

Total monthly income (in Rs.)	*No. of the respondents*	*Percentage*
Below 150	16	5.33
151-300	40	13.33

(Contd.)

Total monthly income (in Rs.)	*No. of the respondents*	*Percentage*
301-450	55	18.33
451-600	18	6.00
601-750	11	3.67
751-900	4	1.33
Not applicable (Nil)	156	52.00
Total	300	100.00
Average:		
Inclusive of nil	170	
Exclusive of nil	354.17	

The table makes it clear that out of 300 respondents only 144 girls have been found doing something of which the largest single group (55 girls) has been earning monthly between Rs. 300 to 450 followed by Rs. 150-300 (40 girls), Rs. 450-600 (18 girls), below Rs. 150 (110 girls), Rs. 600-750 (11 girls) and Rs. 750-900 (4 girls). The average monthly earnings of these working girls has been calculated Rs. 354.17 and in case economically ineffective number of girls is included, the average comes Rs. 170 per month.

Thus it is clear from the table that most of the respondents monthly income ranges from below Rs. 150/- per month to Rs. 450/- per month.

Family Background

In the words of Burgess and Lock "Family is a group of person united by the ties of Blood, marriage, adoption constituting a single house-hold, interacting and communicating with each other in respective social roles of husband and wife, mother and father, son and daughter, brother and sister, and creating and maintaining a common culture." Burgess, E.W. and Lock, Horney. The family is of two types - nuclear and joint. Nuclear family consists of husband wife and their unmarried children. Joint family consists of two or more generations, i.e. husband and wife and married children. Basic future of joint family are common property, common kitchen and common income. So the size of a family is an important factor in an analysis the economic status of a person who is a major source of family income. Therefore to arrive at a two picture of the economic status of the respondents, their family size was studied.

Rural/urban living plays an important role in shaping the personality structure of any human being due to the differential nature in environment as well as social surroundings. This background clearly puts its impact on human being by providing opportunity of different type of quality of life and social setup affecting on the overall attitudes, beliefs and behavior pattern of persons.

Type of Family

Information was gathered in relation to the type of family and is being presented in Table No. 4.8.

Table 4.8
Type of Family of the Respondents

Type of family	*No. of the respondents*	*Percentage*
Joint	124	41.33
Nuclear	176	58.67
Total	300	100.00

The table brings out the fact that more than half of respondents have nuclear family structure (58.67%) followed by joint family structure (41.33%). The reason is being that in urban areas due to rapid westernization and industrialization congestion etc., people are bound to live in nuclear family and in slum areas particularly migrant families are residing which has left their most of family member in rural area.

Number of Family Members

Data pertaining to total number of family members as per nature of family are being tabulated in Table No. 4.9.

Table 4.9
Total Number of Family Members and Type of Family

Total no. of family members	Type of Family: Joint	Type of Family: Nuclear	Total
1-3	5 (4.03)	9 (5.11)	14 (4.67)
4-6	40 (32.66)	98 (55.68)	138 (46.00)
7-9	50 (40.32)	69 (39.21)	119 (39.67)
10-12	14 (11.29)	-	14 (4.67)
13-15	ll (8.87)	-	11 (3.67)
16-18	4 (3.22)		4 (1.33)
Total	124 (41.33)	176 (58.67)	300 (100.00)
Average	7.95	6.02	

The table brings out the fact that the largest single group of respondents (46%) has total family members ranging from 4-6 followed by 7-9 (39.67%), 1-3 and 10-12 (4.67% each); 13-15 (3.67%) and 16-18 (1.33%).

In joint family the largest single group of respondents (40.32%) has total number of family members ranging from 7-9 members followed by 4-6 (32.26%), 10-12 (11.29%), 13-15 (8.8%), 1-3 (4.03%) and 16-18 (3.22%).

In case of nuclear families more than half of the families have family member from 4-6 followed by 7-9 (39.2%) and 1-3 (5.11%).

The maximum number of family members in joint families has been found 18 and minimum 9 in case of joint families.

The average family size of joint families has been found 7.95 i.e. 8 and of nuclear families 6.02 i.e. 6.

In a nutshell it can be concluded that family size of slum areas under study as relatively large in case of both joint as well as nuclear families.

Sex of Family Members

Information pertaining to sex structure of family members is being presented in Table No. 4.10.

Table 4.10
Sex Structure of the Family Members

Sex	*No. of the family members*	*Percentage*
Male	1013	50.73
Female	984	49.27
Total	1997	100.00

The table brings out that family members of slum areas understudy have been found almost equally distributed though the percentage of male members has been found slightly higher as compared to their family members counterpart (male - 50.73% and female-49.27%).

Age and Sex of Family Members

Information related to age and sex of family members is being presented in table No. 4.11.

Table 4.11
Age and Sex of the Family Members

Age (in years)	*Sex*		*Total*
	Male	*Female*	
Below 5	144 (14.21)	142 (14.43)	286 (14.43)
5-14	287 (28.33)	301 (30.59)	588 (29.44)
15-24	141 (13.92)	138 (14.02)	279 (13.97)
25-34	152 (15.00)	148 (15.04)	300 (15.02)
35-44	140 (13.82)	135 (13.72)	275 (13.77)
45-54	81 (8.00)	74 (7.52)	155 (7.76)
55-64	38 (3.75)	29 (2.95)	67 (3.35)
65-74	30 (2.96)	17 (1.73)	47 (2.35)
Total	1013 (50.73)	984 (49.27)	1997 (100.00)
Average	23.89	22.53	23.22

The table clearly presents that the largest single group of respondent family members belong to the age group of 5-14 years (29.44%) followed by 25-34 years (15.02) below 5 years (14.43%), 15-24 years (13.97%), 35-44 years (13.72%), 45-54 years (7.76%); 55-64 years (3.35%) and 65-74 years (2.35%).

Sexwise analysis shows that the largest single group of male members belongs to the age group of 5-14 years (28.33%) followed by 25-34 years (15%) below 5 years (14.21%), 15-24 years (13.92%), 35-44 years (13.82%), 45-54 years (8%), 55-64 years (3.75%) and 65-74 years (2.96%). The largest single group of female family members belongs to the age group of 5-14 years (30.59,%) followed by 15-24 years (7.52%); 55-64 years (2.95%) and 65-74 years (1.73%).

The average age of family members has been found 23.22 years whereas in case of male members 23.89 years and female member 22.53 years. This shows there exists not much difference in the age of male and female members of slum areas understudy.

This average of age brings out another fact that members in families of slum areas understudy have been found young.

Marital Status of the Family Members

Table No. 4.12 presents information pertaining to the marital status of family members in tabular form.

Table 4.12
Marital Status of the Camily Members

Marital status	*No. of the family members*	*Percentage*
Unmarried	1071	53.63
Married	840	42.06
Widower/widow	61	3.05
Separated/divorced	25	1.25
Total	1997	100.00

A close analysis of the information presented in the table brings out the fact that more than half of the respondents are female members (53.63%) and who have been found unmarried followed married (42.06%) widower/ widow (3.05%) and separated/divorced (1.25%).

Thus, it can be concluded that the percentage of married family members of respondents is quite high among relatively young family members.

Educational Status of Family Members

In order to judge literacy level of respondents family members, information has been sought from them and is being tabulated in Table No. 4.13.

Table 4.13
Educational Status of the Family Members

Educational status	*No. of the family members*	*Percentage*
Illiterate	1024	51.28
Literate	106	5.31
Below primary	311	15.57
Primary	116	5.81
Junior High School	67	3.36
High School	49	2.45
Intermedaite	31	1.55
Graduate & above	6	0.30
Not applicable (below 5 years)	287	14.37
Total	1997	100.00

The table clearly demonstrates that more than half of the family members of the respondents have been found illiterate (51.28%) followed by those family members who have been found calculated below primary level (15.57%), primary level (5.81%), just literate (5.31%), Junior High School level (3.36%), High School level (1.55%), and graduate and above level (0.30%). 14.37 per cent of family members has been found of non-school going age.

From the above this can be concluded that level of education in slum area under study is quite low.

Main Occupation of the Family

In order to know the main occupation of the family, the relevant information has been collected and is being tabulated in Table No. 4.14.

Table 4.14
Main Occupation of the Family

Main Occupation	*No. of the families*	*Percentage*
Service	56	18.67
Daily wage earnings	159	53.00
Shop keeping	18	6.00
Petty business	11	3.67
Caste occupation	26	8.67
Domestic servants	30	10.00
Total	300	100.00

The table clarifies that more than half of the families (53%) have been found engaged in daily labour for wage earnings followed by those families which have been engaged in service (18.67%); domestic servants (10%); caste occupation (8.67%); shop keeping (6%); and petty business (3.67%).

This brings out the fact that family occupation in slum areas understudy has generally been found of daily wage earnings by going outside for work daily.

Main Occupation of the Family Members

Table No. 4.15 presents the collected information

regarding main occupation of family members in tabular form in order to know the occupational status of respondent's family members.

Table 4.15

Main Occupation of the Family Members

Main Occupation	*No. of family members*	*Percentage*
Service	80	4.01
Daily wage earnings	649	32.50
Shop keeping	29	1.45
Petty business	12	0.60
Caste occupation	48	2.40
Domestic servants	158	7.91
Household work	46	2.30
Unemployed	243	12.17
Not applicable	732	36.65
Total	1997	100.00

The table brings out that fact that the largest single group of respondents' family members has been found doing service (40.01%) followed by those family members who have been found engaged as daily wage earners (32.50%); domestic servants (7.91%); performer of caste occupations (2.40%); doers household work (2.30%); shop keepers (1.45%); and petty businessmen (0.6%), 12.17 percent family member have been found unemployed and 36.65 per cent of family members have been found of that age who can not do any kind of economic activity.

To conclude, it can be mentioned that main occupation of the respondents' family members have been service, daily wage earnings and rendering of domestic service.

Highest Level of Education in the Family

In order to know about level of education in slum areas understudy, the above mentioned information was sought from the respondents and is being given tabulated Table No. 4.16.

Table 4.16
Highest Level of Education in the Family

Highest level of Education	*No. of families*	*Percentage*
Illiterate	144	38.00
Literate	7	2.33
Below Primary	64	21.33
Primary	33	11.00
Junior High School	30	10.00
High School	25	8.33
Intermedaite	22	7.33
Graduate	3	1.00
Post-Graduate	2	0.67
Total	300	100.00

The table classifies that the largest single group of the respondents families has no education (38%), followed by those families in which highest level of education has been found below primary level (10%); high school level (8.33%); intermediate level (7.33%), graduate (1%); and post graduate level (0.67%), 2.33 per cent of respondent has been found just literate.

The above mentioned analysis clearly brings out the fact that level of education in slum areas understudy has been found very low and majority of respondents' families has been found having no formal educational standard. The number of graduates and postgraduates in these families is almost negligible.

Monthly Income of the Family

The family income of person influences not only the availability of facilities of education and vocational training but also the availability of medical facilities. Family income also affects the availability of aids and appliances to a great extent. Consequently, an attempt has been made in the present study to find out the income of the families of slum adolescent girls. This data have been collected and are being presented in Table No. 4.17 in tabular form for detailed analysis.

Table 4.17
Total Monthly Income of the Family

Monthly income (in Rs.)	*No. of the families*	*Percentage*
Below 500	43	14.33
501-1000	88	29.33
1001-1500	76	25.33
1501-2000	44	14.67
2001-2500	25	8.33
2501-3000	14	4.67
3001-3500	5	1.67
3501-4000	3	1.00
4001-4500	2	0.67
Total	300	100.00
Average	1265	

The above mentioned table brings out that the largest single group of the respondents' families' monthly income has been found in the range of Rs. 500-1000 followed by those respondents' families whose income has been found in the range of Rs. 1000-1500 (25.33%), Rs. 1500-2000 (14.67%); below Rs. 500 (14.33%); Rs. 2000-2500 (8.33%); Rs. 2500-3000

(9.67%); Rs. 3000-3500 (1.67%), Rs. 3500-4000 (1.1%) and Rs. 4000-4500 (0.67%).

The average of family income has been found as Rs. 1265.00 which is quite low. Thus, in a nutshell, it can be concluded that total monthly income of the family is very low.

Total Number of Earning Members in Family

This information was sought from the respondents in order to judge the availability of economically effective persons in each and every family of adolescent girls understudy. The collected information is being tabulated and presented in Table No. 4.18.

Table 4.18
Total Number of Earning Members

Total no. of earning members	*No. of the families*	*Percentage*
1	121	40.33
2	141	47.00
3	23	7.67
4	9	3.00
5	4	1.33
6	2	0.67
Total	300	100.00
Average	1.8	

This table brings out the fact that the largest single group of respondents' families has two earning members (47%), followed by those families which have one earning member (47.33%), 3 (7.67%), 4 (3.00%), 5 (1.33%) and 6 (0.67%). The calculated average comes 1.8 earning member per family. This shows that out of the average size of respondents' families i.e. about 7 persons, 2 have been found economically effective persons or earning members. This establishes the fact that 5 persons per family have been found dependents which is quite high and not helpful in family's development. This may prove detrimental for family's adolescents and other overall development.

Total Number of School Going Children

Existence of the school going child determines the family's interest in education and gives additional responsibility to parents for arranging his/her education for overall development of personality. In order to judge whether parents are performing his role regarding education, the above mentioned information was collected and is being tabulated in Table No. 4.19.

Table 4.19
Total Number of School Going Children

Total number	*No. of the families*	*Percentage*
0	137	45.67
1	67	22.33
2	49	16.33
3	16	5.33
4	11	3.67
5	10	3.33
6	7	2.33
7	3	1.00
Total	300	100.00
Average:		
Inclusive of NiL	1.23	
Exclusive of Nil	2.27	

The table makes it clear that the largest single group of respondent's families (45.67%) has no school going child followed by those families which have one child (122.33%); two children (16.33%); three children (5:33%); four children (3.67%); five children (33.3%); six children (2.33); and seven children (1%). The reason for being the highest number of families having no school going child have been young age of respondents' family members, migratory character of slum population where children generally live in rural area and non-challant attitudes of parents towards education.

The average number of school going children per family comes 1.23 (including those families who have no school going child) and 2.27 (including those families who have no school going child) which is very low.

To conclude, it can be mentioned that most of the respondents' families have no school going child and among those families which have school going children, most of them have one school going child.

Total Number of Non-School Going Children

The existence of non-school going child in the family shows families lack of interest in education or lack of resources for providing education to children on their part. Keeping in view, the information has been collected and is being tabulated in tabular form in Table No. 4.20.

Table 4.20
Number of Non-School Going Children

Total number	*No. of the families*	*Percentage*
0	163	54.33
1	60	20.00
2	48	16.00
3	12	4.00
4	10	3.33
5	5	1.67

(Contd.)

Total number	*No. of the families*	*Percentage*
6	2	0.67
Total	300	100.00
Average :		
Inclusive of zero category	0.89	
Exclusive of zero category	1.96	

A deep probe into the information tabulated in the table brings out that more than half of the respondents (54.33%) have no non-school child. Out of the families having non school going children, the largest single group of families has one school going child followed by those families which have two children (16%), three children (4%), four children (3.33%), five children (1.67%) and six children (0.67%).

The average number of families having non-school children comes 1.96 per family (exclusive of those families having no non-school going child) and 0.87 per family (exclusive of those families having no non-school going child).

Duration of Stay of Family in the City and Present Locality (Slum Area)

Information pertaining to above mentioned aspects was collected from the respondents in order to know their family's duration of stay in the city and in the present locality. This information is being given in Table No. 4.21.

A deep probe into the information tabulated in this table brings out the conclusion that the largest single group of families (26.67%) has been found living in this city since 5 to 14 years followed by those families who have been found living in this city from 25 to 34 years (21.67%); 15 to 24 years (14.33%), 35-44 years (13.67%), below 5 years (11%), 45 to 54 years (10.33%); and 55 to 64 years (4.33%).

Table 4.21
Duration of Stay of Family in the City and Present Locality (Slum Area)

Duration (in yrs)	*City*	*Locality (Slum Area)*
Below 5	33 (11.00)	67 (22.33)
5-14	80 (26.67)	94 (31.33)
15-24	43 (14.33)	59 (19.67)
25-34	65 (21.67)	38 (12.67)
35-44	41 (13.67)	23 (7.67)
45-54	25 (8.33)	15 (5.00)
55-64	13 (4.33)	4 (1.33)
Total	300 (100.00)	300 (100.00)
Average	24.10	17.40

The average duration of stay of the respondents family in this city comes to 24.10 years.

Regarding duration of stay of family in this locality (slum area), it was found that the largest single group of the respondents' families (31.33%), has been residing in this locality since 5 to 14 years followed by those families who have been living since below 5 years (22.33%); 15 to 24 years (19.67%); 25 to 34 years (12.67%); 35 to 44 years (7.67%); 45-54 years (5%); and 55-64 years (1.33%).

The average duration of stay of respondent's family in this locality comes to 14.40 years.

The above description clearly establishes that duration of stay of the respondent's family in the city as well as in this locality has been quite long.

Prior Living Status Coming to This City

Information pertaining to this has been collected in order to know the migration of family to this place. This information is being presented in Table No. 4.22.

Table 4.22
Prior Living Status Coming to This City

Prior living Status	*No. of the respondents*	*Percentage*
Rural	248	82.67
Town	28	9.33
City	16	5.33
Big city	7	2.33
Metropolitan	1	0.33
Total	300	100.00

An analysis of the information tabulated in this table brings out the fact that a dominant majority of respondents' families (82.67%) has been living in rural areas prior to coming to this place followed by those families who have been living in towns (9.33%), city (5.33%) prior to coming to this place. Thus, it can be concluded that most of the families have been migrated from rural areas.

Proper Living Status Coming to This Slum

This information has been collected and is being tabulated in Table No. 4.23.

Table 4.23
Prior Living Status Coming to This City

Prior living status	*No. of the respondents*	*Percentage*
Slum	67	22.33
Rural	195	65.00
Town	20	6.67
City	13	4.33
Big city	4	1.33
Metropolitan	1	0.33
Total	300	100.00

This table brings out the fact that more than half of the respondents' families have been living in rural areas (65%) prior to coming to this place followed by those families who have been living in slum areas (22.33%); in towns (6.67%); in city (4.33%); in big city (1.33%); and in Metropolitan city (0.33%).

Thus, it can be concluded that most of the families of slum areas understudy have been living in rural areas prior to coming to this slum.

Monthly Expenditure of Respondents' Family

Information pertaining to monthly expenditure of respondents' families has been collected and is being presented in Table No. 4.24.

The table brings out the fact out of 300 families understudy 246 (82%) families have been found that they have been expending nothing on housing. 15.77 per cent families have been found expending below Rs. 100 monthly on housing followed by 7 families (2.33%), expending on housing between Rs. 100 to 300 per month.

Table 4.24
Monthly Expenditure of Respondents' Family on the Following Items

Expenditure (in Rs)	*Items of expenditure (n = 300)*				
	Housing	*Fooding*	*Clothing*	*Education*	*Medicine*
Nil	246	-	8	114	3
	(82.00)		(2.67)	(38.00)	(1.00)
Below 100	47	-	228	63	282
	(15.57)		(76.00)	(21.00)	(94.00)
100-300	7	11	52	37	13
	(2.33)	(3.67)	(17.33)	(12.33)	(4.33)
300-500		34	10	80	2
		(11.33)	(3.33)	(26.67)	(0.67)
500-1000		166	2	5	
		(55.33)	(0.67)	(1.67)	
1000-1500		56	-	1	
		(18.67)		(0.33)	
1500-2000		18			
		(6.00)			
2000-2500		9			
		(3.00)			
2500-3000		5			
		(1.67)			
3000-3500		1			
		(0.33)			

Regarding expenditure on food, more than half of the families (55.33%), have been expending monthly between Rs. 500-1000 followed by those families which have been expending between Rs. 1000-1500 (18.67%); Rs. 300-500 (11.33%); Rs. 2000-2500 (3%); Rs. 2500-3000 (1.67%); and Rs. 3000-3500 (0.33%).

Regarding expenditure on clothing, it has been found

that 3/4th of respondents' families (76.1%) have been expending below Rs. 100 followed by those families which have been expending Rs. 100 to 300 (17.33%); Rs. 300 to 500 (3.33%) and Rs. 500-1000 (0.67%), 2.67 percent families have not been expending any money on fooding, may be because of doing domestic work in other families where they have been getting food also.

Regarding expenditure on education, the largest single group of families (38%) has been expending nothing on education followed by those families which have been making expenditure from Rs. 300 to 500 per month (26.67%); below Rs. 100 (21%); Rs. 100-300 (12.33%); Rs. 500-1000 (1.67%); and Rs. 1000-1500 (0.33%).

Regarding expenditure on medicines, the dominant majority of the respondents' families (94%) has been expending below Rs. 100 per month followed by those families which have been expending between Rs. 100 to 300 (4.33%), and Rs. 300-500 (0.67%). One percent respondents has not been expending nil on medicines.

The above analysis clearly establishes that in respondents' families the main item of expenditure is food followed by clothing and medicines.

Chapter V

Housing Needs and Problems of Slum Dwellers

Housing at affordable price is a major issue agitating minds of the public in these days of spiraling prices of flats in major cities, rapid growth of slums, overcrowding and congestion. At present urban population is around 160 million, distributed over about 3,200 urban areas, including 12 Metropolitan cities. It is estimated that by 2000 A.D. the number of Metropolitan cities may go upto 25. Such a big spurt in the growth of urban settlements will aggravate the severe shortage of shelter and basic services and lead to strains in the political and social fabric of cities.

Acute Housing Shortage

Housing shortage in India is estimated 24.7 million including 5.9 million in the urban areas.

As per estimate of the National Buildings Organisation, housing shortage in the country in 1985 was estimated at 24.7 million including 5.9 million in the urban areas. About 13 per cent of the existing housing stock is Kutcha, and about 19 per cent is semi-pucca. Accessibility of basic services like potable water and sanitation is also unsatisfactory due to great pressure on the existing services that the local bodies are able to provide with limited resources. Again, about 50 per cent of the household live in one room units and about 27 per cent in two room units. In Mumbai, as much as 77 per cent households occupy one room houses and many of them live in old dilapidated multi-storied structures with common amenities. About 35 million people are reported to be living in slums in various parts of the country of which over 13 million reside in Metropolitan cities. In Mumbai, about 50 per cent of the population or 4 million persons live in slums.

It has been appreciated from the beginning that the public sector has the basic responsibility of alleviating housing problem faced by the economically weaker sections and certain disadvantaged target groups. The Government of India introduced a scheme in 1952 for construction of dwellings on rental basis for industrial workers having income upto Rs. 500/- per month.

Housing programme for economically weaker sections was later integrated with the scheme. This provided for loan and subsidy to be given by the State Housing Agencies for the construction of houses at subsidised rent for these categories of the public. Till the end of 1977, about Rs. 125 crores were spent on the schemes and over 185,000 houses were constructed. In 1977, it was decided to transfer these tenements to the occupiers at actual cost on hire-purchase basis in view of the problem faced by the housing agencies in maintaining these tenements at low rents and to ensure proper preservation of these buildings by owner cooperatives.

The Government of India introduced a subsidised scheme for plantation workers in 1956 to assist the plantation employers to provide housing for the workers with the help of loan and subsidy from the Central Government. Over 40,000 houses have been constructed under this scheme in a number of States. The Government also introduced a scheme in 1956 to provide for the rehousing of slum-families having income upto Rs. 350/- per month by the construction of single or multi-storied tenements in major cities. Tenements were constructed by the State Housing Agencies or Slum Clearance Boards and these were allotted at subsidised rents to the slum-dwellers. About 1,69,000 dwellings were constructed in many big cities including Mumbai, Pune,

Sholapur, etc. It has been decided to transfer these tenements also on hire-purchase basis to the existing occupiers in view of the problem of maintenance and low rents. Government has given up the concept of slum clearance in view of the sheer inadequacy of effort in relation to the huge magnitude of the problem, organizational and financial constraints, and the inappropriate nature of the solution. Consequently, the Government introduced a scheme for the Environmental Improvement of Slums in 1972. Under this programme, State Governments were provided financial assistance under plan, subject to per capita ceiling cost to provide basic amenities like community water-supply, community latrines, storm-water drains, street-lighting, and paved pathways. The entire expenditure is subsidised by the State Governments and the scheme is implemented by the municipal agencies and State Slum Clearance Board. Per capita cost ceiling has been increased from time to time and Seventh Plan has recently raised ceiling to Rs. 300/-. It is estimated that about 15 million persons have been provided with basic amenities so far out of estimated 33 million population in 1985. A new dimension has been given to this programme recently on account of the decision taken by a number of State Governments to provide tenure to slum-dwellers in non-objectionable slums, with further facility of assistance for home improvement.[1]

Stabilising Land Prices

City Improvements Trusts and Development Authorities, with the cooperation of LIC and HUDCO, have changed the city skylines.

Apart from these schemes for specific target groups, schemes were introduced for various income groups in 1954. Scheme initially provided for grant of loan by the State Government to individuals in different income groups and co-operatives for the construction of houses. It provided for loans to the State Housing Agencies for the construction of houses within a particular ceiling cost. It is estimated that by the middle of 1981, over Rs. 355 crores were spent for the construction of about 5 lakh houses, under the various types of social housing schemes operated in different States. Apart from these schemes for construction of houses, a complementary scheme of acquisition and development of lands was also operated in order to enable large-scale acquisition and development of urban land to make available developed plots to various income groups or to provide sites for construction of houses by the State agencies. It was designed to stabilise land prices and to promote growth of self-contained composite colonies with all community facilities in accordance with the City's Master Plan.

The main plank of urban land policy in India has been large-scale land acquisition and development by public agencies and the ceiling on land ownership in major urban areas introduced in 1976. The entire basis of construction of sufficient number of dwellings at reasonable price by public agencies was the procurement of land in adequate quantity at reasonable price and developing these lands by the provision of necessary infrastructure. Socialistic principle implicit in this policy was further elaborated statutorily by providing for imposition of ceiling on the vacant land holdings of individuals in major urban agglomerations and takeover of the surplus land for housing and other public purposes.

City Improvement Trusts

On the institutional side, a number of Improvement Trusts were set up in major cities before Independence and these were reasonable for the development of housing colonies in cities such as Delhi, Madras, Mumbai and Calcutta. These Trusts confined themselves to the acquisition of land in identified areas, land development and disposal of plots at pre-determined prices. It was decided to set up State-level specialised agencies for housing or slum clearance to concentrate on the construction of houses for various groups with emphasis on the needs of the poor and mobilise funds for various sources. These agencies were assisted by the State Governments and the national financial agencies like LIC and HUDCO through loans at reasonable terms to take up housing schemes on lands to be acquired by them. At present, State level Housing Boards have been set up by practically all the State and some State Governments have set up additional agencies for special groups like slum-dwellers, weaker sections and for rural housing. Development Authorities set up in major cities also undertake area development and housing. Operation of these housing agencies gained momentum after the establishment of the Housing and Urban Development Corporation, through which substantial funds were made available for various types of housing schemes. These agencies operate on the principle of providing houses at cost much less than market rate for the poor income groups and using part of the profits earned on sale of houses to higher income groups, commercial premises to offset loss incurred on housing for the low income groups.

In Maharashtra, housing schemes were initially taken up by the Maharashtra Housing Board and Vidarbha Housing Board. The Government set up MHADA in December 1977 by combining Maharashtra Housing Board, Vidarbha Housing Board, Mumbai, Building Repair and Reconstruction Board and Maharashtra Slum Improvements Board. MGADA was set up in order to integrate the activities and functions performed by these statutory bodies and provide for a comprehensive and co-ordinated approach to the entire problems of housing and area development. MHADA has so far constructed about 1.7 lakh houses and plots in different urban areas of which Mumbai alone accounts for about 1 lakh dwelling units. MHADA operates through five Regional Boards set up for the Greater Mumbai, Konkan Region, Pune Region, Nagpur Region and Aurangabad Region.

It undertakes various schemes for the construction of

houses and developed plots. Income groups have been recently revised by the Government of India and HUDCO as follows:

(a) E.W.S. : upto Rs. 700/-

(b) L.I.G. : Rs. 701/- to Rs. 1500/-

(c) M.I.G. : Rs. 1501/- to Rs. 2500/-

(d) H.I.G. : Rs. 2501/- and above.

Houses are constructed usually on hire-purchase basis for periods ranging from 15 to 20 years at rates of interest ranging from 7 per cent to 13.5 per cent, depending upon income group. Cost of the tenements to be constructed is subject to the ceiling imposed by HUDCO and ranges from 15,000/- for the EWS to Rs. 30,000/- for LIG, Rs. 1 lakh for MIG and Rs. 2.5 lakhs for the HIG. Down payments ranging from 10 per cent of 25 per cent is required to be paid and the balance is recovered in equated monthly installments. Some dwelling units are made available to the public on outright sale basis. Some schemes for the HIG are taken up on advance contribution basis providing for payment of the cost of the flat during the process of construction. Tenements and plots are allotted on the basis of open advertisement and reservations are available for specific categories, such as serving and retired army-men, physically handicapped, State Government servants, journalists, artists, etc. apart from reservation of 20 per cent for Schedules Castes and Scheduled Tribes. Allotments are made only to persons who have continuously stayed in Maharashtra for a period of over 15 years.[2]

Dwelling Sites and not Pucca House

The total number of landless families which have been provided house sites under the sixth plan has been estimated at 13.07 million.

In order to generate larger number of dwelling units and encourage people to construct their own houses on incremental self-help basis, the State Government has decided to shift the emphasis to construction of dwelling sites rather than pucca house. A major project in this regard has been launched with the assistance of the World Bank in Greater Mumbai and Thane. Accordingly, 65,000 sites are being provided during a period of four years starting from 1985-86. These plots will be made available to various income groups at affordable cost with initial down payment and balance price repayable over 20 years. It is proposed to make available cash loans to the allottees through HUDCO or Co-op. Housing Finance Society, under the active supervision of the MHADA to enable them take up construction.

Similar projects for Sites and Services have been taken up in other major cities also. Construction of township to cater to a population of 6000 has been started in Sholapur.

In order to meet special requirements of the people working in industrial areas, and to serve needs of the industries located in areas developed by the Maharashtra Industrial Development Corporation, residential schemes are taken up in the zones identified by the MIDC. Similar schemes are taken up in areas where there are particular groups of workers such as those engaged in beedi-making or handloom weavers. A major project for the construction of about 3000 houses in Sholapur for beedi workers has been taken by the Central Labour Ministry and State Government. Similar scheme for beedi workers are being started in Pune, Jalna and Kamit. A scheme for handloom-weavers has been started in Nagpur and it could be replicated in other areas with handloom-weaver population.

Repair and Reconstruction

In order to encourage people to build their own dwelling units, the State Governments have devised schemes that cater to people of different economic strata.

Apart from the Construction of houses and dwelling

units, the MHADA is also undertaking a major programme of Repair and Reconstruction of old and dilapidated buildings in the Mumbai Island. The scheme has been operated since 1969 and Government set up a Repair and Reconstruction Board to deal with the problem of periodic collapse of these old building with consequent loss of human life and financial hardship. The Repair Board was later merged in 1977 with the MHADA. About 20,000 buildings were identified for inclusion under the scheme and out of the 7800 have been structurally repaired. Repair cost is being levied on the owners and tenants, out of the cost a Repairs Fund is created. Contributions are made to the fund by the State Government and Municipal Corporation. Apart from structural repairs, MHADA also takes up reconstruction of buildings beyond economic repairs after acquiring them.

The MHADA further takes up construction of transit camps for shifting people from collapsed buildings as well as those which are in dangerous condition. About 20,000 tenements are available in various transit camps. The expenditure on the scheme since inception is over Rs. 150 crores. An annual expenditure of about Rs. 25 to 30 crores is being incurred on the scheme. However, considering the magnitude of the problem of reconstruction of all these buildings, there are definite limits to the organisational and financial capacity of the existing agency. Government has, therefore, passed a legislation recently to provide for the transfer of ownership of cessed buildings constructed before 1940 on application by 70 per cent of the tenants and after acquisition of the building. Co-operatives will then by formed, so as to take up repair/reconstruction through financial assistance by Government agency. This is expected to greatly accelerate the process of repair/reconstruction of old buildings. It must be emphasised here that the conservation of housing stock is as important as construction of new housing in the present context of limited resources and the need to avoid relocation of the original inhabitants of the cities.

The Eighth Plan recognises that social housing increasingly tends to the private sector in a variety of ways for taking up housing in a large measure. Activities of the public sector would be to provide developed sites and to set up housing finance institutions at various levels for provision of finance at reasonable rate for the construction of houses.

Housing in the Eighth Plan

Both the article of 21 of our Constitution and the re-structured 20-Point Programme (No. 14) of our Prime Minister lay equal stress on the importance of housing for the houseless. Shelter for the poor millions still remains a serious challenge in free India.

During the Fifth Five Year Plan the Government realised the importance of a comprehensive policy for housing and accordingly social housing schemes were introduced by both the Central and State Governments. However, in proportion to the staggering back-log of dwelling units, particularly in urban areas, the role of public sector housing has remained marginal. Its activity is restricted to the improvement of slums, direct provision of housing to some of the urban poor and schemes for the middle income group. The State-level public bodies like Housing Boards and Development Authorities and other related agencies have been engaged in providing social housing schemes.

The National Building Organisation (NBO) has estimated that in 1991 there was a shortage of around 2.1 crore dwelling units which rose to 2.47 crore units at the beginning of the Eighth Plan (1990—1995) that is 18.8 million in the rural areas and 5.9 million in urban areas. Apart from the existing back-log in housing, the rapid increase in population between 1990-1995 would generate roughly an additional requirement of housing units to the extent of 16.2 million, of which 12.4 million will be in rural areas and 3.8

million in urban areas. Thus, the magnitude of housing problem is gigantic. There is a need for radical revision of our policy on housing from the point of view of both population projection and backlog in housing. There is also need for a high provision of finance for house construction on a large scale, development of suitable land sites in urban areas, provision of house sites in rural areas, developing and applying low-cost technology in house construction and policies relating to rent control.

While all sectors of economy — the Government sector, the public sector, the cooperative sector and the house-hold sector — would have to participate in housing activities in coordinated manner, the major responsibility for house construction, according to the Eighth Plan document, would have to be left to the private sector. The poor sections of the society need subsidization and assistance in house construction from the public sector. The role of public sector would be three fold: first, to initiate steps to mobilize resources for housing sector on an adequate scale; second, to continue the efforts to provide subsidized housing to segments of the rural poor and to other economically weaker sections (EWS) of the community like slum dwellers and dock and plantation workers; and third, to undertake land acquisition and development in urban areas and provide house sites in rural areas.[3]

Investment in Housing

The total outlay for the housing sector in both public and private sectors has been raised to Rs. 31,458 crores in the Eighth Plan from Rs. 12,991 crores in the Seventh Plan (1985—90). This has been done with a view to reducing the shortage of housing in the country. Also, under the 20-Point Programme, the amount of financial assistance for the Rural House Sites-cum-Construction Assistance Scheme for the landless workers has been revised and a provision of Rs. 577 crores made for the purpose during the Eighth Plan period. Of this, Rs. 36 crore will be utilised to provide house sites and Rs. 541 crores for the construction of buildings. Under this scheme, a developed house site up to 100 sq. yards is provided free of charge to the landless workers along with construction assistance. The amount of assistance for the development of plot has been increased from Rs. 250/- to Rs. 500/- and the construction assistance from Rs. 500/- to Rs. 2000/-.

National Housing Bank (NHB)

The total outlay for the housing sector in both public and private sectors has been raised to Rs. 31,458 crores in the Eighth Plan.

National Housing Bank on the lines of National Bank of Agriculture and Rural Development (NABARD) has already been established.

Urban Housing

The role of Government in the field of "Urban Housings" has to be promotional: the major effort will have to come from the private sector. The Government's role will have to be restricted to the improvement of slums, direct provision of housing to the weaker sections of the society, encouragement and support of housing finance institutions that promote channeling of private resource into housing in a constructive way. As in the Seventh Plan, direct public sector investment is proposed for housing the EWS of the community. The public sector would provide sites and services at the cost price to the beneficiaries. In addition, the beneficiaries would be provided a loan of Rs. 5000/- per unit repayable over a period of 20-25 years at the concessional rate of interest. In view of the scarcity of developed urban land and the cost involved, it would be advisable to limit the area of developed land provided to 25 to 30 sq. m. per house. As the economic conditions of the beneficiaries improve, they will be able to develop the quality of accommodation in due course.

The various social housing schemes in the Plan were formally introduced in the fifties. The income limits for eligibility, the ceiling cost of construction as also the ceiling for Government assistance were fixed in the cities and no revision has been made since then. With the substantial rise in cost of construction, real costs have gone up. Thus an EWS house which once cost Rs. 7500/- may now cost Rs. 12000/- and consequently calls for higher installments. It may then become even more out of reach for the EWS category with monthly income up to Rs. 350/-. Therefore, more realistic criteria have to be formulated. A large number of houses are required in urban areas due to large scale migration of people from the rural areas to the urban areas. The migrated people choose urban areas and settle there itself to attend to their jobs. The Metropolitan cities of India have grown so fast due to migration and housing has been lagging much behind and a lot of people are compelled to live in slums and bastis, even on pavements.

Progress on housing in industrial sector too is poor. The percentage of industrial employees provided with accommodation is 9.8 per cent only.

According to a survey, the total housing stock (tenements) during 1991-92 were 6.05 lakhs in the industrial sector. About 368 industrial establishments contributed to the construction or purchase of the tenements during the year. The number of tenements completed and purchased were 15,776 and tenements under construction were 9,018. The survey states that all India average cost of construction of all types of tenements was Rs. 20,220/- per unit during 1991-92.[4]

Hostels for Working Women

Indian women are much more active in all spheres of national life than their counterparts in most other countries. Today in different parts of the country women take up jobs where they live. Economic pressure is making the traditional prejudice against women working outside the home disappear. More and more women are taking up jobs outside the home. One of the main difficulties faced by such women is lack of suitable and safe accommodation. What the working women need is cheap accommodation with adequate supervision. Voluntary Organizations, Christian missions and educational institutions etc. run hostels for the working women. Some organizations like the Y.W.C.A. All India Women's Conference, etc. run hostels for the working girls in the lower income groups who are unable to take advantage of such hostels.

State/Union Territory-wise Number of Working Women's Hostels

Sl. No.	*State/Union Territory*	*No. of Hostels*	*Capacity*	*Hostels with Day-care centres*	
				No.	*No. of children*
1.	Andhra Pradesh	13	661	2	60
2.	Assam	6	425	-	-
3.	Bihar	3	127	-	-
4.	Gujarat	18	802	3	70
5.	Haryana	14	997	6	180
6.	Himachal Pradesh	12	425	-	-
7.	Jammu & Kashmir	1	50	-	-
8.	Kanataka	27	1698	2	110
9.	Kerala	69	6366	24	665
10.	Madhya Pradesh	45	2145	8	225
11.	Maharashtra	32	1940	4	134
12.	Manipur	6	232	4	130
13.	Meghalaya	2	134	1	15
14.	Nagaland	1	126	-	-
15.	Orissa	9	568	1	10
16.	Punjab	8	904	1	30
17.	Rajasthan	27	1204	7	180

Sl. No.	State/Union Territory	No. of Hostels	Capacity	Hostels with Day-care centres	
				No.	No. of children
18.	Sikkim	2	145	1	30
19.	Tamil Nadu	47	2054	11	315
20.	Tripura	1	20	-	-
21.	Uttar Pradesh	21	1341	6	175
22.	West Bengal	8	369	2	40
	Total	372	22760	83	2399
	Union Territories				
1.	Andaman & Nicobar	1	36	-	-
2.	Arunachal Pradesh	1	25	-	-
3.	Chandigarh	4	454	1	30
4.	Dadra & Nagar Haveli	-	-	-	-
5.	Delhi	12	1463	5	130
6.	Goa, Daman & Diu	2	120	-	-
7.	Lakshadweep	-	-	-	-
8.	Mizoram	1	40	-	-
9.	Pondicherry	2	96	-	-
	Total	23	2234	6	160
	Grand Total	395	24994	89	2559

The Central Social Welfare Board and the Ministry of Women and Child Development have sponsored a scheme of aiding working women's hostels throughout the country. Aiding hostils was taken up by the Government as a preventive measure against the possible exploitation of young working girls in urban areas faced with accommodation problem. Under this scheme assistance is provided up to 75 per cent of the cost of construction of building or purchase of a building for starting a working women's hostal. Working women drawing emoluments upto Rs. 2000/- per minth consolidated are eligible for accommodation in the working women's hostels constructed with assistance from Government of India,. An outlay of Rs. 30 crores has been made for this programme in the Eighth Plan. It is proposed to sanction 300 additional hostels during the Eighth Plan period.

A number of voluntary organisation like the All India Women's Conference and the Y.W.C.A. have built up hostels for working women. In some of the big cities working women who are new to the city may find life in the hostel not so smooth sailing with nostalgia for the hometown or village, and soon they would realise that hostel life provides them greater security and a sense of discipline. Working women's hostels are equalisers of social differences and inequalities and help to sharpen the working efficiency of women.

The decision of a girl to stay in a hostel appears to be nothing but a choice of the lesser evil. She will not face so many inconveniences if the hostels are properly equipped, moderately furnished, spacious accommodation with adequate toilet facilities and varied recreational opportunities and good food in sufficient quantity are provided. The hostels play an important role — girls from various diverse socio-economic classes share common facilities and thus become part of an institution which is acting as an equaliser of social differences and inequalities and in fact shape the girls as individuals who are more efficient in playing their roles as members of the social order increasing the work efficiency of the working women.[5]

Housing and Health

The accommodation in the municipal quarters built for slum-dwellers is not worth its name. Each quarter has two rooms. Each room has to accommodate nearly five to six persons and in some cases ten to twelve members of a single family. The built in area is roughly not more than eighteen feet in length and twelve feet in width. There is a six feet payment at the entrance through which one gets into the first room. This room is used for various purposes. Further adjacent to this there is another apartment measuring eight by twelve feet. The huts of the dwellers built by themselves are of the worst type without any proper accommodation. They are built of mud and stone with a roof of miscellaneous articles like tin sheets and gunny sacks. It is a single room tenement, low roofed and without flooring.

Privacy is almost non-existent in these huts. Parents, children, 'in-laws' and their children and parts of a broken family live in these huts. There is little differentiation in the use of rooms. The dilapidated box-like homes contain crude pieces of badly abused furniture usually acquired secondhand or as gifts. The charpoy full of bugs is one of the most common pieces of furniture found in every house. A few houses possess broken chairs and tables. Most of the houses do not possess even a single pieces of furniture.

The two rooms are small and they have to serve all purposes. There is little differentiation in the use of rooms—kitchen, dining room, living room.

There is a direct necessity of a larger number of quarters to be built by the municipality for these people. When the condition of the people living in the municipal quarters is really pitiable, one can imagine the conditions of those living in mud huts. The municipal quarters are very small and they cannot accommodate a family of five or six. It is a fact that the parents have to sleep along with their grown-up children. The room is shared not only by men, women and children but also by the domestic animals like pigs, cows, sheep and buffaloes. They, by force of circumstances, have to live under the most unhygienic conditions. They are helpless and uncared for. During the rains, they have to move away from their huts to take shelter on the pavement of nearby buildings.

All the people of the area complained about the insanitary conditions of the locality. When questioned what measures the people of the locality had taken to improve the sanitary conditions, they rationalised their answers by saying that they had no time for that work. They further stated that it was the concern of the civic authorities to keep the locality clean and neat.

There is an acute shortage of housing in these slums. Houses properly built are totally absent. The huts are not fit for habitation. They are improperly built, unhygienic and dilapidated. For a family of at least five, the municipal quarters are insufficient and accommodation in them is not expansive enough. It is difficult to reach the houses since roads are meandering and filthy. Uneven roads add to the ugly surroundings of the slum area and especially during rainy days one cannot walk across these slushy roads.

The houses of these people are built in the most ill-planned roads. Huts have come up like mushrooms, anywhere and everywhere without proper perspective. Garbage is dumped right in front of the houses. People have no civic sense whatsoever. They spit in front of their own house. Flies are found everywhere. The people of the area live in dungeons, and lead a horrible life. The environment is most disgusting, hopeless and sickening. This has an adverse effect on the younger generation of the area. Even the domesticated animals are ill-fed and not looked after properly.

In spite of these poor conditions of living, they do not want to move from the area. When questioned whether they would like to move to a cleaner part of the city, their answer was in the negative. If at all they would like to move, it should be only when all of them would be provided with houses in one area. They are very much community-minded. They have become desolate and desperate on account of the fact that they have been uncared for by the public and the civic authorities. They have become pessimists. One person remarked that they would be helped and benefited only after their death.

In the formulation of the strategy for urban development, improvement of slums has acquired a special place. As a long term measure, planned house building with particular focus on meeting the needs of the poor sections of society alone holds the key for curbing the twin problems of squatting and proliferation of slums. The development of small and medium towns as well as big towns in the vicinity of large metropolises in regarded as an instrument for regarding migration to large towns. Reservation of sufficient land for provision of affordable shelter in the form of "Sites and Service" and "Core Housing" are important elements of this strategy. There is a Centrally sponsored scheme providing matching assistance to the States/UTs for strengthening the infrastructural facilities and civic amenities in selected small towns. In the short-term, the only practical way of ameliorating the sub-human living conditions in slum areas is to improve their environment by providing basic amenities. The scheme of Environment Improvement of Urban Slums is being implemented under the Minimum Needs Programme. It envisages provision of a package of basic services for removal of unhygienic environment prevalent in the slums and for the provision of minimum civic facilities to the slum dwellers, namely, drinking water, community bathrooms and latrines, street lighting, open sewers, storm water drains and street paving. The cost of providing these services has been revised to Rs. 300/- per capita during the Eighth Plan. The scale of services provided, varies from state to state. The guidelines do not, however specify the quality of services to be provided. A proper mechanism should be evolved for ensuring qualitative assessment of the work done by the state authorities in improving the slums. For this purpose, field visits should be intensified and improvement brought about in the system of reporting progress.

Details of housing have been presented in ensuing paragraphs on the basis of information supplied by the respondents.

Nature of House of Respondents

Information pertaining to nature of house of respondent has been collected from the respondent in order to know the nature of house in which respondents are living. This information is being presented in Table No. 5.1

The table makes it clear that about half of the respondents have been living in houses without any payment (47%) followed by those respondents who have been living in family homes (38.67%) and rented homes (14.33%).

Table No. 5.1
Nature of House of Respondents

Nature of house	*No. of the respondents*	*Percentage*
Family house	116	38.67
Taken on rent	43	14.33
Living without payment	141	47.00
Total	300	100.00

This brings out the conclusion that respondents are generally living either in free houses or in family houses.

Facilities Available in the House

This information has been collected from the respondents and is being presented in Table No. 5.2.

Table 5.2
Facilities Available in the House

Facilities availabity	*No. of the respondents*	*Percentage*
Electricity		
Yes	131	43.67
No	169	56.33
Source of Water		
Well inside house	2	0.67
Well outside house	15	5.00
Public tap	152	50.67
Tap inside house	50	16.67
Hand pump inside house	13	4.33
Hand pump outside house	68	22.67
Latrine		
Flush	2	0.67
Ordinary	56	18.67
Public	94	31.33
Open space	148	49.33
Types of house		
Cemented	28	9.33
Ordinary	47	15.67
Kachcha bricks	83	27.67
Kachcha bamboo mixed	125	41.67
Tenshed	17	5.67

A close scrutiny of the table reveals that facilities available in respondents' house are as follows:

Electricity : Only 43.67 percent respondents' houses have electricity facilities and rest (56.33%) do not have this facility.

Sources of Water : Half of the respondents (50.67%) have told that their families have been taking drinking water from public tap followed by those respondents who use to take drinking water from hand pump outside house (22.67%); tap inside house (5%); hand pump inside house (4.33%) and well inside house (0.67%).

Latrine Facility : About half of the respondents (50.67%) have to go to open place for defecation of the respondents, who have this facility, the largest single group (31.33%) of them has been using public latrines followed by those respondents who have been using ordinary latrines (18.67%) and flush latrines (0.67%).

Type of House : The largest single group of respondents (41.67%) has kaccha bamboo mixed house followed by kaccha brick houses (27.67%); ordinary houses (15.67%); cemented house (9.33%) and tin shed (5.67%).

To conclude, it can be said that houses in slum areas understudy lacks electricity facility, proper drinking water facility and almost no latrine facility. These houses are mainly kaccha bamboo mixed houses.

Space Available in Respondents House

The collected information is being tabulated in Table No. 5.3 in tabular form. This table shows that in slum areas understudy houses have following spaces:

Table 5.3
Space Available in the House

Space availability	*No. of the respondents*	*Percentage*
No. of rooms		
1	202	67.33
2	89	29.67
3	7	2.33
4	2	0.67

(Contd.)

Space availability		*No. of the respondents*	*Percentage*
Varandah			
	Yes	11	3.67
	No	289	96.33
Kitchen space			
	Yes	37	12.33
	No	263	87.67
Storage space			
	Yes	5	1.67
	No	295	98.33

(i) *Number of Rooms* : Majority of respondents (67.33%) has been found having one room space in their houses. 29.67 percentage respondents' houses have two rooms' accommodation. Three rooms' accommodation has been found in 2.33 per cent respondents' houses and four rooms' accommodation has been found in 0.67 percent respondents' houses.

(ii) *Verandah Space* : Only 11 respondents' houses have verandah facility and rest of the respondents' houses (96.33%) do not have this facility.

(iii) *Kitchen Space* : Only 12.33 percent respondents' have kitchen space facility. The remaining houses (86.67%) do not have this space.

(iv) *Storage Space* : Only 1.67 percent respondents houses have separate storage facility.

To conclude, it can be said that most of the houses in slum areas understudy have one room accommodation. A dominant majority of these houses does not have separate space for verandah, kitchen and storage.

(v) *Use of Rooms* : Room accommodation available with houses in slum areas have been used for kitchen, study, sleeping, sitting and storage purposes.

Information about Locality

The collected information is being presented in Table No. 5.4.

Table 5.4
Information about Locality

Information about Locality		*No. of the respondents*	*Percentage*
Type of locality			
Open		34	11.33
Overcrowded		266	88.67
Clean		10	3.33
Not cleaned		290	96.67
Arrangement of Drainage	Yes	31	10.33
	No	269	89.67
Disposal of Waste Water	Yes	29	9.67
	No	271	90.33
Disposal of Waste Material	Yes	28	9.33
	No	272	90.67

An analysis of information tabulated in the table brings out the following conclusions:

(i) *Type of Locality* : The dominant majority of respondents (88.67%) has reported that their houses are located in overcrowded locality. Only 11.33 percent said that their houses have been in open space.

(ii) *Cleanliness of Locality* : 96.67 percent respondents accepted that they are living in uncleaned locality and remaining 3.33 percent responded that their locality is clean which is almost negligible.

(iii) *Arrangement of Drainage* : Regarding drainage, a dominant majority of respondents (89.67%) has accepted that there is no arrangement of drainage system in their locality.

(iv) *Disposal of Waste Water* : There is no arrangement of the disposal of waste water in respondents' locality as reported by 90.33 per cent respondents.

(v) *Disposal of Waste Material* : 90.67 per cent respondents have maintained that there is no arrangement for the disposal of waste materials in the locality of respondents.

In a nutshell it can be said that respondents' houses are located in overcrowded and uncleaned locality having no proper arrangement of drainage and disposal of waste material.

Availability of Facilities and its Distance for the Living Place of Respondents

Information regarding availability of certain basic facilities such as hospital, railway station, city bus station, main market, post office, primary school, police station and sources of drinking water has been sought from the respondents in order to know about their availability and distance so that the respondents and their families may use them as per needs. The same information is being tabulated in Table No. 5.5

Table 5.5
Availability of Facilities and its Distance

Distance (in kms)	*Facility*							
	Hospital	*Railway station*	*City Bus station*	*Main market*	*Post Office*	*Primary School*	*Police station*	*Source of of drinking water*
Below 1	40 (13.33)	10 (3.33)	181 (60.33)	82 (27.33)	83 (27.67)	244 (81.33)	121 (40.33)	300 (100.00)

(Contd.)

Distance (in kms)	*Facility*							
	Hospital	*Railway station*	*City Bus station*	*Main market*	*Post Office*	*Primary School*	*Police station*	*Source of of drinking water*
1	101 (33.67)	18 (6.00)	49 (16.33)	71 (23.67)	137 (45.67)	26 (8.67)	133 (44.33)	
2	149 (49.67)	46 (15.33)	46 (15.33)	79 (26.33)	80 (26.87)	40 (13.33)	27 (9.00)	
3	10 (3.33)	41 (13.67)	24 (8.00)	58 (19.53)			19 (6.33)	
4		29 (9.67)		10 (3.33)				
5		56 (18.67)						
6		67 (22.33)						
7		28 (9.33)						
8		5 (1.67)						
Average	1.5	4.24	1.01		1.61	1.13	0.76	1.01
Total					300			100.00

The table bring out following facts:

(a) *Availability of Hospital* : About half of the respondents (49.67%) have reported that hospital facility is available to them at the distance of 3 kms. followed by those respondents who have reported the distance of the availability of hospital at 2 kms (33.67%); one km (13.33%); and 4 kms (3.33%).

(b) *Availability of Railway Station* : The largest single group of respondents (22.33%) has reported that railway station is available at the distance of 6 kms followed by those respondents who have accepted that railway station is available at the distance of 5 kms (18.67%); 2 kms (15.33%);

3 kms (13.67%); 4 kms (9.67%); 7 kms (9.33%); one km (6%); below one km. (3.33%) and 8 kms (1.67%).

(c) *City Bus Station* : More than half of the respondents (60.33%) have reported that the facility of city bus station is available at the distance of below 1 km followed by those respondents who have told that this facility is available at the distance of one km (16.33%), 2 kms (15.33%) and 3 kms (8.00%).

(d) *Main Market* : As regard this, the largest single group of respondents (27.33%) has revealed that the facility of main market is available at the distance of below one km followed by those respondents who have reported the availability of this facility at the distance of 2 kms (26.33%), one km (23.67%), 3 kms (19.33%) and 4 kms (3.33%).

(e) *Post Office* : The largest single group of respondents (44.33%) has said that post office is available at the distance of one km followed by those respondents who have reported that post office is available at the distance of below one km (40.33%), 2 km (9.00%), and 3 kms (6.33%).

(f) *Sources of Drinking Water* : All the respondents have told that drinking water is available at the distance of below one km.

The calculated average distances for various facilities such as hospital, railway station, city bus station, main market, post office, primary school, police station and sources of drinking water have been found 1.5 kms, 4.29 kms, 1.01 kms, l.61 kms, l.13 kms, 0.76 km, l.01 km and below 1 km respectively.

The above mentioned analysis clearly brings out that the railway station is for away as compared to other facilities.

Availability of Fair Price Shop in the Locality

98.67 percent respondents have reported that fair price shop is not available in their locality. Fair price shop is available only in 1.33 percent of respondents' locality.

Table 5.6
Availability of Fair Price Shop Facility in Respondent's Locality

Availability	*No. of the respondents*	*Percentage*
Yes	4	1.33
No	296	98.67
Total	300	100.00

Thus, the facility of fair price shop is not available in respondents' locality.

Opinion about Lacking of Facilities

Respondents' opinion was sought regarding the lacking of facilities such as road, bus station, school, college, fair price shop, ration shop, hospital, family welfare centre, sanitation, cleanliness, electricity, public reading system, library, cooperative society, bank, security, park and play ground in their area. The collected information is being presented in Table No. 5.7.

Table 5.7
Opinion about Lacking of Facilities in the Locality

Opinion	*No. of the respondents*	*Percentage*
Road	277	92.33
Bus	270	90.00
School	244	81.33
College	280	93.33
Fair Price shop	269	89.67
Ration Shop	202	67.33
Hospital	198	66.00
Family Welfare Centre	126	42.00
Sanitation	186	62.00

(Contd.)

Opinion	*No. of the respondents*	*Percentage*
Cleaniness	245	81.67
Electricity	172	57.33
Public Reading Room	267	89.00
Library	274	91.33
Cooperative Society	256	85.33
Bank	241	80.33
Security	265	88.33
Park	273	91.00
Playground	282	87.33

The table shows that a dominant majority of respondents has reported the lacking of facilities of college (93.33%), road (92.33%), library (91.33%), park (91.00%), bus station (90.0%), fair price shop (89.67%), public reading room (89.1%), security (88.33%), play-ground (87.33%), cooperative society (85.33%), cleanliness (81.67%), school (81.33%), bank (80.33%). More than half of the respondents have reported the lacking of facilities such as ration shop (67.33%), hospital (66%), sanitation (62%) and electricity (57.33%) 42 per cent respondents have mentioned the lacking of the services of family welfare centre.

Chapter VI

Family and Marital Problems of Adolescent Girls in Slums

Family Relationship

Relationship between people rarely remain static. People change and with these changes some changes in their relationship with others, whether this be with members of the family, personal friends, business associates; or social acquaintance. The time where there is the greatest change in interest and attitudes in the time when there is likely to be the most marked change in relationships with others. Because the relationship of parent to child, and of child to parent, in a state of constant flux, it is essential that all involved make adjustments to this change. When they even greater than those of a child. They now want to live an independent life, even though their actual life is one of depending. They make new social, economic and emotional demands, many of which are not only time and energy consuming for their parents but are so unrealistic that their parents feel they must be checked.

The parent in turn, make new demands on the adolescent. As he is no longer a child, they now demand that he acts as per his age and tries to conform to adult standards of behavior. They expect him to shoulder some of the burdens of the home and may even expect him to contribute to its support. They expect him to consider seriously the matter of his future and to prepare himself for it. When he is too serious, they demand that he should have some fun while he is still young. If, on the other hand, he is fun-loving, they demand that he settles down and takes life more seriously. Because there is a delicate interplay in the psychological forces in the relationships of the home, it is possible to upset this relationship should one member of the family be out of stop with the family expectations. As Berman has pointed out, "Any emotional experience that disturbs the psychic equilibrium of one member of the family will bring about a disturbance in the psychological equilibrium of all members of the family".[1]

As children grew older, there is a relative decrease in warmth and intellectual stimulation from their parents and an increase in parental restrictions. One of the important factors in this change is the birth of a younger sibling.[2] The deterioration in family relationships is not all one sided. Children show more interest in their friends than in the members of their families. They not only prefer the companionship of their friends to that of their families, but when there is a conflict between home standards and gang standards, the child will choose the latter and reject the former. With adolescence, the gap widens. Puberty brings a change in behavior which makes the pubescent child moody, irritable, secretive, uncooperative, and quarrelsome. Unless parents recognize the relationship between such behavior and the changes taking place in the child's baby at this time, they are likely to be lacking in understanding and sympathy. This does not help the child to pass through this difficult stage, and it is apt to increase his already present feeling that "No one loves me." That young adolescents feel that their families do not love them may be illustrated by a study of high-school boys attitudes towards their parents attitudes towards them.

Adjustments to other members of the family likewise normally improve as the adolescent grows older. He can now understand younger siblings better and be more tolerant of them than he could when he was just emerging into adolescence. As he develops more praise and self-confidence, he is less annoyed and embarrassed by the behavior of his younger siblings. He may even develop a parental attitude towards them in place of the antagonistic attitude that prevailed when he was younger. Thus, better relationships are established. With older siblings, he is less envious and, as a result, treats them more casually. He is even more gracious to grandparents and elderly relatives than when he was younger. Normally, in late adolescence, family relationships are on a better basis than at any previous time in the individual's life: whether or not this improvement will occur will depend largely upon the way the adolescent is treated by the different members of the family, principally by his parents.

Marital Problems of Adolescent Girls Related to Family Relationship

The pattern of relationships within any family is highly predictable. Typically the baby is the centre of love and attention. Any disturbing behaviour on this part is forgiven on the ground that he is too young to know better. Before he reaches his first birthday, however his relationship with different family members begin to worsen. This deterioration is shown in a decrease in greater parental restrictiveness and punitiveness and in sibling importance, intolerance and jealousy. Improvement depends partly on maturation and partly on environment-how soon family members, especially parents, recognize that the adolescent him. In late adolescence, family relationships are still better. Normally parents treat their almost-adult sons and daughters more like grown ups and the adolescents themselves become more mature both socially and emotionally.

Effect of Family relationships on Home Climate

The home climate - the "Psychological atmosphere" of the home-varies markedly from home to home. Some homes have a good climate, some a poor climate, and some a changeable climate. Even within a home, the climate may very from time to time for any one individual, its certain to vary for the different children of the family. The home climate is most likely to be poor for the young adolescent because friction with family members is at its peak at this period of his life. Few adolescents, unfortunately, feel that their home climate favour good inter-family relationships. As a result, most are unhappy, critical and fault finding.

Overt Expressions of Friction

The emotional climate of the home appeared to be calm and peaceful, even though there may have been hidden smoldering resentments. Under more demicratic child training, hostilities between family members-old, young, and in between - are openly expressed. The young child commonly expresses himself in physical attacks. Parental nagging, fault finding, and other expressions of annoyance provide adolescents with model for expressing their own grievances. As Ellis and Nye[3] have written :

Nagging shows a strong tendency to run in families. If the father nags, one may predict with good accuracy that the mother will nag also... This lends support to the idea that nagging may be a family cultural trait-an approved and expected technique for controlling adolescents.

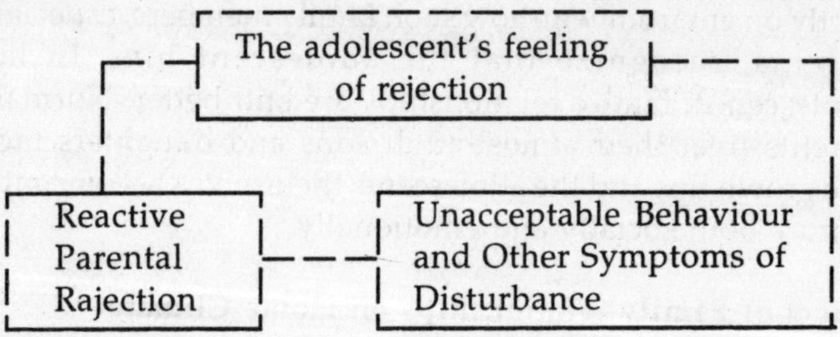

The above figure brings out the vicious circle of parent-adolescent relationships. Adolescents compare their parents unfavourably with the parents of their friends, they nag about being "overprotected" or "deprived" and they find fault with things that are done for them as well as with things that their parents expect them to do for themselves. Boys don't hesitate to tell their brothers or sisters what they think them and why, girls then follow suit.

Effect of Expression of Friction

They are as follows :

? *Parents* : Good parents are deeply hurt by constant criticism from their adolescent children. Mothers are damaged psychologically more than fathers because they come to feel that the years they have devoted to doing things for their children have ended in failure and because they are generally experiencing the physical and emotional crisis of menopause at the time when verbal attacks reach a peak.

? *Adolescents* : The younger the adolescent, more insecure he is and the more ego-deflating any criticism from any source. Expressions of hostility heighten the already existing feeling of most adolescents that they are misunderstood and unloved.

? *Elderly Relatives* : Elderly relatives are hypersensitive to any suggestion that they are out of stop with the times. They are angered by the "impertinence" of young people who say derogatory things to their face. In addition to being hurt, as parents are, they feel indignant.

Conditions Affecting the Home Climate

While family conflicts are more common in every culture at the time when the children of the family reach adolescence, some evidence suggests that they are most frequent and most severe. Of the many conditions and factors that affect the climate of homes in which there are adolescents, the following are the most important :

? *Mutual Understanding* : The home climate during the adolescent year is greatly improved by mutual understanding which is largely determined by the ability of family members to communicate and to enjoy shared experiences.

? *Conflicts over autonomy* : Autonomy is a status symbol of adolescent. It tells his pears that he is no longer a child but has been granted the status of a near adult. Autonomy is also important personally because the adolescent uses it to measure his adequancy to handle his own affairs. If parents deny the adolescent the independence his friends have, he shows his resentment by "parent belittlement". He takes a negative attitude towards his parents. Parents are then likely to reimpose restraints and these will increase the adolescents rebellion.

? *Conflict in Values* : When there is a conflict of values between the adolescent and his parents - and this is especially common when parents are foreign-born or overage-the adolescent tends to reject parental value is favour of peer values. This inevitably leads to family friction with its damaging effects on the home climate.

? *Togetherness* : While togetherness may produce a good home climate when children are young, this does not necessarily mean that it will when the children become more mature. Furthermore, adolescents are under pressure by parents, teachers and peers to be socially active in the school and community. They know that social prestige grow with popularity in the peer group, not with clinging to the family. Young adolescent boys spend more time with their peers and less time with their family than girls. As adolescents become more non-family oriented, outsiders have more influence on their values and decision-making than parents.

? *Parental control* : Studies of the effects of various kinds of parental control reveal that democratic control leads to the least friction in the home while both authoritarian and permissive control tend to be friction instigating

? *Broken Homes* : Parental friction or a breakdown in

family togetherness disrupts the home and friction tends to persist even when the home is broken by parental separation oor divorce. A break caused by divorce or separation is more damaging to the home climate than one caused by dealt.

? *Invasion by Outsiders* : The family is nuclear and adolescents tend to resent the presence of outsiders, be they boarders, part-time domestic helpers, guests, relatives, or step-parents. Thus, homes in which there are outsiders tend to be frictional. Of all outsiders, step-parents and likely to have the most damaging effect on the home climate because adolescents tend to regard them as intruders.

? *Socioeconomic Status of Family* : The socio-economic status of the family is determined chiefly by parental occupations. The mother's occupation has a greater effect on the home climate than the father's. ZIf the parents occupation affects his aspirations if or the adolescents, it will affect the parent-child relationship and thus the home climate.

? *Parental Occupations* : Although the social status of a family is largely determined by the occupation of the father, the working mother is often more important in determining what the home climate will be. The effect of her occupation comes mainly from the disruption it causes in the family's accustomed pattern of living. The employment status of the mother affects various family members differently. The daughter is expected to assume more responsibilities in the home.

? *Parental Aspirations* : When the adolescent comes up to parental expectations, his parents are satisfied and acceptant in their attitudes. This has a favourable influence on the home climate. When the adolescent can't fulfill parental expectations, his parents remind him of the sacrifices they have made and accuse him of not taking advantage of the opportunities they have paovided.

? *Concepts of Family Roles* : When concepts of family

roles change as they do when the child grows older and has wider social contacts, they tend to lead to friction between the adolescent and family members whose appearance, interests, values and behaviour don's coincide with his concept of what they should be. The more unrealistic the adolescent's concept of family roles, the more detrimental they will be to a good more climate.

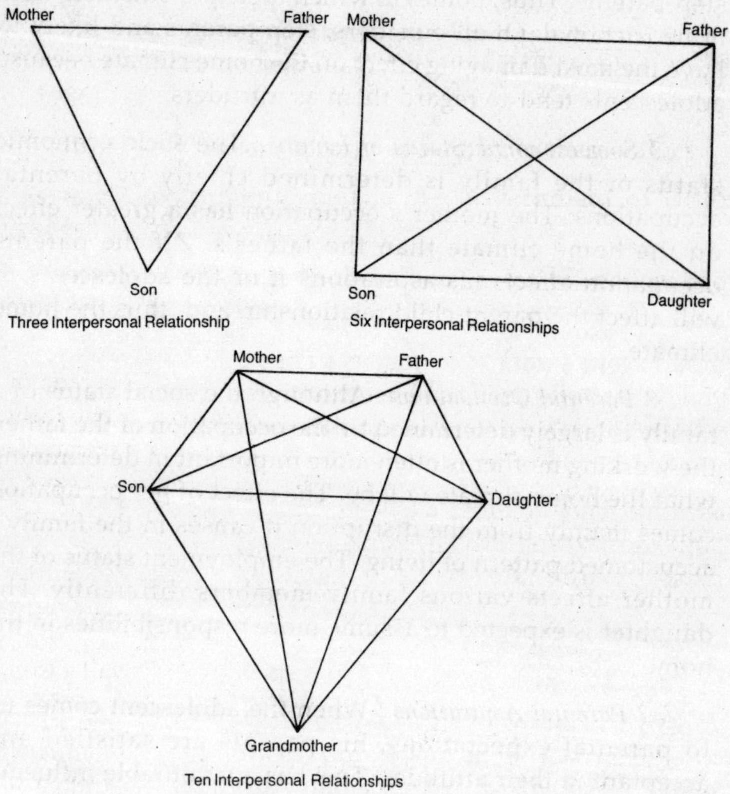

Figure 1 : To determine the number of interpersonal relationships in the family, the formula $X = (Y^2 - Y)/2$, in which X represents the number of interpersonal relationships and Y the number of family members can be used. (Hurlock B, Elizabeth, Adolescent Development, McGrow-Hill Book Company, New York, 1973).

? *Favouritism* : The adolescent's preference for one family member usually causes other members to be resentful, just as parental preference for one child arouses the resentment of the other children. Favouritism contributes heavily to family divisiveness.

? *Family Size and Composition* : How much family size and composition contributes to a frictional home climate depends more on the quality of family relationships than on the number of relationships. Age, sex and status in the family largely deternine the nature of family relationships.

While poor relationships with siblings and relatives may lead to unpleasantness, these relationships have less effect on the adolescent's happiness than an overall unhappy home atmosphere that these poor relationships engender. An unhappy home climate during the adolescents years often causes a permanent rift in the family structure.

Effects of Family Conflicts - Conflicts especially when they are frequent and severe, lead to relationships that are disturbing and deleterious to all concerned and that frequently lead to maladjustments. That is why the large quantity of parent-youth conflicts in our culture today at home were asked why, fully the reasons they gave related to the disagreeable atmosphere of the home created by quarreling. Abnormally frictional have situations lead to maladjustments outside the home as well as in the home. College students who have adjustment difficulties frequently come from homes where the family relationships are bad and where there is excessive friction between parent and child. The individual may become excessively introverted and suspicious of people's motives, he may become an attention-seeker, going to any length to win the attention and affection he feels deprived of at home, are he may even turn to delinquency as a farm of revenge, which comes when he finds that his behavior causes worry or embarrassment to his parents.[5]

While adolescents frequently have as many conflicts with their mother as with their fathers, conflicts with the father come about mainly over matters of great importance to the adolescent, such as his heterosexual relationships and his pending of money. This tends to increase the adolescent's preference for the mother. Even when adolescents are well aware of the preference of mothers for their sons and of fathers for their daughters, this does not seem to change the fact both boys and girls prefer their mothers to their fathers. This may be explained not by the Oedipus complex but by the type of relationship that exists between the mother and the adolescent boy or girl.

The "family field" showing the relationship of boys and girls to family members

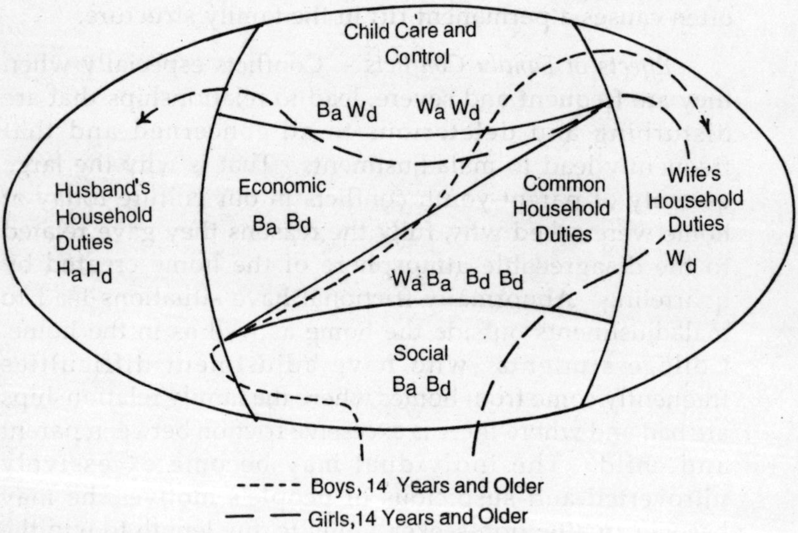

(After P.G. Herbst, 1952)

Relationship between home adjustment & behavior of College Girls.

(After M.D. Woolf, 1943)

Adolescent girls usually have more affection for both parents than do boys, while those who dislike both parents are generally maladjusted. The relationship between the mother and son, during adolescence, is usually stronger than the relationship between mother and daughter, and they, in turn, are stronger than the relationships of either the son or daughter with the father. This may be explained partly on the basis of the mother's preference for the son and partly by the fact that mothers have fewer conflicts with their sons than with their daughter. Strict home training, characteristic of an authoritarian parent, leads to a dislike for that parent, whether it be the mother or the father.

Marriage

Marriage is very directly depicted and defined for the young by the marital relationship of their parents. It is in the home that they first and most continuously encounter marriage, not as a fiction or concept but embodied in the behaviour of their fathers and mothers with and toward one another. Apart from the picture of marriage which the child may build out of inferences from the parent's behaviour, one or both parents may willingly attempt its indoctrinate the child with the conception of marriage as one of the great joys of adulthood or as a status to be warily approached if not altogether avoided.

Some Marital Problems Facing by Adolescent Girls of Slums

- Dowry system
- Lack of employed groom
- Unequal matches - age - difference (25 to 20 yrs) between bride and groom
- Child marriages - in the age of 10 to 12 yrs
- Girl's in-law's bad behaviour
- Separation and divorce are common in slums
- Rigid caste system the choice of marriage partner is strictly endogamous
- Parent's do not give permission of 'love-marriage'
- Parents conservative attitude towards their children embracing new religion through marriage.

Poor parental relationships is a common cause of family friction. Adolescents who feel that their parent's marriage is happy likewise feel that their homes are happy places in which to live. Since deterioration in marital relationships affects the whole family, the home climate may become so emotionally charged that every member is at odds with every other member. It may become so unpleasant for the adolescent that he wants to be out of the house as much as possible.

When parents are preoccupied with their own problems, they give the adolescent the impression that they are disinterested in him. He is hesitant about bringing his periods to his home, not knowing what kind of atmosphere to expect or what sort of reception his friends will get. The most damaging aspect of marital friction is that it is a circular process. The adolescent who is unhappy and disturbed by the emotionally changed atmosphere of his home reacts unfavourably to his parents, his siblings and his relatives, this establishes a frictional relationship with them. Marital friction intensifies, and the circle of bad family relationships grows.

Married people who, as children and adults, had few conflicts with their parents are happier and better adjusted to marriage than those who had frequent conflicts in their homes. The type of adjustment the adolescent makes to his family is going to influence the type of adjustment he makes to his family is going to influence the type of adjustment the type of adjustment he will make to his own family when he is married. Family relationships in the adolescents home also influence his attitude towards children before he becomes a parent.

There are four factors in family relationships which make a happy marriage almost impossible, there are[6] -

1. *Thwarting by Mother,* which makes the boy suspicious of women and distrustful of their motives.
2. *Attachment to mother,* which leads to the selection of a wife as nearly like the mother as possible, or own who is as unlike the mother as possible.

3. *Training,* which results in fear of sex or feelings of guilt about sex matters.
4. *Belittlement of the mother,* by the father, which creates in the boy a contempt for women.

Girls early relationships to their fathers may be more crucial to their adult heterosexual love development than their early relationships with their mothers. Unfavourable relations with their mothers may tend to make them greatly long to be loved by the male they come to have the greatest attachment for, possibly for compensatory reasons. But unfavourable relations with their father may tend to give them decidedly ambivalent attitudes towards their most loved male, to make them want to mother him, on the one hand and to want to hurt him on the other. Unfavourable home relations with both mother and father, it may be hypothesized, may tend to drive girls towards adult love relationships, but tend to make them feel somewhat uncomfortable in these relationships when they are actually experienced.

When a mother, who doesn't love her husband, belittles him continually in the eyes of her daughter, she is doing her best to ensure married misery for her daughter when she grows up.[7]

Attitude of Indians to marriage has come down from the ancient times when it was regarded as a social and religious duty. Even today it is looked up as a sacrament. Indian parents have always considered the marriage of their children as one of their most sacred duties. It's difficult for them to accept the new marriage patterns which are more appropriate for an industrially developed country, such as the right of men and women to choose their own mates, the new emphasis on romantic love and perhaps most difficult of all, breaking down of natural, religious and caste endogamy.

Another factor that is prevailing in the Indian society,

is the parents differential attitude towards the mate selection for sons and daughters. Generally the parents think that they have a greater responsibility of getting daughters married than getting sons married. The view regarding their daughter's marriage is more rigid than for son's.

Whether education has enlightened the parents to change their views towards the mate selection for their sons and daughters and has education been able to break their views on the endogamous nature of marriage for their offsprings.

Traditional arranged marriage is favoured by higher percentage of parents from all the educational level groups for both sons and daughters.

Traditionally arranged marriages are preferred by higher percentage of parents for daughters than for sons whereas allowing children to select their own mate is preferred for sons than for daughters. The similar trend runs to have in all types of families.

Education does not seem to have any impact on the pattern of mate selection by parents for their offsprings. The parents have their own rigid views regarding the marriage of their children whatever may be their educational level. However, it is encouraging to note that from each of the group would allow sons to select their own mates and from each group would allow daughters to select their own husbands.

Selection of mates through advertisement is the recent development in India to attract prospective suitable mates. The parents do not seem to favour it at all.

In India because of the rigid caste-system the choice of marriage partner is strictly endogamous. Due to the impact of western culture and the reforms introduced by social reformers this system is slowly losing ground. Though its pace is very slow, for the city youths who have close contacts with the members of other caste and religion, the rate of their intercaste and inter-religion marriage is gaining ground in the urban areas.

India being a very vast geographical unit with many linguistic groups the people are regional minded. Hence they are rigid about inter-state marriages. A boy from the south getting married to a girl from the north though belonging to the same cost is forward upon by the society. Thus the regionalism is becoming intense even in the selection of mates.

Troughs go to other countries to receive higher education or they migrate in search of better prospects in their career. To avoid inter-religion and inter-national marriages for their children who intend to go abroad the parents get them married before they migrate to other countries.

The tendency of the parents on the whole indicate that the percentage of negative responses to each of the type of inter-marriages is higher for daughters than for sons. Inter-caste and inter-provincial marriages for sons are approved by higher percentage than those who do not. But the negative responses for inter-religious and inter-national marriages even for sons is higher than the affirmative responses. This rigid attitude of the parents can be attributed to their consecutive attitude towards their children embracing new religion through marriages.

Among those who approve of inter-caste marriages for both sons and daughters, college educated parents score higher percentage. However, the percentage for sons are higher than those for daughters in every educational level group.

Percentages approving of inter relations marriages for both sons and daughters are definitely lower than those who approve inter-caste and inter-provincial marriages. The negative response gain majority for both sons and daughters in every group, the highest percentage being found in college educated group. The similar trend in the college educated group is observed among those who say 'no' for the inter-national marriages. The same group shows higher percentage in approving inter-provincial marriages for both sons and daughters.

The better educated are more rigid towards inter-religion and inter-national marriages than towards inter-caste and inter-provincial marriages. The educated parents who may aspire to send their children for higher education to other countries may not want their children to marry a youth of another religion and nationality. They also fear that the children who have gone in for such marriages may not return to their homeland. This may be the reason why most of the educated parents who may have planned for sending their children for higher education abroad don't accept inter-religious and inter-national marriages for their children. The responses of the parents of primary groups and illiterate group though their educational background is poor, show almost nearly equal percentages to that of higher educational level groups of affirmative responses to every type of mixed marriages. These parents may be eager to adopt the reforms based on the Western culture. This may be one of the reasons why these parents are sending their children to English medium schools and also for higher education. They would also prefer all types of inter-marriages, so that they could achieve higher social status. However, the disparity in their attitude towards such marriages for sons and daughters is wider than it was observed in better educated groups.

Parents anticipate that a son will have to become a provider and the daughter will have to become a housekeeper. A modern urban adolescent girl aspires not only to limit herself to be a housewife but also to be a successful earning member of her family. So the adolescent girl equates her role to that of her brother and may not tolerate her parent's differentiation in their function of socialization based on sex role.

Characteristics of the Good Home

Such a home should have the following characteristics[8]-

1. *Affection* - The members of the family like one another and feel tender and loving toward one another. Some homes where affection ebbs and flows, where it flourishes only when the one who is loved is particularly pleasing, or where it is given or withdrawn to reward or punish a child, in the good home this affection is an even, mutual feeling that shows at all times.

2. *Democracy* - In a democratic home there is seldom a condition of subservience to the will of someone else and no feeling that one counts for little in the home organisation. There the adolescent learns self-respect, self-confidence, social responsibility because he is respected and most recognize the needs of others as well as his won and help supply them.

3. *Lack of conflict* - In any home there will be differences of opinion, but in the good home, particularly as the children get older, there will seldom, if ever, be strong, unpleasant emotion arising over conflicting viewpoints or desires.

4. *Comradeship* - The parents come to know their adolescents better the children take joy in doing things with their parents and learn from the ways of adulthood

5. *Good personal adjustment on the part of the parents* - The home where parents are maladjusted will not be the best home for children to grow up in for other reasons as well. For the maladjusted person is usually hard on those he lives with.

6. *Development of the parents* - One can't expect confidence and comradeship between parents and children of the parents are living according to ideas of what is proper, right, or wrong which the children can not in there best judgment accept.

7. *Interest in the children* - Children feel more secure

and more satisfied with their experiences when they know that their parents are interested in them not in any soothing, coddling way, but as one good friend as interested in the ideas and activities of another.

8. *Firm, consistent, fair and objective discipline* - The child will come to understand that there are standards of right action and that there are boundaries for what is right and good. He will know why he should behave in certain ways, and he will realize that punishment is not a matter of the parent but a way of teaching him to do what is right.

9. *A wholesome attitude towards sex and adequate sex instruction* - Parents have made opportunities to give the child sex knowledge gradually and in connection with natural events, such as the birth of a brother and sister. They have answered his questions simply and honestly, without embarrassment and without undue elaboration.

10. *Gradual release of responsibilities to the child* - In the good home, responsibilities are gradually released to the child as he becomes able to assume them. He is given the home duties he is capable of performing and allowed to be on his own wherever this is possible.

11. *It will allow him to take on adulthood as fax as he can handle it* - Parents are used to offering advice which is almost automatically accepted, they are used to protecting the child and to having his full confidence. As a result, it is hard for them to make a sudden change from being parent to the child to being parent to a near-adult.

Every parent should learn early in the life of his children that warm love does not need to carry with it and indeed, should not possessiveness, over-indulgence, complete protectiveness, or authority. The parent of the adolescent must realize that he can love without giving advice, without prying, without being solicitous, and without dominating, and he must remember that such generous love is essential to the adolescent's security.

Respondent were approached to give information and their views related to family and marital problems. The information has been tabulated in tabular forms for the purpose of analysis and making generalization. This analysis is being presented in ensuing paragraphs.

Problems Faced by the Family in case of Marriage

Table No. 6.1 presents these problems. The table shows that the largest single group of respondents (42%) has mentioned dowry as problem of marriage followed by prevalence of child marriage (27.33%), unemployed boys (22%); torture by husband and in laws (17.66%); adjustment problems (10.66%); unstable salary of bridegrooms (8%); and age difference between newly weds (7%).

Table 6.1
Problems Faced by the Family in Case of Marriage of Girls

Problems	*No. of the respondents (n = 300)*	*Percentage*
Dowry	126	42.00
Unemployed boys	66	22.00
Age difference between newly weds	21	7.00
Unstable salary of bridegroom	24	8.00
Torture by Husband and in-laws	53	17.66
Adjustment problem	32	10.66
Prevalence of child marriage	83	27.33

Role of Native in the Marriage of Girls

This information was sought from the respondents for the purpose of knowing the role of natives in case of marriage of girls in slum area understudy. The collected information is being tabulated in Table No. 6.2.

Table 6.2
Role of Natives in the Marriage of Girls

Role	*No. of the respondents (n = 300)*	*Percentage*
Help in searching bridegrooms	33	11.00
Providing stay facility to relatives	35	11.67
Economic help	78	26.00
Help in reception and other work related to marriage party	212	70.67
No role	55	18.33

As per dominant majority of the respondents (70.67%) natives help in reception and other work related to marriage party followed by providing economic help (26.00%), providing stay facilities to the relatives (11.67%) and help rendered in searching bridegrooms (11%). 18.33 per cent respondents have mentioned that natives play no role in case of marriage of girls in their locality.

Thus it can be concluded that natives generally help in the reception of marriage party in case of marriage of girls in slum areas understudy.

System of Marriage

There are various systems of marriage; some marriages are arranged by parents/guardians, some by boys and girls themselves and some are arranged by parents/guardians as per desire of boys/girls. Keeping in this information was sought from the respondents and is being tabulated in Table No. 6.3.

The table clearly establishes that a dominant majority of the respondents (90.33%) has reported that arranged marriages have been performed in their locality may be arranged adult marriage (39.33%) or arranged child marriage (51%). The percentage of responses about child marriages is quite high (57%). 11.67 per cent of the respondents have told about love marriages and five per cent of respondents reported love as well as child marriage.

Table 6.3
Table Showing System of Marriage Prevalent in Slum Locality

System	*No. of the respondents (n = 300)*	*Percentage*
Love marrige	14	4.67
Arranged adult marriage	118	39.33
Love as well as arranged marriage	15	5.00
Arranged child marriage	153	51.00
Total	300	100.00

Opportunity to Express Views about Marriage

This information was collected from the respondents in order to know about the opportunity to express views about marriage. This will establishes that whether adolescent girls are being consulted in case of their marriage or not.

Table 6.4
Opportunity of Expressing Views About Marriage

Opportunity	*No. of the respondents*	*Percentage*
Yes	82	27.33
No	218	72.66
Total	300	100.00

The collected data are being presented in Table No. 6.4 which brings out that a dominant majority of respondent (72.66%) has not been given opportunity to express views regarding their marriage. Only 27.33 per cent of respondents adolescent girls have revealed that they have been given opportunity to express their views regarding their marriage.

Thus it can be concluded that majority of adolescent girls are not being given opportunity to express their views regarding their own marriage.

Reason for not Giving Opportunity to Express Views Regarding Marriage

Information pertaining to these reasons have been collected from the respondent adolescent girls in order to know about main reasons for not giving opportunity to express views regarding the choice of their own life partners. Thus information is being presented in Table No. 6.5.

Table 6.5
Reasons for Not Giving Opportunity to Express Views Regarding Marriage

Reasons	*No. of the respondents (n = 218)*	*Percentage*
Parents' lack of faith in respondent	58	26.60

(Contd.)

Reasons	*No. of the respondents (n = 218)*	*Percentage*
No need of consultation	61	27.98
Traditional values of not consulting girls or boys	24	11.01
Closed nature of society	39	17.88
Prevalence of a view among parents/ guardians that girls can not take right decision	45	20.64
Not giving weight to the opinion of girls	52	23.85
Lack of democratic tradition in family	86	39.44

A close analysis of the table reveals that the largest single group of respondents (39.44%) has mentioned lack of democratic tradition in family as reason for not giving opportunity to express their views followed by no need of consultation (27.98%); parents lack of faith in respondents (26.60%), not giving weight to the opinion of girls in the family (23.85%); prevalence of view among parents/ guardians that girls can not take right decision (20.64%); closed nature of society (17.88%); and traditional views of not consulting girls or boys prevalent in the family (11.01%).

In the nutshell, it can be concluded that main reasons of not providing opportunity to adolescent girls to express views regarding choice of their own partner has been lack of democratic tradition in the families.

Ways of Expressing Views Regarding Marriage

The information pertaining to above subject was collected from the respondents in order to know about those marriages in which respondent girls have to their express views. The information is being presented in Table No. 6.6.

A deep probe into the information contained in table reveals that more than half of the respondent girls (54.82%) have reported that they have expressed their views regarding their marriage through mother or sister. Other ways have been direct conversation with father/guardians (17.07%), through friends/peers (13.49%); and other ways such as neighbors, relatives, elderly person in family etc. (14.63%).

Table 6.6
Ways of Expressing View Regarding Marriage

Ways	*No. of the respondents (n= 82)*	*Percentage*
Direct conversation with father/ gaurdian	14	17.07
Through mother or sister	45	54.87
Through friends/ peers	11	13.41
Other ways such as neighbours, relatives elderly person in family etc.	12	14.63

Thus, it can be concluded that majority of respondent adolescent girls has expressed their views regarding their marriage through mother/sister.

Normal Age of Marriage of Boys/Girls

Respondents were approached about their views regarding normal age at marriage of boys and girls prevalent in their families. The collected views are being presented in Table No. 6.7

A close scrutiny of the information contained in the table brings out that the largest single group of respondents girls (33.66%) has revealed that normal age at marriage of boys and girls in their families has been in the age group of 10-15 years followed by those respondents who have expressed that normal age at marriage of boys and girls has been in the age group of 16-21 years (28.66%); below 10 years (13%) and 22-30 years (9.33%). 12.66 per cent of respondent girls have failed to give response in this enquiry.

Table 6.7
Normal Age of Marriage of Boys and Girls

Age (in years)	*No. of the respondents*			
	For Boys		*For Girls*	
Below 10	28	(9.33)	39	(13.00)
10-15	69	(23.00)	101	(33.66)
16-21	108	(36.00)	86	(28.66)
22-30	42	(14.00)	28	(9.33)
31-44	13	(4.33)	8	(2.66)
No response	40	(13.33)	38	(12.66)
	300	(100.00)	300	(100.00)

Thus, it can be concluded that generally normal age at marriage of boys and girls in respondents families has been from 10 to 15 years.

Age at Marriage of Respondents

The married respondents have been asked to reveal

their age at marriage. These responses have been tabulated in Table No. 6.8.

Table 6.8
Age of Marriage of Respondents

Age at marriage (in yrs)	*No. of the respondents*	*Percentage*
Below 10	16	13.67
10-14	56	47.87
15-19	40	34.18
20-24	5	4.28
Total	117	100.00

An analysis of information contained in the table brings out that the largest single group of respondents has been married between the age group of 10-14 years (47.87%) followed by those respondents who have been married in the age group of 15-19 years (34.18%); below 10 years (13.67%) and 20-24 years (4.28%).

This brings out the conclusion that mostly respondent girls have been married in the age group of 10 to 14 years.

Problems Faced in case of Child Marriage at the Time of Marriage

Table No. 6.9 presents these problems mentioned by respondent adolescent girls. Ignorance of the child has been given as problem faced in case of child marriage at the time of marriage by the largest single group of respondents (47%) followed by other problems mentioned as irresponsibility on the part of parents (20.66%), instability during marriage (19.33%); no legal sanction (18%) and not full marriage due to Gauna and other formalities (15%). 8.66 per cent of the respondents did not response to this question.

Table 6.9
Problems Faced in Case of Child Marriage at the Time of Marriage

Problems	*No. of the respondents (n = 300)*	*Percentage*
Ignorance of the child	141	47.00
Instability during marriage	58	19.33
No legal sanction	54	18.00
Irresponsibility on the part of parents	62	20.66
Not full marriage due to Gauna and other formalities	45	15.00
No response	26	8.66

Problems Faced after Marriage in case of Child Marriage

These problems, as revealed by respondent adolescent girls have been presented in Table No. 6.10.

Table 6.10
Problems Faced After Marriage in Case of a Child Marriage

Problems	*No. of the respondents (n = 300)*	*Percentage*
Adjustmental problems in parents' family	82	27.33
Ignorance about implication of marriage	46	15.33

Mental harrassment and concern	42	14.00
Difficulty in coping up with the new situation	62	20.66
Lack of proper knowledge about married life	51	17.00
Extra burden at tender age	34	11.33
Expectation of maturity at a young age	28	9.33
Improper development of mind and body	35	11.67
Hinderance in education	63	21.00
Early motherhood	74	24.67
The problem of half-married of Vidai has not taken place	34	11.33

According to this table, these problems in order of preference of respondents' have been adjustmental problems in parents' families (27.33%), early motherhood (24.67%); hindrance in education (21%); difficulty in coping with new situation (20.66%), lack of proper knowledge about married life (17.00%), ignorance about implications of marriage (15.33%), mental harassment and concern (14%); improper development of mind and body (11.67%); extra burden at tender age and the problem of half married if Vidai has not taken place (11.33% each) and expectation of maturity at a young age (9.33%).

Expected Age at Marriage in case of Unmarried Respondents

Unmarried respondents are approached to reveal their expected age at marriage in order to know their views about it. The collected information has been tabulated in Table No. 6.11.

Table 6.11
Expected Age of Marriage in Case of Unmarried Respondents

Expected age (in yrs)	*No. of the respondents*	*Percentage*
10-14	39	21.31
15-19	88	48.08
20-24	38	20.76
25-29	14	7.65
No response	4	3.18
Total	183	100.00

This table reveals that about half of respondents (48.08%) expect that their marriage will take place in the age group of 15-19 years followed by those respondents who have told that they expect that their marriage will take place in the age groups of 10-14 years (21.31%), 20-24 years (20.76%), 25-29 years (7.65%). 3.18 per cent respondents have not revealed their expected age of marriage.

This shows that most of the respondents expect their marriage in age group of 15-19 years.

Confidence About Surety of Marriage in Case of Unmarried Respondents

Unmarried respondent adolescent girls were also asked to reveal their confidence about the surety of their marriage. The purpose of this enquiry was to know about the possibility of marriage of all adolescent girls because in slum areas marriage of each and every girl may not take place due to various reasons.

These responses are being tabulated in Table No. 7.12 which shows that majority of respondent unmarried adolescent girls (68.86%) has revealed that their marriage will certainly take place. 18.57 per cent of respondents remained undecided about their response while 12.57 percent of respondents have reported that their marriage will not take place.

Table 6.12
Confidence About Surety of Marriage in Case of Unmarried Respondents

View	*No. of the respondents*	*Percentage*
Yes	126	68.85
No	23	12.56
Can not say	34	18.57
Total	183	100.00

Hindrances in Way of Marriage

Respondents, who have reported that their marriage is not sure, were approached to elaborate causes for this state of affairs. These respondents have been tabulated in Table No. 6.13. This table reveals that a dominant majority of respondents (86.96%) have given dowry as hindrance for their marriage. The other hindrances as reported by respondents have been poverty (52.17%), non-challant attitude of parents about marriage (39.13%), non-availability of suitable bridegroom (34.78%); unmarried elder brother/sister (30.43%); lack of seriousness of marriage due to joint family (26.09%); bad physical appearance (17.37%); and social hindrance due to previous marriage of elders (13.04%).

Table 6.13
Hindrance in Way of Marriage

Hindrances	*No. of the respondents (n = 23)*	*Percentage*
Poverty	12	52.17
Non-availability of suitable bridegroom	8	34.78
Dowry	20	86.96
Non-challant attitude of parents	9	39.13
Social hindrances due to previous marriage of elders	3	13.04
Bad physical appearance	4	17.39
Unmarried elder brother/sister	7	30.93
Lack of seriousness of marriage due to joint family	6	26.09

Problem of Dowry Faced by Family

Table No. 6.14 present information pertaining to above subject in tabular form. The table reveals that a dominant majority of respondent adolescent girls (87.66%) has reported that their family faced dowry problem in marriage. Only 12.34 per cent of respondents have said that their families have not faced dowry problems.

Table 6.14
Problem of Dowry Faced by Family

	No. of the respondents	*Percentage*
Yes	263	87.66

No	37	12.34
Total	300	100.00

Nature of Problem Regarding Dowry

These problems have been presented in Table 6.15. The table reveals that demand for more money has been given by the largest single group of respondents (37.33%) as nature of problem. Other problems have been mentioned as demand for particular things such as cycle, wrist watch, TV, etc. (28.66%); lack of proper arrangement of marriage party (25%), parents' inability to meet the required dowry (24.67%), quarrel about ornaments (23.95%) and no readiness on the part of parents to pay mutually agreed dowry (10.33%).

Table 6.15
Nature of Problem Regarding Dowry

Nature of Problem	*No. of the respondents (n = 263)*	*Percentage*
Demand of more money	112	37.33
No readiness to pay mutually agreed dowry by parents of girls	31	10.33
Demand for particular thing such as cycle, wrist watch, T.V.	86	28.66
Parental inability to meet the required dowry	74	24.67
Lack of proper arrangement for marriage party	75	25.00
Quarrel about ornaments	63	23.95

Initiation of Dowry Problem

Respondents were approached to elaborate the initiation points of dowry problems. These responses are being presented in Table No. 6.16 in tabular form.

Table 6.16
Initiation of Dowry Problem

Initiation	*No. of the respondents*	*Percentage*
At the time of Tilak	83	27.66
After reaching the marriage party	22	7.33
At the time of presentation of ornaments	68	22.66
At the time of Kalewa	56	18.66
After the departure of marriage party	34	11.33
Total	263	100.00

The table reveals that the largest single group of respondents (27.16%) has revealed that dowry problem was initiated at the time of Tilak followed by at time of presentation of ornaments (22.66%), at the time of Kalewa (18.66%), after the departure of marriage party (11.33%) and after reaching of the marriage party at home (7.33%).

Result of the Dowry Problem Faced

Responses regarding results of the dowry problem are being presented in Table 6.17. This table brings out the fact that the largest single group of respondents has reported the presence of little friction (32%) between families of bride and bridegroom, followed by tension between two parties (27.33%) and delay in Vidai of bride (24.66%). 3.66 per cent respondents have reported the breaking of marriage also.

Table 6.17
Results of the Dowry Problem Faced

Problem	*No. of the respondents*	*Percentage*
Marriage is broken	11	3.66
Tension between two parties	82	27.33
Little friction	96	32.00
Delay in Vidai of bride	74	24.66
Total	263	100.00

Existence of Custom of Child Marriage in the Family

This information was sought from the respondents for knowing the prevalence of child marriage in respondents' families which also create a lot of marital problems. The collected information is being presented in Table No. 6.18.

Table 6.18
Existence of Custom of Child Marriage in the Family

Response	*No. of the respondents*	*Percentage*
Yes	141	47.00
No	159	53.00
Total	300	100.00

The table reveals that child marriage has been found prevalent in 47 per cent of respondents' families which is quite significant number.

Reasons for Existence of Custom of Child Marriage

Responses regarding these reasons have been tabulated in Table No. 6.19. These reasons, as revealed by respondents have been backwardness (34.04%); less expensive (29.79%); family belief (20.07%); marriage before puberty (25.53%); following of old traditions (18.43%); and parents feel free from their major obligation of life (15.60%).

Table 6.19
Reasons for the Existence of Custom of Child Marriage

Reasons	*No. of the respondents (n = 141)*	*Percentage*
Parents' feel free from their major obligation of life	22	15.60
Following of old traditions	26	18.43
Backwardness	48	34.04
Family belief	41	29.07
Marriage before puberty	36	25.53
Social pressure	39	27.65
Less expensive	42	29.79

Prevalence of System of Gauna (Vidai After Sometime) of Marriage

This information is being tabulated in Table No. 6.20.

This table reveals that a dominant majority (83.67%) of respondents have reported the existence of the system of Gauna after marriage.

Table 6.20
Prevalence of System of Gauna After Marriage

Response	*No. of the respondents*	*Percentage*
Yes	251	83.67
No	49	16.33
Total	300	100.00

Period After Which Gauna Took Place

The responses pertaining to above mentioned subject have been presented in Table No. 6.21.

Table 6.21
Period After which the Gauna usually Took Place

Period (in months)	*No. of the respondents (n = 251)*	*Percentage*
Immediately after marriage	53	21.11
Below -24	48	19.12
25-48	43	17.13
49-72	39	15.53
73-96	28	11.15
97-120	18	7.17
121-144	22	8.76
Total	251	100.00

The table reveals that the largest single group of respondents has revealed that Gauna ceremony in their family usually takes place immediately after marriage (21.11%), followed by those respondents who have report that this ceremony usually takes place within 24 months after marriage between 24 to 48 months (17.13%); between 48 to 72 months (15.53%); between 72 to 96 months (11.15%); between 120 to 144 months (8.76%); and between 96-120 months (8.76%).

Chapter VII

Educational Problems of Adolescent Girls in Slums

Education for women seems necessary for various reasons. Since in our country, the role of women in household activities is most important and total burden of household duties rests upon women who perform duties like members of the family. Therefore for the development of family, society and the nation, it is highly desirable and inevitable to educate the women. Education is a primary and powerful tool for a person to develop his ability and perform all duties given by the family, society and even the nation. A child's education starts from his mother at the home. Hence, mother's education must be compulsory so that she could understand all the things in right way and direct her children in correct direction. In Mahatma Gandhi's words: "If you educate a man you educate an individual. But if you educate a woman you educate entire family".[1]

The nature of education in India during the ancient period was sacred and informal. Its door was closed for women of common families. It had elite orientation. From the very beginning of the 19th century, the importance of education, as the most significant instrument for changing women's status, was realised. Social reformers also emphasized the crucial importance of female education to improve their status in society. However, the main purpose of women's education was not to make them efficient and active units in the process of socio-economic and political development but to make them more capable of fulfilling their traditional roles in society as wives and mothers. In other words, education for women was regarded as a means to improve their status within the family and not to equip them to play any role in the wider social context. The absence of any economic compulsion was in fact, one of the main reasons for the slow progress of women's education in this country during the pre-independence period. But in the post-independence era women were given equal status and importance of their education as realized. After independence there has been de-elitization of educational facilities. The education of women at various levels has expanded more rapidly but is still far from satisfactory. Under the new education policy (1986) perhaps for the first time Government of India has accepted that the development of female education in the country was inadequate. It observes: "It is clear that despite considerable acceleration in the recent years because of deliberate measures to facilitate their (Girls) education, they are still very behind the boys. To a great extent this disparity is more the result of economic and cultural biases of society than the accessibility of educational facilities. Many parents still hesitate in sending girls to educational institutions and are particularly averse to those in which there are no women teachers. Even though the performance of girls compares favourably with that of boys, relatively fewer girls seek admission to professional courses, other than those pertaining to medicine, teachers' training and nursing."[2]

Since measures such as mid-day meals, free supply of uniform and books and even central assistance to nine educationally backward states for the appointment of women teachers in single teachers schools have not yielded significant results as yet. Consequently, certain new approaches, such as the setting up of part-time schools and non-formal education centres, payment of opportunity cost, compensation to parents who forego the support of children while they are at school, effective management of schools and exercise of evaluation control on teachers have been taken up. *Aganwadi scheme* has also been launched. In this scheme girls would be able to come to the school with siblings and *Anganwadi* will take care of them.

Adolescent Boys and Girls

It seems a good idea to start with a list of problems that trouble adolescents. Many of these problems are at least partially solved, one way or another, during the high school years. Some of them are so troublesome that pupils cannot make much academic progress, even when they very much wish to do so. The list that will be presented on the next pages is based upon a number of studies concerning the typical problems is detail. It has been made so purposely in order that one may see the problems in as concrete form as possible. The figures in Table-A are percentages and are taken from several different sources. Some items were mentioned in one study, in only which case the figure comes from that one other items appeared in two or more reports, in such instances, the per cent from all of them have been averaged. These figures are only approximations of frequency and are included because they provide a rough estimate of how common a difficulty is among adolescents. An average student in high school will have at least a dozen such problems, many will have more of which however, only two or three are basic, the rest being pyramided on top of the fundamental ones. The list includes problems mentioned by more than 25 per cent of the adolescents.

Table A - Outstanding Problems of Adolescents

I. Adjustment to School Work:

1. Not spending enough time in study
2. Worrying about examinations
3. Afraid to speak up in class discussions
4. No interest in some subjects
5. Just can not get some subjects
6. Afraid of failing
7. Wanting advice on future plans
8. Worrying about grades/numbers

9. Trouble with oral reports
10. Often feel restless in class
11. Don't like to study
12. Trouble with mathematics
13. Not getting assignments in one time
14. Can't kept mind on studies
15. Unable to express self in words

II. Social—Psychological Relations :

1. Wanting to improve appearance
2. Trouble in keeping a conversation going
3. Wanting to be more popular
4. Too few dates
5. Worrying how I impress people
6. Wanting to learn how to dance
7. Wanting more time to self
8. Getting into arguments
9. Not being attractive to the opposite sex

III. Personal—Psychological Attitudes:

1. Wanting a more pleasing personality
2. Worrying
3. Feelings too easily hurt
4. Losing temper
5. Forgetting things
6. Afraid of making mistakes
7. Day-dreaming
8. Can't forget some mistakes that have made
9. Getting embarrassed too easily

10. Taking something too seriously
11. Being nervous
12. Not taking something seriously enough
13. Sometimes wishing never to have been born

IV. Finances :

1. Wanting to earn some of own money
2. Needing to learn how to save money
3. Having to ask parents for money
4. Needing a job during vacations
5. Wanting to buy more of own things

V. Health :

1. Poor complexion or skin trouble
2. Being overweight
3. Weak eyes

VI. Home and Family :

1. Talking back to parents

Money became slightly less important for boys but lightly more so far girls. Personal problems are judged to be one step more important for boys and one step less so far girls. Health as a centre for concern dropped out of the boys' first five choices and reappears for the girls being approached; this particular worry will recede still further. The outstanding change, however, is in the realization of both boys and girls that they have to study and that study involves a number of problems they have not yet solved.

As can be appreciated from the nature and number of the problems listed in Table A, adolescence is a period of great insecurity and instability. If a teacher keeps these problems in mind, he can contribute to their solution through his procedures and assignments. The main force however, that cures an adolescent of his difficulties is more growth and more living. Often a pupil does not realize that his difficulties are not permanent. He sees no end to them nor does he sense their relation to his stage of development. A teacher can often relieve a good deal of strain merely by telling a pupil that his troubles will soon pass. He does not need to add that the present problem will be replaced by another.

Mental Health in the School Room

The secondary school teacher of today is responsible for teaching subject matter, just as teachers have always been, but in addition he is responsible for improving his pupil's mental health. This section contains suggestions for the maintenance of a serene emotional atmosphere in the class-room.

Adolescent's Problems in the School[3]

Children regularly showing more than one or two such behaviour tracts as those to be listed are showing clear symptoms of emotional or nervous difficulty. These are the danger signals. The teacher's task is to make sure that they are not flown in vain.

Physical Symptoms : Frequent headaches, attack of nausea, dizziness, loss of weight, loss of appetite, habitual twitching of muscles, grimacing, nail biting, stammering, lack of coordination, sudden blushing or paling, frequent complaints of aches or pains, obesity, mannerisms, rigidity, constant restlessness, chronic fatigue, nervousness, affectations or posturings, jumping at sudden noise, inability to stop talking.

Symptoms of Emotional Immaturity : Dependence on teacher, frequent requests for help, efforts to attract teacher's attention, crushes on teachers, efforts to curry favour with teacher, behaviour too young for age, irresponsible behaviour, mischievousness, frequent interruptions in class, unwillingness to state an opinion, preoccupation with marks.

Symptoms of Social Inadequacy : Excessive shyness, lack of self-confidence, preference for remaining alone, overt rejection by other pupils, lack of friends of either sex, avoidance of members of opposite sex, absence from school parties, homesickness, chronic attitude of insecurity or anxiety, refusal to take part in games, tendency to stay alone at recess or to go home alone from school, refusal of rewards, expectations of special privilege as a right, snobbishness, efforts to join groups where not wanted.

Symptoms of Abnormal Emotionalism : Frequent absorption in day-dreaming, irrelevant answers to question, tendency to worry unduly, lack of voluntary participation in class, absent mindedness, neediness, melancholy or apathy, unusual sensitivity to annoyances, tendency to have feeling hurt, extravagant expression of any emotion, marked distress over failures, frequent bad dreams, hang dog attitude of guilt.

Symptoms of Exhibitionism : Teasing other pupils, pushing them, effusiveness, exaggerated courtesy, constant bragging about exploits, frequent attempts to dominate younger pupils, frequent blaming of failures on accidents, frequent bluffing, attempting either far too little or far too much work, showing off.

Symptoms of Intellectual Involvement : Marked pressure of ideas that crowd forward so fast that one sentence is left unfinished as another is begun, marked slowness of answers to questions, frequent breaking off of speech in the middle of sentence, apparent blocking of ideas, explosive tone in argument, inability to grasp the basic ideas of a course, false interpretations and accusations of others, constant negative criticism of others, rationalization and projection of failures, "chip-on-the-shoulder: attitude, marked suspiciousness of other people's motives, interest in school work to the exclusion of everything else.

Symptoms of Antisocial Tendencies : General attitude of aggressiveness in all relations, insolence, frequent loss of temper when corrected, destructiveness of school property, defacing of books, bullying, abusive or absence language, undue interest in sex, dirty-stories, writing obscenities on walls, showing phonographic pictures, fierce resentment of authority, bad reaction to discipline, "hoodlum" behaviour whenever unsupervised, irresponsibility, lying, cheating, swiping things - profound dislike for school work, delight in non-intellectual competitions.

Fears Caused by School Work : Three fears are so common that they sometimes seem natural and unavoidable accompanishments of school work: fear of teachers, fear of examinations, and fear of talking before class. None of these is necessary, all are destructive to either progress in school or normal personal development, and all are learned from experiences in school. Moreover, the whole atmosphere of the examination room is likely to be gloomy. It is not the current notion that examinations should be fun and should challenge the interest and abilities of the students. Fear of talking in class is common among adolescents, especially among boys, perhaps because their voices are changing. If pupils are required to stand when talking, they may be embarrassed by their own awkwardness. Except for the occasional student who is shy in nature, a good teacher should be able to eliminate this fear by making class work informal and by giving special help to those who are apprehensive.

Control of the Class : Class control should be constructive i.e. it should lead the pupils to control themselves. Its objective is not quietness but the creation of an environment in which pupils can grow in both achievement and personality. The modern theories of control condemn the use of fear or intimidation in any form and not only on humanitarian grounds. Fear leads to rigidity, not relaxation, it introduces a destructive emotion into what ought to be a constructive relationship, it prevents learning, it does not lead to a healthy attitude of mind, it favours the growth of all manner of escape mechanisms. In short, except for producing quiet, it is useless. The latest way of describing the best form of control is to call it "permissive", "accepting" and "nondirective". A teacher is "permissive" if he has few rules and if he doesn't demand routinized school room manners from his pupils. He is "accepting" if he lets the pupils act naturally and if he remains unruffled in the face of whatever conduct the natural behaviour produce. He is "nondirective" if he does not tell his pupils what to do but sets before them a problem and then lets them derive their own solutions. The good modern class-room is not especially quiet. It is a hive of industry in which most of the pupils are engaged in doing something useful and in minding their own business.[4]

Over 30 years ago, an extremely important investigation was made into the attitudes of teachers of clinical psychologist toward common types of misbehaviour; including whispering, inattention, careless work; impertinence, defiance, temper, day-dreaming, over activity, cheating, laziness and rudeness. The total comes to 51 different forms of offensive or kinds of personal traits that interfere with peace and order of the class-room. The average boy showed ten of these reactions or characteristics, the average girl six. The most maladjusted children averaged 17, the chronic liars and thieves averaged 19, and the aggressive delinquents 21. The investigator asked several teachers as well as a group of mental hygienists to rate the seriousness of each offense. The two sets of rating almost contradicted each other, as indicated in Table B. The correlation between the two rating was -0.05. It was suggested that the teachers were rating as most serious the traits and reactions that were annoying to them rather than those that were worst for the pupil is development. The hygienists felt that there was always hope for the younger who fought back but not nearly as much for those who had already withdrawn from life. The investigation with some minor variations, has been repeated at least three times. Presumably the ratings of hygienists and teachers should not correlate perfectly, since they are estimating the importance of a given reaction by different criteria and each has something to add to the others evaluation. The teachers have probably become less interest in maintaining order and more interested in developing normal personalities among their pupils.

Table B
Misdemeanors in school

	Teacher's ratings	Mental Hygienist's ratings
	Immorality	Shyness
	Dishonesty	Lack of participation
	Impertinence	Oversensitiveness
	Defiance	Suspicion
More serious	Temper	Day-dreaming
	Rudeness	Imaginative lying
	Shyness	Impertinence
	Lack of participation	Defiance
Least Serious	Oversensitive-ness	Temper
	Suspicion	Rudeness
	Day-dreaming	Whispering
	Imaginative lying	Restlessness

Application of Mental Hygiene : Although the actual instruction in mental hygiene is the responsibility of one or two teachers who are especially equipped for giving it, every teacher needs to make what contributions he can make to the solution of typical problems and to the maintenance of mental health. A pessimistic outlook about the future does nothing to improve learning, and it is an unnecessary emotional load for a lad to be carrying around with him.

One of the writers was once in a class in Calcutta when she decided that the whole subject was impractical and useless, but it was too late to withdraw without the teacher's permission. Some teachers are in a position to make assignments that will throw light upon such perennial problems as the antagonism between generations or the intense youthful love affair. Many novels present these problems, with or without solution in readable and interesting form. If a social studies teacher finds a good deal of prejudices and misunderstanding in the class, he can organise any of a half-dozen projects that are aimed at the decreasing of ignorance - which is a considerable element in the creation of unfavourable attitude. Each teacher should apply the principles of mental hygiene to his own instruction and should use assignments, as and when possible, to aid in the normal development of the pupils and in the solution of their problems.

Provisions for Emotional Outlets[5] : Another important contribution of the school to emotional stability is the provision of adequate outlets for the easily aroused emotions of adolescents. It is better for all concerned if, by providing frequent outlets, the school allows emotions to be expressed as they are generated so that a feeling that must in the interest of others be temporarily suppressed, will soon be worked off. Such outlets are of various types.

Fortunately for mental hygiene, man is a talkative creature and finds it possible to work off much of his tension by merely talking. Modern school methods provide adolescents with abundant opportunities for conversation. Much work is done by committees of students who plan their assignment, talk over what each has to contribute; and work out a joint report. These informal groupings produce relatively little tension and provide an excellent means for the draining off of destructive emotion and the expression of integrative feelings. Since emotions generate muscular tension, practically anything that requires exertion acts as a relief. Games of all sorts give excellent opportunity to work off pent up feelings generated either in or out of class. If every pupil in a high school has some agreeable form of exercise during his last period in school, or after school, he is automatically provided with an outlet of a socially accepted sort. Kicking a football is just as good as kicking a chair and much better than kicking the cat. Games may also act as compensatory activities for those pupils whose academic work is poor but whose athletic skills are superior. Any kind of extracurricular activity may also function in the same way, even though little or no physical exertion is involved. Such developments distract the pupils mind from his worries, provided the activities are interesting to him and he does not find them too competitive or too difficult. Then, too, they offer such opportunities for emotional expression as singing, acting, or pursuing an emotionally satisfying hobby. If a boy has a lively interest in electronics, for instance, he may be able to work off during the time he spends with the electronics club, the feelings of inferiority and discouraged he has developed earlier in the day because his English composition was unsatisfactory. A girl may be able to express her drives for domination and prestige by making a stunning poster to support an appeal for funds on behalf of some charity - fierce resentment of authority, unwillingness to conform to regulation, bad reaction to discipline, "hoodlum" behaviour whenever unsupervised, irresponsibility, frequent minor delinquencies - lying, cheating, swiping things—profound dislike for school work, inability to profit from experience, delight in non-intellectual competition.

Adolescents as a group have a great many problems, and even individual boys and girls have more than a few the school should certainly help them in solving those that are most pressing. As time goes on, teachers are becoming more and more concerned with the needs of their pupils and with the importance of the emotional atmosphere within their classrooms. They are developing a mental hygiene point of view that should contribute a good deal to the normal growth of their pupils. Whenever possible, the regular assignments should be selected to help student in either expressing or solving their difficulties.[6]

Majority of the parents in all types of families seem to adopt the method of advising when the child is wrong and reward by praising when he is right. This psychological approach of disciplining the children is a strong link in a healthy parent adolescent relationship. The analytical study on the goals of education as viewed by adolescent revealed that majority of them on the whole, agreed to each of the four different goals suggested to them - to provide for economic security, to achieve higher status in society, to be a cultured man, to turn into a good citizen. But a comparative analysis of their responses to different goals revealed that overwhelming majority of them agreed that the goal of education as to turn one into a good citizen.

The views of the adolescents of the parents of different educational levels on different goals of education showed negligible difference and the pattern of their views was almost similar. This may be due to the fact that adolescence is a period when idealism is natural and materialistic goals are despised. Parent's education does not seem to hold any influence on adolescent's views on goals of education as their views show a uniform pattern.

Since goal of citizenship has evoked such massive response from the students, this should be fruitfully used for nation building. If we emphasize socially responsible behaviour, we will be more likely to have a larger preparation of good citizen in the future. "A citizenship between project" can be established by parent - teacher associations to harness this goals of adolescents.

The Basic Needs

The school should give each boy and girl[7] a sense of:

Security : The school has at least three major ways of

contributing to the adolescent's sense of security, accepting him, ensuring him to freedom from mistreatment and enlarging his experiences. These are the adolescent's due and no school can be called a proper school for the adolescent if it fails him in these.

Acceptance : We all know what is meant when it is said that a young person is rejected by his parents or by his group-they don't like him, they don't want him around. Such rejection may be expressed very plainly in action; or it may be felt but outwardly concealed. In either case the rejected person is likely to be aware of his status, far even when those who reject him endeavor to hide their feelings, there are usually many subtle indications of the true attitude.

Fair Treatment : Just as the adolescent has a right to acceptance by the adults who work with him, so he also has a right to fair treatment from them. He does not always get it when one group of people have absolute jurisdiction over another group, there is always possible the misuse of authority and in school this takes the form of "picking on" a student, sarcasm, harsh punishment, and discrimination of various kinds.

Rich Experiencing : The adolescent boy of long ago knew what the elements of his life were. He knew the people he would associate with outside the family, indeed he had known them all his life. He knew how he would spend each day, for the pattern of daily living changed little from year to year. He knew what his reactions would be like. The unknown often appears frightening and hazardous even though it actually may have no harm in it whatever. It is for this reason that we say that it contributes to the adolescents sense of security to become as widely acquainted as possible with the many friendly and pleasant aspects of living which are available to him. The school too often depends almost entirely on giving the adolescent "book-learning" experiences and little else.

The School Should Give the Adolescent a Sense of Worth: The school must let the adolescent group. It often forgets how many times there are when the adolescent can be treated as an adult. Instead they tend to treat him with protectiveness and circumvent him with restrictions as they would a child, and he reacts to the frustration of his desire for importance with rebellious behaviour. The adolescent feels similarly mistreated when he is reduced to a state of childhood which he has actually grown beyond. It is easiest for the teacher to teach traditional subject matter in the traditional manner, letting the students adjust as best they can to the method and material used, rather than making a careful adjustment to the needs and abilities of the students.

The School Should Help the Youth Secure Companionship and Affection : Cannot stress too much the importance to the adolescent of happy social relationships, both with adults and with his own age group. Teachers should be friendly and interested in every one of their students, and opportunity should be given to boys and girls to be together in many different kinds of informal situation. A class can be socialized through whole class discussion, small group discussions, committee work, and group or whole class projects or through the class's having lunch together; dinner together, a picnic or something similar. Noon-time is usually an occasion for informal social activity, which is good in itself, though some schools feel it wise to provide organised games and dancing at this time for those who have their lunch at school The cafeteria too, should be made attractive for it is another place where students can enjoy each other's companionship; particularly if they may eat at leisure in pleasant surroundings.

The School Should Provide Variety : There are so many worth-while interesting activities for the adolescent to engage in and so many methods of learning - trips, group work, movies, panel discussions, demonstrations, wire recording, actual participation in community affairs, dramatizations, individual projects - that every boy and girl should look forward to the day at school as something interesting and even exciting.

The School Must Promote Physical Well-Being : Yearly health examinations, a health counsellor, medical and dental care without cost and without publicity to those who need it but cannot afford it, physical education that is helpful and appealing enough to establish lasting interests and habits, a cafeteria with healthful foods very attractive all of this and more might be considered in helping the adolescent be and stay healthy and vigorous.[8]

The future career of the adolescents depend upon their educational plans which are chalked out by them under their parent's guidance. These plans are based on the degree of interest of the parents and of the adolescents towards the career they aspire. Their interest is to a great extent influenced by the social background of the family.

Educational plans depend on the adolescent's self-concept which is the product of interaction, among others, between parents and himself. It is generally accepted that an individual's concept of himself originates in the perceptions and expectations of his parents. Parents have expectations not only for their children but also of themselves as parents. The expectations, values and goals of the parents which are the product of their educational standard are among the important factors which have an influence on the self-concept of the adolescents.

To study the goals of education as viewed by adolescents, it is essential to know the cultural perspective of the family in which he is reared. The parents are the transmitters of cultural to their offsprings. They orient the child with the values of education. Based on this assumption, the adolescents were asked to give their views on each of the goals of education suggested to them. The four goals are given below[9] :

(1) The goal of education is to provide economic security.

(2) The goal of education is to achieve higher status in society.

(3) The goal of education is to be a cultured person.

(4) The goal of education is to turn into a good citizen.

Majority of parents agree that the goal of education should be to make the children good citizens. An almost equal number of them said that education should be aimed at making the children cultured persons. In the comparative study of the views of the parents of different educational levels on the goals of educations, one significant factor observed was that higher percentage of the parents of higher educational level agreed to the three goals - to provide economic security, to achieve higher status in society and to be a cultured person. Comparatively, the lower educated group showed lower per cent for the above mentioned three goals. But the some group showed higher percentage for the goal — to turn children into good citizen. Similar views expressed by the adolescents of the parents of low educational levels were observed, majority of them said that education should make them into good citizen. A citizenship education project if established with the cooperation of the parents and their adolescent children, can prove to be a successful programme for bringing out a generation of good citizens.

The expectations of the parents about the future of their sons and daughters also supported the fact that they want them to be respected citizens. The same trend was observed among those who wanted their children, both sons and daughters, to reach a high social standing in life. At the other end, it was observed that higher percentage of the parents of higher educational level than that of lower educational level wanted their children to lead a financially secure life and also be outstanding in their chosen field in life. The educated parents, already having social position, are for materialistic achievement of their children whereas the attitude of the illiterate and low educated parents is for a socially respected life for their children because they lack it themselves.

Neither the parents nor the teachers can singly succeed in their efforts to help adolescents students attain their developmental goals. Through regular school visits by the parents and through parent-teacher associations and conferences, parents and teachers may becomes more understanding of adolescent problems in school education. Many programmes can be arranged to discuss the progress of children and ways and means a guiding them on proper scientific lines. Apart from discussing the children's progress, such programmes may enrich the parents' own lines. Though the main functions of parent-teacher association would be to assess student's progress and solve student's problems, they can accomplish several other social purposes such as [10] -

(1) establish a friendly relation between the parents and the teacher.

(2) help the parents understand their own child better,

(3) help the parents understand what the school is trying to do for the child,

(4) Acquaint the teacher with home conditions that may be affecting the child's behaviour and progress in school.

(5) Enable the parents and teachers to plan together who they can make the home, the school and the neighbourhood environment conductive to the best development of their children.

Apart from the interest of the parents in the school education of their children, the extent of their interest in their children's participation in extra-curricular activities is considered essential for the social development of the adolescent children. The analysis of this aspect revealed that majority for the parents preferred both their sons and their daughters to participate in debates and other literary competitions. But a wide difference was observed in the parent's attitude towards sons and daughters participating in activities like going for picnics and outstation camps. Daughters are not encouraged to participate in these activities as sons are. The parents should also see that differentiation is minimised between son's and daughter's participation in extra-curricular activities, otherwise, it may lead to personality problems due to sex discrimination by the parents.

If education is the ladder for upward social mobility in a democracy, if it increases the level of economic and social competence of our youth, if it makes them more intelligent voters and more useful citizens, then our society, might well consider, subsidy of college education as a device not only for equalizing opportunity but also for strengthening its own future by having more educated youths as citizens.

Problems of Adolescent Girls Living in Slums

Girls living in slum areas have to face many educational problems, they are -

- Lack of money
- Parent's ill-attitude towards education of girls.
- Their society is very backward so most of them don't educate their daughter because they think no one could go against society.
- Parent's illness (any chronic disease)
- Illiterate parents don't know the importance of girls education at present time.
- No free-educational aid for poor girls
- No extra time for studies because they work outside the house.

The analysis of responses gathered regarding educational problems has been presented in the ensuing paragraphs.

Incidence of Going to School

This information was sought from the respondents in order to know the extent and incidence of the prevalence of education in respondents. The collected information is being presented in Table No. 7.1.

Table 7.1
Incidence of Going to School

Incidence	*No. of the respondents*	*Percentage*
Yes	118	39.33
No	182	60.67
Total	300	100.00

A close security of the information presented in the table brings out the fact that majority of adolescent girls (60.67%) understudy has accepted that they have not been going to school. Only 39.33 per cent girls have been going to school.

This shows that in slum areas understudy most of the girls are not going to school.

Age of Joining the School

This information was sought from those respondents who have accepted joining of school. The collected information is being presented in Table No. 7.2.

Table 7.2
Age of Joining the School

Age (in yrs)	*No. of the respondents*	*Percentage*
5-7	55	46.61
8-11	49	41.53

(Contd.)

Age (in yrs)	*No. of the respondents*	*Percentage*
12-14	11	9.32
15+	3	2.54
Total	118	100.00

The table shows that the largest single group of respondents (46.61%) has told that they joined school in the age group of 5-7 years (16.67%) followed by those respondents who have accepted the joining of school at the age of 8-11 years (41.53%), 12-14 years (9.32%) and more than 15 years (2.54%).

Thus, it can be concluded that mostly respondents have joined school for study in the age group of 5 to 7 years.

Class of Joining School

The information is being presented in Table No. 7.3.

Table 7.3
Class of Joining School

Class	*No. of the respondents*	*Percentage*
1	92	77.97
2	14	11.86
3	8	6.78
4	2	1.69
5	1	0.85
6	1	0.85
Total	118	100.00

The table clearly mentions that more than 3/4 of the respondents (77.97%) have told that they have joined school in Class I followed by those respondents who have told that they joined school in Class II (11.86%), Class III (6.78%). Class IV (1.69%), Class V and VI (0.85%) each.

This clearly establishes that a dominant majority of adolescent girls understudy joined the school in Class I.

Reasons not Joining School

Information pertaining to these reasons was sought from those respondent girls who failed to join the school. The collected information is being presented in Table No. 7.4 in tabular form.

Table 7.4
Reason for Not Joining the School

Reasons for not joining the school	*No. of the respondents (n = 182)*	*Percentage*
Due to poverty	154	84.61
Conservative attitude of parents	29	15.93
Earning of livelihood	42	23.08
Early marriage	22	12.09
Ignorance towards education	21	11.54
Unsuitable atmosphere	10	5.49

The above table brings out the fact that a dominant majority of respondent girls (84.61%) could not join the school due to poverty. Other reasons mentioned by these respondents have been: earning of livelihood (23.08%); conservative attitudes of parents (15.93%); early marriage (12.09%), ignorance towards education (11.54%) and unsuitable atmosphere (5.49%).

Thus, it can unequivocally be mentioned that adolescent girls understudy could not join school due to poverty which can be labelled as an important and foremost reason of not joining school by adolescent girls understudy.

Reasons for Leaving the School

Sixty-one respondent girls have accepted that they joined school and later on left the school. The collected information pertaining to reasons for leaving the school is being presented in Table No. 7.5.

Table 7.5
Reasons for Leaving the School

Reasons for leaving the school	*No. of the respondents (n = 61)*	*Percentage*
Belief in traditional values	11	18.03
Burden of earning small children in the family	25	40.98
Illness of parents	9	14.75
Economic problem	37	60.66
Low income of family	30	49.18
Ignorance towards education	19	31.15
Narrow minded	6	9.84
Early marriage	20	32.79
More distance of school	5	8.20
Uninteresting syllabus	11	18.03
Lack of good company	12	19.67
Unsuitable atmosphere	7	11.48

This table brings out that more than half of the respondents (60.66%) have told that they left school due to economic problems. About half of them (49.81%) have given low income of family as reason for leaving the school. Other reasons, as told by respondents, have been burden of earning small children (40.98%); early marriage (32.79%); ignorance towards education (31.15%), lack of good company (19.67%), belief in traditional values (18.03%); boring nature of syllabus (18.03%); illness of parents (14.75%), unsuitable atmosphere (11.48%) and more distance of school (8.20%).

Thus, it can be concluded that the main reasons for leaving the school has been economic problems, low income of the family, burden for caring small children in the family, early marriage and ignorance towards education.

Difficulties Faced in Going to School

Fiftyseven respondent girls elaborated their difficulties which are being presented in Table No. 7.6.

Table 7.6
Difficulties Faced in Going to School

Difficulties faced	*No. of the respondents (n = 57)*	*Percentage*
Distance of school	18	31.58
Conveyance problem	23	40.35
Lack of good company	22	38.60

The table shows that the largest single group of respondents (40.35%) has reported conveyance problems in going to school. The other reported difficulties have been lack of good company (38.68%) and distance of school (31.58%).

Desire to Go to School

Information pertaining to the desire to go to school was

sought from those respondent girls who have reported not joining of the school. The collected information is being presented in Table No. 7.7.

Table 7.7
Desire to Go to School

Desire	*No. of the respondents*	*Percentage*
Yes	59	24.28
No	184	75.72
Total	243	100.00

A close look into the information presented in the table brings out that 3/4th of the respondents (75.72%) have been found having no desire to go to school. Only 24.28 per cent of the respondents have expressed their desire to go to school.

Thus, it can be concluded that mostly non-school going adolescent girls have no desire to go to school.

Reasons for not Having Desire to Go to School

Information pertaining to these reasons have been presented in Table No. 7.8.

Table 7.8
Reasons for Not Having Desire to Go to School

Reasons	*No. of the respondents (n = 184)*	*Percentage*
Uninteresting syllabus	39	21.19
Economic problem	124	67.39
Distance of school	82	44.56
Unsuitable atmosphere	74	40.21

(Contd.)

Reasons	*No. of the respondents (n = 184)*	*Percentage*
Traditional values of family	79	42.93
Engagement in household work	86	46.73
Working outside	62	33.69

The table makes it clear that majority of respondents (67.39%) has told economic problems behind not going to school. The other mentioned reason have been: engagement in household work (46.73%); distance of school (44.56%); traditional values of the family (42.93%); unsuitable atmosphere (40.21%); working outside (33.69%); and uninteresting syllabus (21.19%).

Condition of Performance of Respondents in Respect to Study

The relevant information is being presented in Table No. 7.9.

Table 7.9
Condition of Performance of the Respondents in Respect to Their Study

Condition of performance	*No. of the respondents*	*Percentage*
Good performance	30	52.63
Bad performance	27	47.36
Total	57	100.00

The table brings out the fact that about half of the respondents (52.63%) have told that they perform good at school. However, 47.36 percent have accepted bad performance in their study.

Reasons for Bad Performance in Studies

Information pertaining to these reasons have been presented in Table 7.10.

Table 7.10
Reasons for Bad Performance in Studies

Reasons	*No. of the respondents (n = 27)*	*Percentage*
Disinterested in studies	12	44.44
Heavy curriculum	9	33.33
Irregularity in attending the school	14	51.85
Lack of proper guidance	10	37.03
Lack of study material	11	40.74
Lack of time	6	22.22
Unsuitable atmosphere	5	18.50
Lack of good company	7	25.92

The table brings out that more than half of the respondents (51.85%) have accepted that reason for their bad performance in studies has been irregularity in attending school. The other reasons have been: disinterested in studies (44.44%), lack of study material (40.79%), lack of proper guidance (37.03%), heavy curriculum (33.33%), lack of good company (25.95%), lack of time (22.22%) and unsuitable atmosphere (18.50%).

The Presence of Desire to Study but Could not Study

The relevant information is being tabulated in Table No. 7.11

Table 7.11
The Presence of Desire to Study But Could Not Study

Desire	*No. of the respondents*	*Percentage*
Yes	94	51.64
No	88	48.35
Total	182	100.00

The table shows that more than half of the respondents (51.64%) have reported that they had the desire to study but could not study. 48.35 percent of respondents have reported that they had no desire to study.

Reasons for Failure to Study Irrespective of Desire to Study

Information pertaining to these reasons have been collected and is being presented in Table No. 7.12.

Table 7.12
Reasons for Failure to Study Irrespective of Desire to Study

Reasons	*No. of the respondents (n = 94)*	*Percentage*
Poverty	43	45.74
Traditional values of family	11	11.70
Care of siblings	13	13.82
Engagement in household chorus	20	21.27
Family restrictions	32	34.04
Preference to Boys in Education	14	14.89

(Contd.)

Reasons	*No. of the respondents (n = 94)*	*Percentage*
Lack of interest of parents regarding their studies	29	30.85

According to the analysis of the information poverty has been mentioned as main reason by the largest single group of respondents (45.74%). Other reasons, as mentioned by the respondents, have been family restrictions (34.04%), lack of interest shown by parents in the respondents' studies (30.85%), engagement in performing household chorus (21.27%), preference to boys in education as compared to girls (14.89%), care of siblings (13.82%) and traditional values of family (11.70%).

Encouragement by Family Members for Getting Education

Information pertaining to this encouragement has been collected and tabulated in Table No. 7.13.

Table 7.13
Encouragement by Family Members for Getting Education

Encouragement	*No. of the respondents*	*Percentage*
Yes	169	56.33
No	131	43.66
Total	300	100.00

The table brings out the fact that more than half of the respondents (56.3%) have reported that they have been encouraged by their parents for getting education. However, 43.66 percent of the respondents also felt that they have not been encouraged by their parents for getting education.

Methods Used by Parents for Encouraging Respondents to Get Education

Information pertaining to these methods is being presented in Table No. 7.14.

Table 7.14
Methods Used by Parents for Encouraging Respondents to Get Education

Methods	*No. of the respondents (n = 161)*	*Percentage*
Admitting to school	69	42.85
Meeting all study requirements	42	26.08
Giving time for study	30	18.63
Providing guidance	15	9.31
Making aware about the need and importance education	13	8.07
Adjusting themselves according to their child's requirements	27	16.77
Sacrificing their own needs	14	8.69

The table brings out that the largest single group of respondents (42.85%) has told that their parents encouraged them for education by admitting them to school. The other methods used by them have been meeting all study requirements (26.08%), adjusting themselves according to their child's requirement (16.77%), providing guidance (9.31%), sacrificing their own need (8.69%) and making aware about the need and importance of education (8.07%).

Reasons for Not Encouraging for Education

These reasons have been tabulated in Table No. 7.15.

Table 7.15
Reasons for Not Encouraging for Education

Reasons	*No. of the respondents (n = 139)*	*Percentage*
Economic problems	54	38.84
Parents need for helping hands in their work	24	17.26
Ill health of parents	15	10.79
Responsibility for look after young children	17	12.23
Prevalence of traditional and backward ideas in family	20	14.38
Priority for education of boys	34	24.46
Conservative attitude	22	15.82

The table lists the reasons for not encouraging by parents for education of their children. These reasons have been mentioned as economic problems (38.85%), priority for education of boys (24.46%), parents' need for helping hand in their work (17.26%), prevalence of traditional and backward ideas in the family (14.38%), responsibility for looking after young children (12.33%) and ill health of parents (10.79%).

Preference of Boys as Compared to Girls in the Matter of Education

Information pertaining to the above subject is being presented in the Table No. 7.16. The table brings out the fact that 2/3rd of respondents have reported that there exists a feeling on their part that boys are preferred as compared to girls for providing education and the remaining 1/3rd of respondents have felt vice-versa.

Table 7.16
Existence of Feeling on the Part of Respondents that Boys are Preferred as Compared to Girls for Providing Education

Preference	*No. of the respondents*	*Percentage*
Yes	203	67.66
No	97	32.33
Total	300	100.00

Reasons for Preference of Boys as Compared to Girls in the Matter of Education

The reasons are being tabulated in Table No. 7.17.

Table 7.17
Reasons for Preference

Reasons	*No. of the respondents (n = 203)*	*Percentage*
Traditional values of family having conservative outlook	92	45.32
No future for girls	42	20.68
Girls are for marriage only	38	18.71

Sick mentality	31	15.27
Need of helping hands for household works	27	13.30

The table shows that the largest single group of respondents has mentioned traditional values of family having conservative outlook as main reason for preferring boys for education as compared to girls. The other reasons have been mentioned as no future for girls (20.68%); girls are for marriage only (18.71%); sick mentality (15.27%); and need of helping hand for household work (13.30%).

Reasons Responsible for Blocking Education of Respondents

The collected information is being tabulated in Table No. 7.18. The reasons given by respondents have been poverty (55.73%), conservative attitudes (36.06%), ignorance (31.14%), lack of time due to household work (22.95%), preference to boys as compared to girls (11.47%) and early marriage (9.83%).

Table 7.18
Reasons Responsible for Blocking Education of Respondents

Reasons	*No. of the respondents (n = 61)*	*Percentage*
Poverty	34	55.73
Conservative attitude	22	36.06
Ignorance	19	31.14
Lack of time because of household work	14	22.95
Early marriage	6	9.83
Preference to boys as comapred to girls	7	11.47

Preference for Girls Coming Forward in the Matter of Education

Information pertaining to preference for girls coming forward in the matter of education has been sought from respondents in order to know about preference for education for girls. This information has been tabulated in Table No. 7.19.

Table 7.19
Preference for Girls Coming Forward in the Matter of Education

Preference	*No. of the respondents*	*Percentage*
Yes	214	71.33
No	86	28.66
Total	300	100.00

The tabulated information in the table makes it clear that majority of respondents (71.33%) preferred for the education of girls.

Reasons for Preference

The reasons given by the respondents have been presented in Table No. 7.20. These reasons have been the present policy of liberalization and modernisation (26.16%); job security (25.70%); female education brings education to whole family (19.62%); formation of future generation (19.15%); reducing family burden (18.22%); economic independence to girls (16.35%); girls education is the need of hour (11.20%) and equal chance of education to all (9.81%).

Table 7.20
Reasons for the Preference

Reasons	*No. of the respondents (n = 214)*	*Percentage*
Formation of future generation	41	19.15
Female education brings education to whole family	42	19.62
Equal chance of education to all	21	9.81
The present policy of liberalisation and modernisation	56	26.16
Girl's education is the need of the time	24	11.21
Job security	55	25.70
Lessening family burden	39	18.22
Economic independence to girls	35	16.35

Facilities Needed in the Matter of Education

Respondents have been asked to list those facilities which are needed by them for accessibility to education. The Table No. 7.21 lists out these facilities as free education (27.33%), school should be opened (23.63%), establishment of adult education centre (20.33%); supply of free study material (17.66%), easy admission procedure (14.68%); awareness campaign should be organised (8.66%), and scholarships should be widely sanctioned (4%).

Table 7.21
Facilities Needed in the Matter of Education

Facilities	*No. of the respondents (n = 300)*	*Percentage*
Free education	82	27.33
Establishment of adult education centre	61	20.33
Scholarships should be widely sanctioned	12	4.00
Schools should be opened	71	23.66
Supply of free study material	53	17.66
Easy admission procedure	44	14.66
Awareness campaigns should be organised	26	8.66

Availability of Separate Space for Study

Separate space for study is important for smooth and good study because in a crowded atmosphere studies cannot be properly managed. Keeping in view this, information was sought from respondents and is being tabulated in Table No. 7.22.

Table 7.22
Availability of Separate Space for Study

Availability	*No. of the respondents*	*Percentage*
Yes	171	57.00
No	129	43.00
Total	300	100.00

According to this table more than half of the respondents (57.1%) have maintained that for study purpose they used to get separate space but quite a sizable number of respondents (43%) have no separate space for study.

Meeting the Problem of Lack of Space for Study

This information was sought from those respondents who have reported lack of separate space for study. This information is being tabulated in Table No. 7.23.

Table 7.23
In Which Manner Respondents Manage the Problem of Lack of Space for Study

Methods	*No. of the respondents (n = 129)*	*Percentage*
Making adjustment of time	54	41.86
Going to other place for study	28	21.70
Study in late night	15	11.62
Try to finish other chores early	49	37.98
Take some one's help to finish other responsibilities	32	24.80

The table makes it clear that respondents solve the problem of lack of separate space for study in several ways such as making adjustment of time (41.86%), try to finish other chores early (37.38%), take someone's help to finish other responsibilities (24.80%), going to other place for study (21.70%) and study in late night (11.62%).

Chapter VIII

Employment Problems of Adolescent Girls in Slums

The history of female employment in gainful professions outside the family in India is recent one. Their role since the Vedic period has been traditional. During Rig Vedic period status of women was high but they were supposed to bear sons, be good house-wives and were also supposed to tolerate every thing quietly and do their duties towards their husbands, home and children. During the Buddhist period also their role was traditional. According to Thomas view, the role of women during ancient India was confined to inside the four walls.[1]

The modern adolescent in the slum area is an irresponsible, carefree, illiterate youth. A common complaint of the adolescents is that the parents expect them to perform the same work around the home as parents do and they deny the right to select their own way of life. The dominant conditioning factor in the choice between school or work, as well as the combination of school with part-time work, is the family's and the adolescent's need for money. To the adolescent, money comes from out of his own income. The more severe the strain of economic conditions on the family, the more likely that boy or girl is to choose or be forced by circumstances to find a job. Constant questioning of the child, when money is required by him leads to friction between the father and the child. The healthy solution to the problem from the point of view of the adolescent is to earn his own money.

The world of the adolescents and his family is centred in the struggle for the basic necessities of life and in a search for pleasure to break the monotony of work, unemployment and insecurity. Family life, is punctuated with quarrels followed by fights and physical violence. Money is a scarce commodity. Therefore, an essential conditioning factor in the slum-dweller's childhood is the desire to grow up and get a job. It's noticed that the adolescents particularly girls suffer from inferiority complex. Steps, therefore, must be taken to spot out talent among them and give all possible encouragement to individuals with special talents. Correctional schools are to be opened in slum area which could transform the adolescent's and help them to develop their personality.

Since the role and responsibilities of Indian Women were traditional. They were not supposed to seek any gainful employment outside the family. This hindered economic development, which further reduced the chances of improvement in their social position.

But after the industrial revolution the social situation has changed through out the world. Due to rapid growth of industrialisation, urbanisation, development in the field of transportation and communication, science and technology, new roles have emerged and new social norms and values have come into existence. It has created a new situation in the society. Job opportunities outside the family, economic hardship, and favourable social and cultural situation have encouraged women to seek employment outside the family. Now in India women have entered in different fields of employment as teaching, medicine and law, etc.

Women at Work

In 1991 Census the total population is divided into three broad categories : 1. Main worker, 2. Marginal workers and 3. Non-workers. Main workers are those who have worked for the major part of the year preceding the date of enumeration and whose main activity was in either cultivation or as an agricultural labour or in household industry or in other work. In the 1991 census 222.52 million (33.45 percent) of the Indian population were main workers, of which 44.97 million (13.99 percent) were female.

Marginal workers are those who have not worked for the major part of the preceding year concerned but nevertheless have done some work during any time in the reference period. Of the total marginal workers (22.09 million) in India 83.92 per cent (18.55 million) were female.[2]

In our society and also in almost all the societies in the world, the son not only inherits the family property but he also inherited the family's title, status and other encumbrance. Soon after he matures and starts earning, the responsibility of the family is gradually shifted on him. It's obligatory on his part to support his parents in their old age and other dependent members of the family if there are any. Hence the investment on the son's education is preferred by the family with an expectations of good dividends in future. Whereas to spend on daughter's education may not be preferred by those parents who expect in return by way of their earnings. Once the daughters are married, the parents will not have the benefit of their income. So the parents may not take the risk of taking loan to educate daughters. To marry the daughter, the parents would not hesitate to take loan if their financial position is not sound. The parents consider it their responsibility to get the daughters married in a way, society demands this from them.

The urban parents may be intended to take loan to educate their daughters with a view that they could get good spouses. Modern young men would like to marry educate girls and some of them even prefer to marry only employed girls, so these educated employed girls can financially help the family for some years till they get married.

General Employment Problems of Slum Dwellers with Particular Reference to Adolescents

The slum-dwellers have taken up different occupations. They are sweepers, collies, cobblers, beggars, DDT sprayers.

Mostly there is only one bread-earner for the family and all others are dependents on him. There are also instances where the youth particularly male in the family is working but is not helping the family, whatever she/he earns, she/he spends on himself.

The grave problem of unemployment and their inability to get jobs even when they apply through the Employment Exchange, has frustrated them. They have no belief in the words of the civic authorities. Their apathy towards the employment exchange is very clear in their own remarks.

Laziness is a factor responsible for their misery. There is a small section of the population in slum area who are unwilling to work. One can see the youths idling away their time gossiping under the shade of the tree. They roam about in the street, gamble and are addicts to several vices. When asked how they could get money for smoking and gambling, they avoided answering such questions, but their parents said that they threatened to leave houses and run away, if they were not paid a few coins. Afraid of this, the parents had to pay them whatever they could. Absence of fair treatment of children in the family, in the neighborhood and lack of proper social environment have made them develop indifferent attitudes towards work. Poverty stricken conditions, and lack of proper training have made them unsuited for many occupations. Though they are not properly trained and equipped they think they are fit for all jobs. These are the causes for their unemployment.

Some slum-dwellers do not like wholeheartedly the idea of women and girls going out for work. It's true that most of the women go out for work to add to the better economic status of the family. But in certain cases where women and daughters who are adults and have not been able to secure some job or the other, the head of the family is not worried about their unemployment. The head of the family are more particular about their sons and male members of the family getting jobs than their daughters and wives.

The very outlook of all the slum-dwellers has been pessimistic. They occupy the lowest ranking station in the prestige structure. Its further looked down upon as the scam of the city by the higher classes. It is believed that nothing beyond charity can be done for these people. They work at manual jobs only. They have no interest in health and medical care. These people are very lazy to work or do odd jobs around the city. They believe that they are at the bottom and can be nothing to improve their position. They complain that they are always asked to obey. They feel that they are forced to accept a life of frustration and defeat in society. This attitude makes them remain in eternal poverty.

The uncertain nature of their employment results in long periods of idleness, and illness which may result in a voluntary lay off for a few days. The persons in the higher class consider this to be laziness. These people are more irregular in their employment than any others in our society.

Adolescents have little faith in their own capacities to do anything. Although they feel dependent on the local authorities, they are antagonistic towards the local government because situations are seldom improve and they do little to cooperate with the municipal authorities. Economic frustrations, unemployment and under-employment are always there. Though poor, they are not happy to live in filthy surroundings or remain illiterate and they are aware of the contrasts between their own lives and those of many others they have seen in the city. But their attitude towards the authorities, jobs and themselves in harried. Thus the universal characteristics of the slum is the poverty of its inhabitants. Misery is writ large on their faces.

The slum is a poverty-stricken area. These factors have contributed to their misery.

Adolescents of lower income group are frequently required to help parents in the household work after their school hours. This cuts down on the time available for activities related to his educational pursuits. Furthermore, money and time needed to pursue certain interests of his own also depends on the economic condition of the family. Membership in a family whose socio-economic level is low sometimes prevents an adolescent's acceptance in a socially better placed peer group. If he is not able to keep up the standard of peer group, he is deprived of the status and support outside the family that are so important in the development of his social personality. In financially handicapped families, the elder child has often to sacrifice his education to help and support the family or to send younger brothers and sisters to school. Thus, the socio-economic status of the adolescent's family will influence not only what interests are possible for him to develop but also what shape these interests will take. Economic status of the family effects the aspirations of the school going children and those of higher socio-economic strata have nurtured high aspirations, particularly for technical education and technical profession. Socio-economic status of the family has a dominant impact on the educational and occupational aspirations of adolescents and as well as those of parents, for their children. This study deals with the impact of the income of the family on the educational and occupational aspirations of both the adolescents and their parents. The different aspects studied are [3].

1. Educational aspirations of adolescents
2. Parent's aspirations for their children
3. Occupational preferences as viewed by the family
4. Study facilities available to the adolescents
5. Factors that hinder study habits at home.

Recent studies have divided social classes into five categories, thus covering the in between income groups. The classification thus followed is as under[4]:

	Annual Income	*Categories*
1.	Upto Rs. 3000	Very low income group
2.	From Rs. 3001 to 6000	Low income group
3.	From Rs.6001 to 9000	Middle income group
4.	From Rs. 9001 to 12,000	High income group
5.	From Rs. 12,001 & above	Very high income group

Based on this criteria the families under this study have been classified and different aspects of aspirations of both parents and adolescents have been analyzed and studied on this variable.

Adolescence is a time when important choices have to be made. Socio-economic background of the family influences adolescent's plan of continuing or discontinuing his studies for higher education or to take up a job suitable to him or to learn and earn for which this industrial city has a very wide scope. Majority of the adolescents on the whole intend to continue studies and only a small percentage of them say they have to launch on an earning expectation. Adopting the 'earning and learning' scheme is favoured by them. The parents of lower income groups may not want their children to be aware of their financial position. Though they can not afford, they may intend to educate their children so that they can move up in an economic structure of the society and thus the family can achieve an upward social mobility.

Parental Occupation of Adolescents

Children do not fully appreciate the relationship between the father's occupation and the social status of the family. As a result, they are likely to be proud of any parental occupation that seems glamorous to them. By adolescence, the child's concept of occupational values has completely changed. Now he recognizes the prestige value associated with certain occupations and the social status that is automatically accorded to his contemporaries whose fathers are in prestige occupations. He is the influenced greatly in his attitude towards his father's occupation, an attitude that affects markedly his attitude toward his father, toward his family, and toward his home.

By the adolescent age, there is a clear relationship between social class and choice of friends. Socio economic status plays a more important role in friendship selection in cities or rural district than in suburban areas. In a study of a suburban community, there was no evidence that the occupation of the father was a factor in determining the friendship of adolescent students. When there is a crossing of class lines in friendship choices, it is most often found among middle class adolescents who strive to form friendships with those of the higher class.

Because communities are, to a certain extent, segregated by income, an adolescent is more likely to come in contact with other adolescents of his socio-economic group than with those of higher or lower groups. The pattern of behavior varies with the social class, and this tends to encourage friendships with members of the same social group. Furthermore, friends must, within limits, be able to afford much the same kind of clothing and recreation if they are to remain as friends. This is more possible when they are from a similar economic status than when there is a marked difference. And finally, adolescents of different socio-economic backgrounds want different traits in their friends. When two high school groups of marked differences in socio-economic backgrounds were compared for expressed preferences for certain characteristics of classmates of their own sex, it was found that both groups preferred friends who had many friends, who were friendly well-mannered, cooperative with a group, who enjoyed hearing or telling jokes, and who were loyal to their friends.

Adolescents of the higher socio-economic group prefer as friends individuals who are serious minded, talkative, talented in arts and crafts, enthusiastic, and who enjoy working on their own hobbies as friends individuals who are good listeners, attractive, enjoy practical jokes, peppy, neat in appearance grown up in looks and behavior, and are of the "hail-fellow-well-met" type.

If the mother works when the children are young, she provides some care far them. When mother of adolescents works, by contrast, no such provision is made. As a result, more home duties are assigned to the adolescent children of the family, home duties are often neglected, and meals are irregular. The recreational and social activities of the whole family are, of necessity, curtailed, largely unplanned, and in most cases make use of community resources, such as the movies.

Adolescent daughters often are unhappy and lonely when their mothers work, and as a result they stay out of the home. If antisocial activities prevail in the neighborhood, they are especially susceptible to them and become delinquent. When both the mother and father are away from home most of the time and are tired, busy, and preoccupied when they are at home, the adolescent resents this, even when his parents engage in occupations that have prestige value and that improve the family's social and economic status. The type of adjustment they make ranges from quid submission to better resentment.

The adolescent's adjustments to the parents and the home climate in general are better when the mothers work part time than when they work full time or not at all, especially in the case of adolescents need something to keep them busy and interested, which also keeps them from interfering in their children's affairs too much. In addition, mothers gain status in their own, their husband's and their children's eyes, if they make some money. By contrast, working full time means neglect of the home, of social life, irritations, and other factors which are detrimental to the home climate.[5]

Occupational Preferences as Viewed by the Parents and Adolescents

As children mature and approach adulthood they become more and more conscious of the need for choosing their vocation. Sooner or later every young person has to choose his future occupation. Such choices may involve decision as to whether or not to continue in school. They may involve selection of appropriate study courses. In making these choices, some adolescents blending to the bidding of their parents, others calmly weigh the possibilities and a number of them drift along aimlessly, putting off any serious consideration. The ability to look into the future and to think independently reflect personality factors which evolve from the family situations in which children are reared. If training is required for one's occupation the choice of an occupation should be made by the time of adolescence at the latest, because this period represents the last stage of really rapid learning. In order to plan their education, young adolescents must have a general vocational goal. Parents may want their adolescents to enter a certain line of work that they themselves had always wanted to enter, but for one reason or other they were unable to do so. The child is, thus to compensate for some parental wish that was thwarted, forced into a career.

Occupational Values of Adolescents

By adolescence, her concept of occupational values completely changes. Adolescent student's attitude toward their father's occupation showed that those whose father's were in higher occupations respected their father's because the occupation provided a good living for the family. Those whose fathers had very low type of occupations were ashamed of their father's occupation because of the level of work done by them. Thus the adolescents relate their occupational status of the father to their social status and inevitably this attitude of the adolescents does have an impact on their own vocational aspirations.

Many adolescent girls highly educated, just educated or illiterate have realized the need of their contribution to the family income, though the husbands can maintain the family, some of the wives may still want to earn so that they can raise the economic status of the family by contributing to the family income. Its apparent that several interacting variables such as economic aspirations, intellectual and social status etc. make women enter the labour market. So it is quite reasonable to assume that because of wives' contribution to the family income, though the husband's occupational status and income is low, the income level of such family will be at the higher level.

Vocational Choices of Adolescents

A uniform pattern of influences enters into each adolescent's vocational development. The pattern of vocational choices is very well described by Ginzberg and Ginzberg which is as follows:

1. Upto eleven years of age: Period of fantasy choices, when the child's occupational aspirations are indiscriminate and unreal. Instead of being governed by such occupational realities as abilities and training, the child makes fantasy attempts to play adult roles.
2. From eleven to seventeen years of age: Period of tentative choices, when occupational preferences are based first on like and dislikes or interests, but later on aptitudes and capacities and still later, on personal values and ideals.
3. After the age of seventeen years: Period of realistic choices, when there is a consideration of occupational opportunities and other realities.[6]

The adolescents of lowest income group may not be having high hopes because of the inability of the parents to finance their education which is essential to enter the prestigious occupations. Adolescents say it is their cherished wish may be confident in their own capacity to achieve the occupation of their choice.

The adolescent's family plays a major role in the development of the adolescent's interest in occupations. Father's occupation determines the social status of the family, which in turn influences their values towards their children's occupations. Parents of low economic status aspire in good numbers for such occupations which demand high expenses and long period of training, and they may not hesitate to raise loan for the education of their children. This shows that the parents struggle to raise their social status through their children's achievements.

Employment Problems of Adolescent Girls

Specifically the employment problems of adolescent girls in slums are as follows :

- Prevalence of unemployment and underemployment.
- Casual employment
- If employed are meager earnings/salaries
- Physical exploitation by employers
- Difference in income between boys and girls
- Dissatisfaction with the job
- Alone bread-winner in the family
- Illiterate and irresponsible adolescents
- Eternal poverty
- Due to laziness, they are unwilling to work
- Unable to get secured employed like governmental jobs

- Lacks specialised or technical work
- Does menial jobs
- Mostly maid servants
- Unskilled jobs
- Irregular income
- Not expanding earning on his own expenses
- Unplanned working and expenditure
- Expenditure on unproductive work.

Incidence of Involvement of Respondent's in Work Outside the Family

Information pertaining to the above mentioned subject was collected from the respondents and is being presented in Table No. 8.1 in the tabular form.

Table 8.1
Incidence of Involvement of Respondents in Work Outside Family

Response	*No. of the respondents*	*Percentage*
Yes	115	38.33
No	185	61.66
Total	300	100.00

The table makes it clear that the majority of respondents (61.66%) have reported their non-involvement in work outside their family. However, 38.33 percent of respondents has told that they remained involved in work outside their family.

Thus, it can be concluded that more than 1/3rd of the respondent adolescent girls have been found involved in work outside their families.

Nature of Work Done

The information pertaining to above subject was taken from those respondents who were involved in work outside their family. Thus information is being tabulated in Table No. 8.2.

Table 8.2
Nature of Work Done by Respondents

Nature	*No. of the respondents*	*Percentage*
Involvement in making handicrafts such as Jhavai, Rassi, envelopes, etc.	16	13.91
Labourers	23	20.00
Tailoring	15	13.04
Cottage industry like making Papad, candles, etc.	12	10.43
Caring of others' small children	6	5.21
Doing household work at others place	19	16.52
Maid servants	14	12.17
Total	115	100.00

The table clearly indicates that the largest single group of respondents (20%) has been working as labourers outside their families followed by those respondents who have reported that they have been involved in doing household work at other place (16.52%); in making handicrafts such as Jhavai, rassi, envelop etc. (13.91%); in tailoring (13.04%); as maid servants (12.17%); in cottage industry like making of

Papad, Candles, etc. (10.43%) and caring of others small children (5.21%).

Age at which Started Working

The collected information is being presented in Table No. 8.3. This table indicates that more than half of the respondents (55.65%) have started working outside their families between the age group of 8-12 years followed by those respondents who have started working at the age of 12 or more than that age and below 8 years (20.87%).

Table 8.3
Age at which Started Working

Age in years	*No. of the respondents*	*Percentage*
Below 8 years	24	20.87
8-12	64	55.65
12 and above	27	23.48
Total	115	100.00

This shows that respondent adolescent girls have started working outside their family at a very young age.

Person for whom Adolescent Girls work

The related information has been tabulated in Table No. 8.4.

The table makes it clear that the largest single group of respondents adolescent girls (46.09%) work for the satisfaction of their own as well as their family members needs followed by those respondents who have mentioned satisfaction of members needs only (22.61%); and satisfaction of own needs only (20.87%), 10.43 percent of respondents did not respond to above mentioned question.

Table 8.4
Persons for Whom Adolescents Girl Work

Persons	*No. of the respondents*	*Percentage*
Satisfaction of their own as well as their family members' needs	53	46.09
Satisfaction of own needs only	24	20.87
Satisfaction of family members' needs only	26	22.61
No response	12	10.43
Total	115	100.00

In this way, it can be concluded that most of the respondent adolescent girls have been working for the satisfaction of their own as well as family members' needs.

Persons Motivation Adolescent Girls to Work

The collected information is being presented in Table No. 8.5. According to this table, the largest single group of respondents have reported that their parents (27.83%) have been motivating force for their involvement in work followed by those respondents who have mentioned self (21.74%); neighbours (15.65%), relatives (13.04%), family members other than parents (12.17%), and peers (7.83%) as motivators for taking up work. 1.74 per cent of respondents did not respond to the above mentioned question.

Thus, it is clear that respondent adolescent girls have generally been motivated to take up work either by their parents or they have taken up work on their own.

Table 8.5
Persons Motivating Adolescent Girls to Work

Persons	*No. of the respondents*	*Percentage*
Self	25	21.74
Parents	32	27.83
Relatives	15	13.04
Neighbours	18	15.65
Peers	9	7.83
Family members other than parents	14	12.17
No response	2	1.74
Total	115	100.00

Reason for Working

The adolescent girls have been asked to elaborate reasons responsible for taking up work outside. The family in order to know the circumstances under which they have been pressed to age for work. Thus collected information is being tabulated in Table No. 8.6.

Table 8.6
Reasons for Working

Reasons	*No. of the respondents*	*Percentage*
To supplement family income	33	28.65
Death of parent(s)	8	6.96
Not liking for dependence on others	11	9.56
No body to support	7	6.09

(Contd.)

Reasons	*No. of the respondents*	*Percentage*
Managing out of pocket allowance	12	10.43
Fulfilment of own needs	24	20.87
To learn some work	3	2.61
Will of parents	17	14.78
Apathy towards studies	12	10.43
Weakness in studies	8	6.96
Liking for doing work	16	13.91
No other employment opportunities	15	13.04
Total	115	100.00

An analysis of above information tabulated in the table makes it clear that the largest single group of respondents (28.65%) has taken up work for the purpose of supplementing family income followed by other reasons such as fulfillment of own needs (20.87%), will of parents (14.78%), liking for doing work (13.91%), no other employment opportunities (13.04%), managing of out of pocket allowance and apathy towards studies (10.43% each), no liking for dependence on others (9.56%) death of parents and weakness in studies (6.96% each), no body to support (6.09%) and for learning of some work (2.61%).

Average Duration of Engagement in Works in a Year

The related information has been tabulated in Table No. 8.7 which brings out that about half of the respondents (47.83%) have reported that they remained engaged in work for half of the year followed by those respondents who have mentioned their engagement in work for three months in a year (19.13%), whole year (17.39%) and less than half year (15.65%).

Table 8.7
Average Duration of Engagement in Work in a year

Duration	*No. of the respondents*	*Percentage*
Whole year	20	17.39
Three-fourth year	22	19.13
Half year	55	47.83
Less than half year	18	15.65
Total	115	100.00

Thus it can be concluded that most of the respondents have been able to get work upto six months only in a year.

Per Day Hours of Work

The collected information has been presented in Table No. 8.8. The table brings out the fact that in case of those respondents who work outside their family about half of them (48.69%) have reported that they work from 3 to 5 hours in a day followed by those respondents who have reported working from 5 to 7 hours (24.35%), more than seven hours (10.43%) in a day.

Table 8.8
Per day Hours of Work in Case of Working Outside

Hours of Work	*No. of the respondents*	*Percentage*
Below 3	12	10.43
3-5	56	48.69
5-7	28	24.35
7+	19	16.52
Total	115	100.00

Thus, it can be concluded that majority of respondents work from 3 to 7 hours in a day.

Behaviour of Employer

The adolescent girls were approached to spell out the behaviour of their employer in order to know about the condition under which they have been compelled to work. The relevant information has been tabulated in Table No. 8.9.

Table 8.9
Behaviour of Employer

Behaviour	*No. of the respondents (n = 115)*	*Percentage*
Cooperative	15	13.04
Sensitive towards respondents problem	8	6.95
Exploitative	22	19.13
Rude	18	15.65
Helping	16	13.91
Uncooperative	25	21.73
Autocratic	11	9.56

The table brings out the fact that the largest single group of respondents (21.73%) has mentioned that they have to work with uncooperative employer (21.73%) followed by those respondents who have mentioned their employers as exploitation (19.13%), rude (15.65%), helping (13.9%), cooperative (13.04%), autocrat (9.56%) and sensitive towards respondents problems (6.95%).

On the basis of above it can be concluded that most of the respondent adolescent girls work with uncooperative, exploitative and rude employer.

Person Supervising the Work of Adolescent Girls

The relevant information has been tabulated in Table No. 8.10. The table shows that in case of about half of the respondents (48.69%) employer himself/herself used to supervise their work followed by those respondent in whose case employers' family members (20.87%); senior worker (19.13%); and employers' representative (11.30%) used to supervise their work.

Table 8.10
Persons Supervising Work of Adolescent Girls Who Work Outside Family

Persons	*No. of the respondents*	*Percentage*
Employer himself /herself	56	48.69
Employer's family members	24	20.87
Employer's representative	13	11.30
Senior workers	22	19.13
Total	115	100.00

Sex of Supervisors

This information was collected from the respondents for the purpose of knowing that whether working adolescent girls have been supervised by male/female. This information has been tabulated in Table No. 8.11. This table makes it clear that more than half of the working adolescent girls (58.24%) have been supervised by males followed by females (42.74%).

Table 8.11

Sex of Supervisors of Respondents Who Work Outside Family

Sex of supervisor	*No. of the respondents*	*Percentage*
Male	67	58.26
Female	48	41.74
Total	115	100.0

Method of Supervision of Work

The collected information has been tabulated in Table No. 8.12, which brings out the fact that the largest single group of the respondents (39.13%) has been supervised by assigning work in the morning and evaluating in the evening followed by those respondents who have been supervised by explaining and doing work (29.56%); verbally explaining the work (18.24%) hurling abuses (6.96%) and even beating (6.09%).

Table 8.12

Methods of Supervision of Work

Methods	*No. of the respondents*	*Percentage*
Explaining and doing work	34	29.56
Assigning work in morning and evaluating it in evening	45	39.13
Verbally explaining the work	21	18.26
Hurling abuses	8	6.96
Beating	7	6.09
Total	115	100.00

Step Taken for Getting Maximum Work

The collected information is being presented in Table No. 8.13. This table makes it clear that the largest single group of respondents (29.50%) has reported that their employer takes no steps for getting maximum work from them followed by those respondents who have mentioned that their employer used to take maximum work from them by paying extra wages/benefits (21.74%), paying extra benefits only (18.43%) paying extra wages only and exercising strict control (15.65%) each, and hurling abuses (6.96%).

Table 8.13
Steps Taken for Getting Maximum Work

Step	*No. of the respondents*	*Percentage*
No steps	34	29.56
Paying extra wages only	18	15.65
Paying extra benefits only	12	18.43
Paying extra wages and benefits	25	21.74
Strict control	18	15.65
Hurling abuses	8	6.96
Total	115	100.00

This shows that in most of the cases employers pay extra wages and benefits for taking up maximum work from the respondents.

Wages Earned Per Day in Case of Working Outside Family

This information is being tabulated in Table No. 8.14.

The table makes it clear that the largest single group of respondents (34.78%) has reported that they earn wages from Rs. 26 to 35 per day for their work followed by those respondents who have told that they earn wages per day from Rs. 16 to 25 (22.60%); Rs. 36 to 45 (15.65%), Rs. 5 to 15 (13.91%), Rs. 46 to 56 (9.56%) and Rs. 56 to 75 (3.47%).

Table 8.14
Wages Earned in Case of Working Outside Family

Wages (Rs./Day)	*No. of the respondents (n = 115)*	*Percentage*
5-15	16	13.91
16-25	26	22.60
26-35	40	34.78
36-45	18	15.65
46-56	11	9.56
56-75	4	3.47
Total	115	100.00

This shows that dominant majority of respondents earn wages from Rs. 16 to Rs. 45 per day.

Feeling of Satisfaction with the Nature of Work Behaviour of Employer, Supervision of Work, Facilities Available at Work Place and Status Compared to other Working People

The collected information about above mentioned subject has been presented in Table 8.15. The analysis of the table is being presented in ensuing paragraphs.

(a) *Satisfaction from Nature of Work*

More than half of the respondents (56.52%) have been found satisfied with their nature of work. Remaining 43.47

percent of the respondents have been found dissatisfied with their nature of work.

Table 8.15

Feeling of Satisfaction with Nature of Work, Behaviour of Employer, Supervision of Work, Facilities Available at Work Place, Status Compared to other Working People

Response	*Nature of work*	*Behaviour of employer*	*Supervision of work*	*Facilities available at work place*	*Wages*	*Status compared to other workers*
Yes	65	59	42	49	41	56
	(56.52)	(51.30)	(36.52)	(42.60)	(35.65)	(48.69)
No	50	56	73	66	74	59
	(43.47)	(48.69)	(69.47)	(57.39)	(64.35)	(51.30)

(b) *Satisfaction from Behaviour of Employer*

More than half of the respondents (51.30%) have been found satisfied with the behaviour of employer. 48.69 percent of respondents have been found dissatisfied with the behaviour of employer.

(c) *Satisfied with Supervision of Work*

More than 2/3rd of the respondents have been found dissatisfied with the supervision of their work.

(d) *Facilities Available of the Work Place*

More than half of the respondents (57.39%) have been found dissatisfied with the facilities available at work place. 42.60 percent of the respondents have been found satisfied with facilities available at the work place.

(e) *Wages*

About 2/3rd of respondents (64.35%) have been found dissatisfied with their wages. Only 35.65 percentage of respondents have been found satisfied with their wages.

(f) *Status compared to Other Workers*

More than half of the respondents have been found dissatisfied with the status compared to other workers.

Thus it can be concluded that relatively more respondents have been found satisfied with their nature of work and behaviour of employer as compared to their dissatisfied counter parts and large number of respondents have been found dissatisfied with their supervision of work and wages as compared to their satisfied counterparts and relatively more respondents have been found dissatisfied with facilities available at work place and status enjoyed by respondents as compared to other workers while seen in comparison to their satisfied counterparts.

Activities Performed at Home in Case of Nonworking Respondents

This information was collected from those respondents who are not going for work outside the family, but they perform certain works in their family. The collected information is being tabulated in Table No. 8.16.

Table 8.16
Activities Performed at Home in Case of Non Woking Respondents

Activities	*No. of the respondents (n = 185)*	*Percentage*
Bringing water	52	28.10
Cleaning utencils	63	34.05
Cooking	60	32.43
Looking after young ones	39	21.08
Buying domestic things	63	34.05

(Contd.)

Activities	*No. of the respondents (n = 185)*	*Percentage*
Watching the house	42	22.70
Accompanying other senior house hold lady when going out	38	20.54

The table brings out the fact that the largest single group of respondents (34.05% each) have reported cleaning of utensils and buying domestic things as activities performed in their families, followed by those respondents who have reported cooking (32.43%), bring water (28.10%), watching the house (22.70%), looking after young ones (21.08%) and accompanying other senior household lady when going outside (20.54%).

Problems Faced by Adolescent Girls Regarding Work and Employment

Table No. 8.17 presents respondents views regarding problems faced by them in the matter of their work and employment. These problems have been non-availability of regular work (44%), no satisfaction of basic need (39.33%); non-availability of adequate and proper work (38.33%); low earnings (29%); exploitation by employer (28%); unskilled work (26%); no proper development of skills (21.33%); bad supervision (15.33%), long hours of work (14%); unsuitable work (11.67%), lack of facilities at work place (10.67%) and no opportunity for education and development (10.33%).

Table 8.17
Problems Faced by Adolescent Girls Regarding Work and Employment

Problems	*No. of the respondents N = 300*	*Percentage*
Non-availability of adequate and proper work	115	38.33
Non-availability of regular work	132	44.00
Low earnings	87	29.00
Exploitation by employers	84	28.00
Bad supervision	46	15.33
Heavy work	55	18.33
No proper development of skills	64	21.33
Unskilled work	78	26.00
No satisfaction of basic needs	118	39.33
Long hours of work	42	14.00
Unsuitable work	38	12.67
No job security	35	11.67
Lack of facilities at work	32	10.67
No opportunity for education and development	31	10.33

Chapter IX

Attitudes and Beliefs of Adolescent Girls in Slums

Dread of adolescence has been intensified by the traditional belief that it is characterized by 'Storm and Rang' a label which received the scientific stamp of approval from G Stanley Hall when he called adolescence a "period of storm and stress". The word "storm" suggests that anger with its accompanying temper outbursts, is a prominent, if not the dominant emotion at this age. "Stress" suggests the existence of factors, emotional and physical, which disrupt normal functioning. It implies a generally upset condition which leads to deterioration of both physical and psychological function.[1]

Attitude Towards Marriage

Marriage is celebrated for the girls in early teens and for the boys either in late teens or early twenties. This has an effect upon the size of the family and the population in the locality. Most of these women have their first child before they complete the teens. This traits has made the family life more complex on account of this early motherhood, the size of the family has gone up owing to the large number of children. There is little pre-natal or post-natal care of either the mother or the child. The child is generally delivered at home or at the Government hospital. There are a number of instances of mother giving birth to children in a private hospital situated very near the area.

Divorce among the slum-dwellers is fairly easy. They need not go to the court of law. They live separately and that means the marriage is broken off. The husband and wife lead separate lives in their own way. Widow-remarriage is permitted. There are many instances of widows who have married again.[2]

Attitudes and Beliefs Towards Employment

The modern adolescent in the slum area is an irresponsible, carefree, illiterate youth. A common complain of the adolescents is that the parents expect them to perform the same work around the home as parents do and they deny the right to select their own way of life. The dominant conditioning factor in the choice between school or work, as well as the combination of school with part-time work is the family's and the adolescent's need for money. To the adolescent, money comes from out of his own income. The more severe the strain of economic conditions on the family, the more likely the boy or a girl is to choose or forced by circumstances to find a job. Constant questioning of the child, when money is required by him leads to friction between the father and the child. The healthy solution to the problem from the point of view of the adolescent is to earn his own money.

The world of the slum-dweller and his family is centred in the struggles for the basic necessities of life in a search for pleasure to break the monotony of work, unemployment and in security. Family life is punctuated with quarrels followed by fights and physical violence. Money is a scarce commodity. Therefore, an essential conditioning factor in the slum-dweller's childhood is the desire to grow up and get a job.

A modern urban adolescent girl aspires not only to limit herself to be a housewife but also to be a successful earning member of her family. So the adolescent girl equates her role to that of her brother and may not tolerate her parent's differentiation in their function of socialization based on sex role. This attitude of the adolescent girls may weaken their relationship with their parents.

The parents expect that school going adolescents would do this job of supervising the studies of their siblings better than looking after infant siblings.[3]

Attitude Towards Extra-Curricular Activities

As the child grows into adolescence his interest changes. Generally the adolescent child is more interested in the outside social activities in his peer world than in the household duties. He tries to loosen the clutches of his parents by breaking away from the routine domestic work. His/Her interests are centered around the recreational activities extra-curricular activities of the school and other social activities with his/her friends. He/she may not find enough time to attend to household duties after returning from school where he/she is required to spend nearly six hours per day. He/she is also required to study at home for some hours to keep up the study up to date.[4]

Attitudes Towards Family

The slum dwellers have each a fairly big family. There are instances of eleven to twelve persons living together with a single-bread-winner. Their attitude towards the employing family planning measures, is indifferent. This poverty, low income or misery have not encouraged them to limit size of the family. They attributed the birth of the children in the family to God. They reported that God is responsible for the birth of children and hence this sort of artificial birth control is unwanted and unnecessary. Though the slum-dwellers know that a large family is a burden, no attempt to decrease the size of the family has been made.

For the slum-dwellers sex is also one of the major recreational activities. Being fatigued and tired the slum-dwellers either drinks alcohol or when he has no money for it - enjoys sex with his wife. It is very rare that the men folk of the area go to prostitutes. The only extra-marital relationship he could think of is with a girl of the same locality. Hence he has to go to his wife only. This has been one of the reasons for the fast birth rate in the area. There are instances of the absence of proper spacing between births. It often happens in the area that the woman becomes pregnant again, when the former child is hardly a year old. Pre-natal and post-natal care is totally absent. Pregnant women are seen sweeping the streets. They do not get proper food. Their health is neglected. Hardly a month will have passed after the birth of the child when the mother will be seen at work on the streets with the small child in her arms feeding on her breasts. This has been another cause for the large number of children born in the area.[5]

Attitudes and Beliefs Towards Religion

Most adolescents want a religion that meets their needs, though needs vary markedly among adolescents, depending on the religious atmosphere of their homes, religious affiliation, peer, attitudes, sex, environment, socio-economic status, religious denomination and personality. Five developmental processes are essential to make a religion fit the needs of adolescents : religious awakening, religious doubt, changes in religious beliefs, changes in religious participation, and increased tolerance toward the belief and practices of others. Modern adolescents are not as irreligious as in popularly believed is shown by their interest in talking about religion, their study of religions in colleges and universities and their participation in religions that deviate from the traditional patterns. Religious awakening, which means an increased interest in religion leading to a reconstruction of religious beliefs and attitudes, may be gradual or catastrophic. Changes in religious beliefs are most frequent in those beliefs based upon specific concepts; such as the childish concept of God, of prayer, or of Heaven; such changes have four effects: decreased interest in religion, religious reconstruction, acceptance of the family faith or of a new faith and agnosticism or atheism. When changed beliefs lead to decreased interest in religion, the adolescent's religious observances also affected. Increase in religious tolerance is generally gradual, it accompanies the pattern of religious doubt. Overt expressions of religious tolerance in adolescence include a decrease in prejudice, change of religious faith, and interfaith dating and marriage. The transitional changes in religious beliefs, attitudes and observances may have temporary or permanent effects on religious attitudes and activities; depending on how the adolescent resolves his religious doubts.[6]

Attitude and Beliefs Towards Education

Slum-dwellers economic backwardness has been a factor coming in the way of the education of children. Parents want them to work for the family and help the family. The children study under hardships and that too for just a year or two. They have a hostile environment. They have felt that education imparted at schools has not been quite utilitarian as it is a long process. These factors dissuade them from continuing their studies. Another reason for this kind of apathy towards education is the non-availability of government schools. The children were just playing in the dirty streets of the locality and picking up all bad habits. With the cooperation of the municipality the Bharat Sevak Samaj people have been trying to create interest among the inhabitants in improving living conditions.

The problem of illiteracy is acute in the area. There has been no attempt on the part of the slum-dwellers to eradicate illiteracy among them. They are not inspired by education. The youth of the area are spending their time recklessly. They are lazy and careless. This sort of irresponsibility on their part has created slums have not got any formal training.

They are either trained as cobblers or masons either through apprenticeship or they are in pursuit of their hereditary occupations. The education of the children is not appreciated. The parents are also indifferent towards education. Hence most of the children abstain from attending the schools. Because of differences in aspirations, backgrounds and many other factors, adolescents have markedly different attitudes towards education. They enter high school or college with either favourable or unfavourable attitudes and they change very little.[7]

Factors Affecting Attitudes Toward Education

They are -

- *Cultural Values* : While most Americans put a very high value on education, some subcultural groups do not, feeling that it will not help them to get ahead.

- *Social Class Value* : In general attitudes toward education become more favourable as one goes up the socio-economic ladder.

- *Parental Attitudes* : Middle-class parents, anxious to have their children rise in the world encourage them to take part in academic and extracurricular activities. Lower-class parents as a group show little interest in education and permit their children to drop out of school if they want to go to work.

- *Ordinal Position* : First borne especially in middle and upper class families are likely to receive more encouragement and more educational advantages than later born siblings.

- *Peer Group Attitudes* : Boys tend to develop more favourable attitudes towards education when they recognize its value to their future. Girl's attitude become less favourable after the high school sophomore year.

- *Sex Roles* : Boys as a group, think of education as preparation for their vocation and girls as a group, for their home making and social roles.

- *Vocational Plans* : Adolescents who aspire to go into

work that requires higher education have a more favourable attitude towards academic and extracurricular activities from those who aspire to do skilled labour.

- *Social and Academic Success* : Success or failure in extracurricular activities in more important in determining attitudes towards school than success or failure in academic work.

-*Attitudes Towards Teachers* : Even when an adolescents likes a teacher, his attitude toward school may be unfavourable if he dislikes the subject she teaches, if he does poorly in those if he feels it has no practical value for him.

- *Teaching Techniques* : In contrast to the glamour of excitement of movies and television, teaching techniques seem boring and classroom work dull.

- *Antiwork Attitude* : Adolescents who are used to having help from parents and teachers dislike subject that require work. They may develop a general dislike for school[8].

Attitudes Towards Discipline

The role of discipline in moral development is to help the adolescent develop socially approved moral concepts, to reward him for socially approved behaviour, to punish him for intentional wrong doing and to provide consistent social expectations as an aid in building moral values. Of the three systems of discipline commonly used in controlling adolescent behaviour - authoritarian, democratic and permissive - the democratic product the best results from the point of view of the adolescent's personal and social development. Discrepancies between moral knowledge and moral behaviour in adolescence are due most commonly to peer group pressures, confusion about moral values, immature control of strong urges, decisions based on expediency and emotional factors and striving for independence.

Attitudes Towards Morality

In making the transition from childish to mature morality, the adolescent must learn what the social group expects of its members and then assume responsibility for his own behaviour. The most common obstacles the adolescent faces in making the transition are inadequate preparation for making moral decisions being confronted with a number of moral alternatives, conflicts in moral values, and pressures from the peer group to conform to peer rather than adult standards. To make a successful transition to adult morality, the adolescent must (1) change the attitudes and values which made up his childish moral concepts so that they will conform to adult standards and (2) assume control of his own behaviour. The conscience is the inner controlling force that makes external restraints unnecessary. Guilt and shame act as deterrents to behaviour that does not meet social expectations.

Girls on the whole have less difficulty making the transition to an adult morality than boys, primarily because their early training has been stricter and they have learned that adhering to cultural values enhances their prestige. Boys, by contrast, know that violating rules and even laws gives them greater prestige, especially in the peer group, than being law-abiding citizens.[9]

Attitudes Towards Leisure

Gambling among the slum-dwellers is essentially a male activity. Gambling is often defined as a deliberate wagering of money on some test of skill or strength or on the outcome of a game. These forbidden pleasures are very common in these slum areas. Gambling, drinking liquor, roaming about, regular attendance at the theaters to see motion pictures, smoking, taking intoxicants are a few of their leisure time activities. These have become the most unwholesome forms of recreation among the slum-dwellers. Taverns are prohibited by law to sell alcoholic beverages to the people and so all taverns now have shifted to the homes from which these liquors are being sold at fancy rates. Hence the leisure time activities have become commercialized. Business men have long since learned than even poor people are willing to pay for pleasure. Motion picture theaters consistently attract a significantly higher percentage of patrons than any other form of recreation. Practically all boys smoke irrespective of age. Smoking is a symbol of manhood and independence to the boys. Use of alcoholic beverages is rampant in both the sexes. The youngsters learn this from their parents quite early in life.

Further, these slum-dwellers do not take part in community activities. Leisure is expanded in loafing around in neighbourhood. The family is so loosely organised that the members go their own way in search of amusement or pleasure. Traveling for pleasure is practically absent. Lack of money among slum-dwellers denies them this privilege of making travel a pleasure. Perhaps this monetary inability has incapacitated them in a number of ways from having wholesome recreation to spend their leisure hours. Even the little money they have, are present on unhealthy forms of recreation to degenerate them both physically and socially. This has been largely responsible for the degraded state of affairs among the slum-dwellers in these areas. They are very backward culturally too. They are physically weak, mentally subnormal and inefficient and morally wrecks. Taking intoxicants is common among the slum-dwellers. They rationalize this drinking habit by telling us that they drink to 'drown their miseries' and forget everything in life for a while. Smoking among the men-folk is common. Gambling among the youths is a diversion. Visiting theaters to witness motion pictures is a common week-end programme among the slum-dwellers inspite of their poverty. In addition to all these pleasures during leisure time, there are people who reside in these slum areas spending their spare time in 'Ram Bhajan' and others keep idle and gossip. The younger generation dress themselves in all sorts of colours and roam about aimlessly. Loafing itself is a leisure time activity.

These recreational activities in the slum areas, are not found during a specific time. Most of the youths who are unemployed gamble at all hours of the day. The elders also have witnessed; serious fist fights and brawls among to some hitch in these gambles. The elderly residents of the areas are disgusted with the behaviour and movements of the present day youths of the locality. Many a time elders have intervened to stop these fights. The use of vulgar terms, tearing each others clothes and fist fights are a few of the results of gambling.

The residents in the area spend their time gossiping also. This is true especially in the case of women. They gossip for hours together, when their men folk are away at work. They are not interested in politics. As is evidenced, the moment they meet a stranger the only topic which they would like to discuss is about their plight. They express their miseries by cursing the civic authorities. Apathy usual habit with them is to discuss their neighbours and talk a very peevish way. Sex matters occupy an important place in their gossips. Their discussions are not healthy. The youths tease teenage girls. They even follow them. The moral tone is at a low ebb. This degeneration is attributed to their loose sexual standards. Women too are least concerned about the changing scene in society.

Slum dwellers have been interested in witnessing wrestling bouts. Just as they spend money to visit films, once in a way, they go to the wrestling stadium, where generally wrestling bouts are conducted twice or thrice a month. The spectators on the ground in these bouts will be partly the inhabitants from the slum areas. This is mainly a masculine activity. The youths and the middle aged men attend these bouts and enjoy themselves.

Superstitious practices like sacrifices to the village deities. Unclean habits like carrion eating must be discouraged gradually, this could be achieved only through education. Intensive propaganda to educate them in the personal hygiene sanitation is also required. Film shows and speeches on health would go a long way in making them conscious of health factors. The health units, which could prevent the spread of communicable diseases, must start working in these areas. Further knowledge about family planning should be made available in order to check the rapid growth of their population. This indirectly could encourage them to raise their standard of living.[10]

Opinion Regarding Slum Dwellers

In the present investigation, adolescent girls understudy are the residents of slum area and so is appropriate to enquire from the about their opinion regarding slum dwellers, keeping in view the above fact information was sought from the respondent regarding their opinion about slum dwellers. The collected information is being presented in tabular form in Table No. 9.1.

Table 9.1
Opinion Regarding Slum Dwellers

Opinion	*No. of the respondents (n = 300)*	*Percentage*
The condition of slum dwellers is very poor	92	30.66
The condition of slum dwellers is satisfactory	48	16.00
Slum dwellers are backwards	84	28.00
Slum dwellers are medium class people	51	17.00
Slum dwellers are in a developing stage	46	15.33

(Contd.)

Opinion	*No. of the respondents (n = 300)*	*Percentage*
Slum dwellers are exploited on several counts	74	24.67
Slum dwellers consist of respect in society	65	21.67
Slum dwellers have to engage themselves in illegal practices for earning livelihood	38	12.67
Slum dwellers should have not migrated from their native villages	42	14.00
Slum dwellers have anti-social elements also	39	13.00

It is clear from the data presented in the table that the largest single group of respondents (30.66%) has opined that the condition of slum dwellers is very poor followed by those respondents who have expressed the view that slum dwellers are backward (28%); slum dwellers are exploited on several counts (24.67%); slum dwellers have no respect in society (21.67%); slum dwellers are medium class people (17%), the condition of slum dwellers is satisfactory (16%); slum dwellers are in developing stage (15.33%); slum dwellers should have not migrated from their migrated villages (14%); slum dwellers consist of anti-social elements also (13.00%) and slum dwellers have to engage themselves in illegal practices for earning livelihood (2.67%).

Opining Regarding Fulfillment and Sufficiency of Different Need

Table No. 9.2 presents information collected from

respondents related to their opinion regarding above mentioned subject.

Table 9.2

Opinion Regarding Fulfilment and Sufficiency of Different Needs

No. of respondents; N = 300

Incidence	*Food grains*	*Clothes*	*Residential accommoda-tion*	*Medical care*	*Education*	*Recreation*
Yes	256 (85.33)	192 (64)	216 (72)	102 (34)	116 (38.66)	88 (29.33)
No	44 (14.66)	108 (36)	84 (28)	198 (66)	184 (61.33)	212 (70.77)

A close scrutiny of the table brings out the following facts:

1. Regarding fulfillment of the need and sufficiency of food grains, a dominant majority of respondent adolescent girls (85.33%) have reported that they have been able to manage food grains sufficiently, hence able to fulfill this need. However, 14.66 percent of respondents have failed to manage sufficient food grains.

2. Regarding clothing, it was found that majority of respondents (64%) has been able to manage sufficient cloths, but 36 per cent of respondents have also reported their inability to manage sufficient cloths.

3. Regarding residential accommodation, majority of respondents (72%) have reported the sufficiency of residential accommodation, may be because of most of the slum dwellers have migrated from the villages/small towns and whatever accommodation they have been able to manage, they are satisfied with this.

4. 2/3rd of Respondents (66%) have expressed that they have not been able to arrange sufficient medical care.

5. Majority of respondents (61.33%) has also expressed their inability for education.

6. Majority of respondents (70.77%) have also reported their inability to arrange proper and sufficient recreation for them and for their family.

Thus, it is clear that as per opinion of respondents, majority of them has been able to manage sufficient food grains and sufficient clothes and they have felt that their residential accommodation is sufficient. But, majority of them have expressed their failure to arrange medical, educational and recreational facilities.

Opinion Towards Taking up Work in Place of Study

This information have been tabulated in Table No. 9.3 which brings out the fact that the largest single group of respondents has reported about taking up of work in place of study as a good step (47.33%) followed by those respondents who have mentioned this as a bad step (35%). However, 25.33 percent of respondents failed to answer the question.

Table 9.3
Opinion Towards Taking up Work in Place of Study

Opinion	*No. of the respondents (n = 300)*	*Percentage*
Good step	142	47.33
Bad step	105	35.00
No response	76	25.33

Opinion Towards Education of Children

Adolescent girls, understudy, were approached to give their opinion regarding education of children for the purpose of know their preference for education. The collected information is being tabulated in Table No. 9.4.

Table 9.4
Opinion Towards Education of Children

Opinion	*No. of the respondents (n = 300)*	*Percentage*
Should be made compulsory	118	39.33
Should be voluntary	64	21.33
Shoud be academic	36	12.00
Recalling oriented	28	9.33
Consisting of manual labour	21	7.00
Should be limited to those boys/girls who are good at studies	18	6.00
To both boys and girls without any discrimination	72	24.00

The table clearly brings out that the largest single group of respondents (39.33%) has expressed the view that education of children should be made compulsory followed by those respondents who have opined that education should be given to both boys and girls without any discrimination (29%), should be voluntary (21.33%), should be academic (12%), should be recalling oriented (9.33%), should be consisted of manual labour (7%) and should be limited to those boys and girls who are good at studies (6%).

Opinion Regarding Dowry

In India, dowry is one of the most important social problem which has taken away lives of many young brides and has created problems for parents arranging marriage of their daughters. The worst affected and the girls of marriageable age, keeping in view the information was sought from the respondents in Table No. 9.5.

Table 9.5
Opinion Regarding Dowry

Opinion	*No. of the respondents (n = 300)*	*Percentage*
Very bad	141	47.00
Common problem in every group of people	62	20.66
All worries of parents are due to Dowry	46	15.33
A part of social custom	28	9.33
All right if not insisted	36	12.00
Distructive in outlook	41	13.66
Unavoidable	39	13.00

An analysis of the information presented in table brings out that about half of the respondents think dowry as very bad (47%), followed by those respondents who think dowry as common problem in every group of people (20.66%); all worries of parents are due to dowry (15.33%); destructive in outlook (13.66%); unavoidable (13%), all right if not insisted (12%), and dowry is a part of social custom (9.33%).

Opinion Regarding Social Tensions

Presently Indian scene plagued with castism,

communalism and regionalism. The caste conflict and communal strife are every day affair.

Poverty, discrimination, unemployment, under-employment, corruption and dowry are major social problems of contemporary India. These situations have established a social system full of social tensions, keeping in view the above mentioned circumstances in mind, respondents were approached to give their opinion regarding these tensions. The relevant information is being presented in Table No.9.6.

Table 9.6
Opinion Regarding Social Tensions

Opinion	*No. of the respondents (n = 300)*	*Percentage*
Causing Fear of life	51	17.00
Unavoidable	48	16.00
Destructive	71	23.66
Cause of backwardness	89	29.66
Part of life	38	12.66
Based on vested interests	42	14.00
No response	36	12.00

A deep probe into the data tabulated in above mentioned table leads to the conclusion that the largest single group of respondents (29.66%) has mentioned these tensions as cause of backwardness followed by those respondents who have labeled them as distractive (23.66%), causing fear of life (17%), unavoidable (16%), based on vested interests (14%) and part of life (12.66%). 12 percent respondents did not respond to this question.

Feeling of no Development as Long as Living in Slums

The related information is being tabulated in Table No. 9.7 which shows that more than half of the respondents (59%) have been in agreement that one can not develop as long as one lives in slum followed by 23 percent respondents who have been of the opposite view that one can develop while living in slums. 19 per cent of respondents have been found in partial agreement to the above mentioned statements, i.e. one can not develop as long as one lives in slum.

Table 9.7
Feeling that One Can Not Develop as Long as One Lives in Slum

Responses	*No. of the respondents*	*Percentage*
Yes	177	59.00
No	69	23.00
Partially	54	18.00
Total	300	100.00

Approval of Discrimination Between Boys and Girls

Indian society is marked with the discrimination between boys and girls in their daily life because boys are counted as assists while girls are taken as liability leading to the establishment of such system which is discriminative for girls on several counts as compared to boys. Keeping this in view, the information was sought from the respondents regarding the above mentioned subject and is being presented in tabular form in Table no. 9.8.

An analysis of data presented in the Table brings out the fact that more than half of the respondents (51.33%) have reported their approval for this discrimination may be because of the circumstances prevailing in their slum where ignorance, illiteracy, lack of access to media etc. are rampant.

The most of the respondents (48.67%) have not approved this discrimination.

Table 9.8
Approval of Discrimination Between Boys and Girls

Response	*No. of the respondents (n = 300)*	*Percentage*
Yes	154	51.33
No	146	48.67
Total	300	100.00

Reasons for the Approval of Discrimination Between Boys and Girls

The adolescent girls who have approved the discrimination between boys and girls have been asked to elaborate reasons for their opinion. The collected information is being presented in Table No. 9.9.

Table 9.9
Reasons for the Approval of Discrimination Between Boys and Girls

Reasons	*No. of the respondents (n = 154)*	*Percentage*
Male dominant society	52	33.77
Traditional importance to boys as compared to girls	34	22.08
Earners	68	44.16
Dependence of family on Boys	46	29.87

(Contd.)

Reasons	*No. of the respondents (n = 154)*	*Percentage*
Expectation of support from boys in old age	48	31.17
Boys are physically strong as compared to girls	50	32.47
Boys bring dowry for parents	69	44.80
Salvation can be achieved with the help of boys	45	29.22

The Table shows that the largest single group of respondent (44.16%) has approved this discrimination because according to them boys bring dowry for parents (44.8%), followed by those respondents who have mentioned boys are earners (44.6%), male dominate society (33.77%), boys are physically strong as compared to girls (32.47%), expectation of support from boys in old age (31.17%), dependence of family on boys (29.87%), salvation can be achieved with the help of boys (29.22%) and traditional importance to boys as compared to girls (22.08%).

Reasons for Disapproval of the Discrimination Between Boys and Girls

These have been tabulated in Table No. 9.10. According to this table the dominant majority of respondents (84.33%) has reported that they disapprove this discrimination because both boys and girls have equal importance followed by the respondents who have been of the view that approval of this discrimination means unnecessary approval for dominance of male (81.51%), and this discrimination should be socially unacceptable (57.53%) and irrational (32.19%).

Table 9.10
Reasons for the Disapproval of the Discrimination Between Boys and Girls

Reasons	*No. of the respondents (n = 146)*	*Percentage*
Both have equal importance	124	84.93
Unnecessary approval for the dominance of man	119	81.51
Socially unacceptable	84	57.53
Discrimination is irrational	47	32.19

Opinion Regarding Abolition of Slums

Table No. 9.11 brings out that only 1/3rd of respondents have been of the opinion that slums should be abolished. Rest 2/3rd of the respondents (65.33%) have been found against the abolition of slums may be due to the fear that in case of abolition of slums, there will be problem of accommodation to slum dwellers.

Table 9.11
Opinion Regarding Abolition of Slum

Response	*No. of the respondents (n = 300)*	*Percentage*
Yes	104	34.66
No	196	65.33
Total	300	100.00

Reasons for Giving Opinion in Favour of Abolition of Slums

Respondents in favour of abolition of slums have given reasons for that information pertaining to these reasons has been tabulated in Table No. 9.12

Table 9.12
Reasons for Giving Opinion in Favour of Abolition of Slums

Reasons	*No. of the respondents (N = 104)*	*Percentage*
Development rate in slums is very slow	44	42.30
Chances of improvement and upliftment of slums are almost negligible	48	46.75
Unhygienic atmosphere	32	30.76
Congested ways	49	47.11
Lack of basic amenities	58	55.76
Prevalence of slum mentality	46	44.23
Place of hiding for anti social elements	32	30.77
Exploitation by politicians	34	32.69
Prevalence of various diseases and bad habits among slum dwellers	42	40.38

The table makes it clear that lack of basic amenities has been given by more than half of the respondents (55.76%)

as reason for abolition of slum. The other reasons spelt out by these adolescent girls have been congested ways (47.11%); chances of improvement and upliftment of slums are almost negligible (46.75%); prevalence of slums mentality (44.23%); development rate in slum is very slow (42.30%) prevalence of various diseases and bad habit among slum dwellers (40.38%); exploitation by politicians (32.69%); unhygienic atmosphere and place of hiding for anti-social elements (30.77% each).

Reasons for Giving Opinion Against the Abolition of Slums

The collected information is being presented in Table No. 9.13. The respondents have listed fair reasons for giving above mentioned reasons. These have been—slums are shelter for poor people (41.83%); slum dwellers incapability of leaving slum areas (40.30%); lack of resources for proper housing (37.75%) and making stay arrangements and newly migrants in the city (34.18%).

Table 9.13
Reasons for Giving Opinion Against The Abolition of Slums

Reasons	*No. of the respondents (n = 196)*	*Percentage*
Shelter for poor people	82	41.33
Lack of resources for proper housing	74	37.75
Making stay arrangement of newly migrants articles in the city	67	34.18
Incapability of leaving slum area	79	40.30

Possibilities of Improving Your Working/Living Conditions

This information is being presented in Table No. 9.14 which brings out the fact that more than half of the respondents (53.66%) have expressed hope that there are possibilities of improving working/living condition of respondents. 37.66 per cent of respondents have given pessimistic opinion of no possibilities of improvement. 8.66 percent of respondents have failed to respond to this query.

Table 9.14
Possibilities of Improving Your Working /Living Conditions

Possibilities	*No. of the respondents (n = 300)*	*Percentage*
Yes	161	53.66
No	113	37.66
No response	26	8.66

Reasons for Lack of Possibilities of Improving the Living and Working Conditions

This information was sought from those respondents who have expressed no possibilities of improvement in the living and working conditions of slum dwellers. This information is being presented in Table No. 9.15.

This table makes it clear that the largest single group of respondents (46.90%) has exploitation by the employers as reason for the absence of possibilities of improvement in living and working conditions of slum dwellers followed by other reasons which have been ignorance and unawareness among slum dwellers about slum improvement programme (46.10%); increasing population (38.05%); lack of interest by Government officials (27.43%)

and prevalence of vested interests even in providing help and support to poor people (25.66%).

Table 9.15
Reasons for the Possibilities of Improving the Living and Working Conditions

Reasons	*No. of the respondents (n = 161)*	*Percentage*
Increasing awareness among the people	44	27.32
Governmental efforts	58	36.02
Rise in salary	44	27.32
Rapid socialization	46	28.57
Efforts for educating people	68	42.23
Vocational education	48	29.81
Concentration of voluntary agencies for solving the problems of slum	52	32.30

Reasons for Possibilities of Improving Living and Working Conditions

Information pertaining to these reasons has been sought from those respondents who have expressed possibilities of improvement in living and working conditions. These reasons have been listed in Table No. 9.16.

According to this table, the largest single group of respondents (42.23%) has been of the opinion that these are possibilities of improvement in the living and working condition of slum dwellers because of efforts done for educating people. The other reasons have been : Governmental efforts (36.02%); concentration of voluntary agencies for solving the problems of slum (32.30%);

vocational education (29.81%); rapid socialization (28.57%); increasing awareness among the people and rise in salary (27.32% each).

Table 9.16
Reasons for Lack of Possibilities of Improving the Living and Working Conditions

Reasons	*No. of the respondents (n = 113)*	*Percentage*
Lack of interest by Government officials	31	27.43
Ignorance and unawareness among slum dwellers about slum improvement programmes	52	46.01
Exploitation by the employers	53	46.90
Increasing population	43	38.05
Lack of concern shown by the slum dwellers	32	28.31
Prevalence of vested interests even in providing help and support to poor people	29	25.66

Suggestions Offered by Respondents for Improving the Life and Living Conditions of Slum Dwellers

The information has been tabulated in Table No. 9.17. The table brings out that more than half of the respondents (62.33%) have suggested for the arrangement of minimum basic facilities such as potable water, drainage, lights, mean of accessibility, etc. The other suggestions have been opening of fair price shop in slums (37.33%), launching of awareness campaign among slum dwellers about health and hygiene (35%), arrangement for hand pump in the area (34.67%); arrangement for immunization (29.67%); arrangement for training of women in different trades in order to make them economically effective (28.33%); Balwadis and school should be opened and prenatal and post-natal help and nutrition education should be arranged (27.67% each); security to slum dwellers by granting clear titles of the land (25.33%), organization of literacy campaign and classes and propagation as well as information about poverty alleviation programmes (21.33% each); regular health checkup of the slum dwellers (16%) drive against drug addiction (15.33%); regular cleanliness of the area (15%); drive against anti-social elements (13%); facilities to the handicapped person (11.33%) and opening of consumer stores in slums (8%).

Table 9.17
Improvements Suggested by Respondents For Improving the Life and Living of Slum Dwellers

Improvements	*No. of the respondents (n = 300)*	*Percentage*
Launching of awareness campaign among slum dwellers about health and hygiene	105	35.00
Arrangement of minimum basic facilities such as potable water, drainage, lights, means of accessibility, etc.	187	62.33
Balwadis and schools should be opened	83	27.67

(Contd.)

Improvements	*No. of the respondents (n = 300)*	*Percentage*
Play ground for children should arranged	43	14.33
Regular cleanliness of the area	45	15.00
Security to slum dwellers by granting clear title of the land	76	25.33
Organisation of literacy campaign and classes	64	21.33
Drive against drug addiction	46	15.33
Arrangement of immunization	89	29.67
Facilities should be provided to handicapped persons	34	11.33
Regular health check-up of slum dwellers	48	16.00
Arrangement for handpumps in the area	104	34.67
Opening of Fair price shops in slums	112	37.33
Opening of consumer stores in slums	24	8.00
Prenatal and postnatal help and nutrition education should be arranged	83	27.67

(Contd.)

Improvements	*No. of the respondents (n = 300)*	*Percentage*
Arrangement for training of women indifferent trades in order to make them economically effective	85	28.33
Propagation and implementation of poverty alleviation programmes	64	21.33
Drive against anti-social elements should be launched	39	13.00

Chapter X

Conclusions and Suggestions

CONCLUSIONS

In every research investigation, it becomes the duty of researcher to gather various findings of the investigation for the purpose of making them useful for prospective consumers i.e. expert, experiment and masses who generally want to know about it by going through its main conclusions. Findings in clear and concised form prove to be of considerable use to the researcher also as they not only make him aware of the extent to which he has been able to obtain his research objective but also pave the way for suggesting a plan of action for the betterment of the lot of area of the study. Findings of the present are being presented chapter-wise in ensuing paragraphs.

Chapter I consists of the analysis of urbanization incorporating urbanization processes in historical perspective, migration and urbanization, rural urban integration, trends in urbanization in whole country as well as in Uttar Pradesh including regional variation in urbanization and mushroom growth of slums due to the phenomenon of urbanization. This is significant to note that population living in slum areas has been found around 38 percent of the urban population which is quite large.

Chapter II deals with programmes and services for urban poor with particular reference to slums. The programmes of slum clearance, provision of housing and improvement; environmental improvement of urban slum in VIIIth Plan (1992-97), Nehru Rozgar Yojna, Prime Minister's Rozgar Yojna for self-employment, Shelter related programme; nutrition supplement programmes, child development programme, employment generation and employment oriented training programmes, support to training and employment projects, training-cum-employment-cum-production centres, socio-economic programmes, Mahila Samriddhi Yojna, Rashtriya Mahila Kosh, Programmes and services for urban poor in Uttar Pradesh such as Integrated Development Programme, Nagar Vikas Yojna, Environmental Improvement of Slums, Integrated Development of small and medium towns, Kanpur Urban Development Project, Urban Basic Services, U.P. Urban Development and Water Supply Project and Urban Transport Scheme have been discussed.

Research, Design and Methodology have been discussed in *Chapter-III*, hence there are no conclusions in this chapter.

Profile of adolescent girls has been presented in *Chapter IV*. The main findings are as follows :

1. Majority of adolescent girls belongs to the age group of 12-14 years and their average age has been found 13.1 years.
2. More than half of the respondent adolescent girls (57.7%) have been found married leading to the conclusion that adolescent girls in slum areas go for an early marriage.
3. Slum areas understudy have been found dominated by Muslims and lower caste Hindus.
4. Majority of adolescent girls has been from urban areas.
5. Most of the adolescent girls of slum areas have been found illiterate and they have very low level of education because the maximum level of educational status has been found upto high school level only.

6. Majority of adolscent girls has been found economically ineffective because they have been either non-workers or unemployed. Among earning adolescent girls, the largest single group has been working as daily wage-earners.
7. Average monthly income of working adolescent girls has been Rs. 354.17 per month which comes to about Rs. 11.8 per day which is very low.
8. More than half of the respondents (58.67%) have nuclear family structure and the average family size of joint families has been found 7.95 i.e. 8 and of nuclear families 6.02 i.e. 6 which is relatively large in case of both joint and as well as nuclear families.
9. Regarding sex, it was found that family members of slum areas understudy have been found almost equally distributed as males 50.73% and females 49.27%.
10. The average age of family members of adolescent girls understudy has been found 23.22 years. Whereas in case of male members 23.89 years and female members 22.53 years bringing out the fact that members in families of slum areas understudy have been found young.
11. The number of married family members of respondents is quite high among relatively young family members.
12. The educational status of family members is quite low.
13. Family occupation in slum areas understudy has generally been found of daily wage learning.
14. The main occupations of family members have been service, daily wage earnings and rendering of domestic service.

15. The level of education in slum areas understudy has been found very low and majority of respondents' family members has been found having no formal educational standard. The number of graduates and postgradaute in these families is almost negligible.
16. The average income of respondents' families has been found as Rs. 1265.00 per month which is quite low.
17. It was found that average number of earning members per family comes to 1.8 i.e. 2 members out of the average family size of 7 members, hence dependence rate in respondents' families is quite high.
18. It was found that most of the respondents' families have no school going child and among those families which have school going children, most of them have one school going child.
19. The average number of families having non-school children has been 1.96 i.e. 2 per family.
20. Regarding duration of stay of family in the city and present locality (slum areas), it was found that duration of stay of respondent's family in the city as well as in this locality has been quite long (average 24.10 years in case of stay of respondents' families in the city and 14.40 years in case of stay of respondents' families in this locality).
21. Most of the families have been migrated from rural areas prior coming to this city as well as to this slum.
22. Regarding monthly expenditure of respondents' families, it was found that the main item of expenditure on which most of these families expend their monthly income has been found, food followed by clothing and medicines.

Housing Needs and Problems of Slum Dwellers have been discussed in *Chapter V*. Main findings of this chapter are :

1. Most of the respondent adolescent girls have generally been living either in houses involving no rent or in family houses.
2. It has been found that most of the houses in slum areas lack electricity, potable drinking water facility and almost no proper latrine facility. Their houses are mainly Kachha - bomboo-mixed houses.
3. It has been found that most of the houses in slum areas understudy have one room accommodation and the dominant majority of these houses does not have separate space for varandah, kitchen and storage. Consequently, room accommodation available wtih these houses has been used for kitchen, study, sleeping, sitting as well as storage purposes.
4. It can also be concluded that respondents' houses are located in over-crowded and uncleaned locality having no proper arrangement of drainage and disposal of waste material.
5. Regarding availability of facilities and its distance, it has been found that the average distances for various facilities such as hospital, railway station, city bus station, main market, post office, primary school, police station and sources of drinking water have been found 1.5 kms, 4.29 kms, 1.01 kms, 1.61 kms, 1.13 kms, 0.76 km, 1.01 kms and below 1 km respectively bringing out the fact that railway station is far away as compared to other facilities.
6. The facility of fair price shop is not available in respondents' locality.

7. As regards opinion of respondents about the lacking of facilities, it has been found that a dominant majority of respondents has reported the lacking of facilities of College (93.33%), road (92.33%), library (91.33%), park (91.00%), bus station (90.00%), fair price shop (89. 67%), play ground (87.33%), cooperative society (85.33%), cleanliness (81.67%), school (81.33%), bank (80.33%) and more than half of the respondents have reported the lacking of facilities such as ration shop (67.33%), hospital (6%), sanitation (62%), and electricity (53.33%). 42 per cent respondents have mentioned the lacking of the sources of family welfare centre.

Chapter VI deals with Family and Marital Problems of the adolescent girls. The main findings have been :

1. The adolescent girls understudy have listed dowry (43%), prevalence of child marriage (27.33%), unemployed boys (22%), torture by husband and in-laws (17.66%), adjustment problems (10.66%), unstable salary of bridegrooms (8%) and age difference between newly weds (7%) as problems faced by the family in case of marriage.
2. A dominant majority of respondents (70.67%) has revealed that natives help in the reception and other work related to marriage party followed by providing economic help, providing stay facilities to the relatives and help rendered in searching bridegrooms. A handful number of respondents (18.33%) also revealed that natives do not provide any help during marriage.
3. Regarding system of marriage, it has been reported by majority of respondents that generally arranged marriages are performed in their locality. More than half of the respondents (57%) have also

reported about the prevalence of child marriage.

4. As regards opportunity to express views about marriage it has been found that majority of these girls are not being given opportunity to express their views regarding their own marrige. The reasons have been lack of democratic tradition in family, lack of faith of parents in respondents; not giving weight to the opinion of girls in the family, prevalence of a view among parents/guardians that girls can not take right decision, closed nature of society and traditional views of not consulting girls/boys prevalent in the family.
5. Among respondents who have opportunity to express their views regarding marriage, majority of respondent adolescent girls has expressed their views regarding their marriage through mother/sister.
6. As regards normal age at marriage of boys/girls prevalent in respondents' families, largest single group of respondent has revealed it from 10 to 15 years leading to the conclusion that child marriages are prevalent in slum areas understudy.
7. This fact is also supported by the married respondent girls because most of them have been married between the age group of 10 to 14 years.
8. In case of child marriage, respondent adolescent girls have reported many problems as evident from the following :
   (a) Problems faced at the time marriage have been ignorance of child, irresponsibility on the part of parents, instability during marriage, no legal sanction and not full marriage due to Gauna and other formalities.
   (b) Problems faced after the marriage have been revealed as adjustmental problems in

respondents' families, early motherhood, hindrance in education, difficulty in coping with new situation, lack of proper knowledge about married life, ignorance about implications of marriage, mental harrassment and concern, improper development of mind and body, extra burden at tender age, problem of half married and expectation of maturity at a young age.

8. Most of the respondent adolescent girls expect their marriage in the age group of 15-19 years.

9. Majority of unmarried adolescent girls have been found sure about their marriage. However, 12.57 percent of respondents have reported that their marriage will not take place.

10. Dowry, poverty, non-challant attitude of parents about marriage, non-availability of suitable bridegroom, unmarried elder brother/sister, lack of seriousness of marriage due to joint family, bad physical appearance, and hindrance due to previous marriage of elders have been given as hindrances coming in way of marriage.

11. A dominant majority of respondent adolescent girls has accepted that their family faced dowry problem in marriage in the forms of demand for more money, desired for particular things such cycle, wrist watch, TV etc., demand for ornaments, etc. The main initiation points of dowry problems have been at the time of Tilak, at the time of the presentation of ornaments, at the time of Kalewa, after the departure of marriage party and after reaching of the marriage party at home.

    The dowry problem has resulted into little friction between families of bride and bridegroom in largest number of cases (32%) followed by tension (27.33%), delay in vidai (24.66%) and even breaking of marriage (3.66%).

12. Child marriage has been found prevalent in about half of the respondents' families (47%). The reasons, as reported by the respondent adolescent girls, for the prevalence of child marriage have been backwardness, less expensive, family belief, marriage before puberty, following old traditions and parents' feel free from their major obligation of life.

13. A dominant majority of respondents has revealed the prevalence of Gauna ceremony in their families which either takes place immediately after marriage of within 24 months to 120 months as the case may be.

Chapter VII deals with Educational Problems of Adolescent Girls. The main conclusions have been presented in the following paragraphs:

1. Most of the girls are not going to school in slum areas understudy.

2. The respondent adolescent girls, who have joined school, have joined the school between the age group of 5 to 7 years generally in Class-I.

3. Poverty has been given as main reason responsible for not joining the school by adolescent girls.

4. The main reasons for leaving the school after joining have been economic problems, low income of the family, burden for caring small children in family, early marriage and ignorance towards education.

5. Conveyance problem, lack of good company and distance of school have been mentioned as difficulties faced in going to school.

6. Most of the non-school going adolescent girls have no desire to go to school mainly due to the

economic problems, engagement in household work, distance of school, traditional values of the family, unsuitable atmosphere, working outside and uninteresting syllabus.

7. Quite a significant number of adolescent girls (47.36%) has accepted bad performance in their studies due to their irregularity in attending school, lack of interest in studies, lack of study material, lack of proper guidance, heavy curriculum, lack of good company, lack of time and unsuitable atmosphere.

8. More than half of the respondents (51.64%) have accepted that they had the desire to study but could not study because of poverty, family restrictions, lack of interest shown by parents in respondents' studies, engagement in performing household chorus, preference to boys in education as compared to girls, care of siblings and traditional values of family.

9. A significant number of respondent adolescent girls has reported that they have not been encouraged by their parents for getting education. However, in case of those respondent adolescent girls who got encouragement for study from their parents have revealed that parents encourage them for education by admitting them to school, meeting all study requirements, adjusting themselves according to their child's requirements, providing guidance, sacrificing their own need and making aware about the need and importance of education.

   Reasons for not encouraging for education have been economic problems, priorty for education of boys, parents' need for helping hand in their work, prevalence of traditional and backward ideas in family, responsibility for looking after young children and ill health of parents.

10. About 2/3rd of respondents have reported that there exists a feeling on their part that boys are preferred as compared to girls for providing education. The reasons for this preference have been mentioned by these respondents as conservative outlook of family, sick mentality and need of helping hands for household work.
11. Poverty, conservative attitude, ignorance, lack of time due to household work, preference to boys as compared to girls and early marriage have been mentioned as reasons responsible for blocking education of respondent adolescent girls.
12. Majority of respondent adolescent girls (71.33%) preferred for the education of girls because of the present policy of liberalization and modernisation, job security, female education brings education to whole family, formation of future generation, reducing family burden, economic independence to girls and equal chance of education for all.
13. Adolescent girls understudy have suggested free education, opening of schools; establishment of adult education centre, supply of free study material, easy admission procedure, awareness campaign, and arrangement of scholarships as facilities needed in the matter of education.

Chapter VIII describes Employment Problems of Adolescent Girls. The main findings of this chapter are as follows:

1. More than 1/3rd of the respondent adolescent girls have been found involved in work outside their families and engaged as labourers (20%), household workers (16.52%), in making handicrafts such Jhavia, Rassi, envelops etc. (13.19%), in tailoring (13.04%), as maid servants (12.17%), in cottage industry like making of papad, candles etc. (10.43%), and caring of others' small children (5.2%).

2. Adolescent girls understudy have started working outside their family at a very young age.
3. Most of the respondent adolescent girls have been working for the satisfaction of their own as well as family members' needs.
4. Most of adolescent girls understudy have generally been motivated to take up work either by their parents or self-motivated.
5. Supplementing the family income, fulfilment of own needs, fulfilment of will of parents, liking for doing work, no other employment opportunities, managing of out of pocket allowance, apathy towards studies, no liking for dependence on others, death of parents, weakness in studies, no body to support and for the purpose of learning some work have been mentioned as reasons for working by respondent adolescent girl.
6. As regards average duration of engagement in work in a year, it has been found that most of the respondents have been able to get work upto six months only in a year.
7. Regarding hours of work per day, majority of respondents has reported that they work from 3 to 7 hours per day.
8. Most of the respondent adolescent girls work with uncooperative, exploitative and rude employer.
9. The working adolescent girls understudy have generally been supervised by employer himself/herself. Regarding sex of supervisors, it has been found that more than half of them have been supervised by males (58.26%); by assigning work in the morning and evaluating it, in the evening, by explaining and doing work, by verbally, explaining the work, hurling abuses and even beating.

10. In most of the cases, employers pay extra wages and benefits for taking up maximum work from the respondents.
11. It has been found that dominant majority of respondent adolescent girls, who is engaged in work earns wages per day ranging from Rs. 16 to Rs. 45.
12. Regarding feeling of satisfaction with nature of work, behaviour of employer, supervision of work, facilities available at work place and status compared to other working people, it has been found that relatively more respondents have been found dissatisfied with their nature of work and behaviour of employer as compared to their dissatisfied counterparts and large number of respondents have been found dissatisfied. With their supervision of work and wages compared to their satisfied counterparts and relatively more respondents have been found dissatisfied with facilities available at work place and status employed by respondents as compared to other workers while seen in comparison to their satisfied counterparts.
13. Non working respondent adolescent girls have mentioned cleaning of utencils and buying domestic things; cooking; bringing water; watching the house; looking after young ones; accompanying other senior household lady when going outside as activities performed by them in their families.
14. The respondent adolescent girls have reported various problems faced by them regarding work and employment. These have been : non-availability of regular work, no satisfaction of basic needs, non-availability of adequate and proper work, low earnings, exploitation by

employer, unskilled work, no proper development of skills, bad supervision, long hours of work, unsuitable work, lack of facilities at work place and no opportunity for educational development.

Respondents' Attitude and Beliefs have been discussed in *Chapter IX.* The main conclusions of this chapter are as follows :

1. Regarding slum dwellers, respondents have expressed the opinion that the condition of slum dwellers is poor, they are backwards and exploited on several counts leading to no respect in the society.
2. Most of the respondent adolescent girls have mentioned that their family is way able to manage sufficient foodgrains and cloths only but they are unable to manage medical, education and recreational facilities.
3. The longest single group of respondents has reported about taking up of work in place of study as a good step (47.33%).
4. Regarding education of children, the respondent adolescent girls have opined that education of children should be made compulsory followed by the suggestion that education should be given to both boys and girls without any discrimination.
5. Most of the respondents think dowry is bad, though it is a part of social custom.
6. Regarding social tensions, the respondent adolescent girls have opined that these tensions are as cause of backwardness, destructive, causing fear in life and based on vested interests.
7. Most of respondents have been found in agreement to the statement that one can not develop as long as one lives in slum.

8. Regarding approval of discrimination between boys and girls, it has been found that more than half of the respondents (51.33%) has approved this discrimination may be due to the circumstances prevailing in slum areas where ignorance, illiteracy and lack of access to the media etc. are rampant. The reasons behind this, approval have been mentioned by respondents as 'boys bring dowry for parents', 'male dominant society', 'boys are physically strong as compared to girls', 'expectation of support from boys in old age', 'dependence of family on boys', 'salvation can be achieved with the help of boys' and 'traditional importance of boys as compared to girls'.

   However, 48.67 percent respondents disapprove this type of discrimination because they opined that 'both boys and girls have equal importance', 'approval of this discrimination means unnecessary approval for dominance of male', and 'this discrimination is irrational'.

9. 2/3rd of the respondents have been of the opinion that slums should not be abolished because they have felt that slum are shelter for poor people; slum dwellers are not capable to leave the slum and lack of resources for housing.

   1/3rd of the respondents have advocated for the abolition of slums and reasons behind such advocacy have been: lack of basic amentities in slum areas, conjusted ways; negligible chance of improvement and upliftment of slum dwellers, slow development rate of slum people, prevalence of various diseases and bad habits among slum dwellers; exploitation of politicians and place of hiding for anti-social elements.

10. Regarding possibilities of improvement in working/living conditions in slums, it has been

found that more than half of the respondents (53.66%) have expressed the hope for possibilities of improvement. As per respondents, these possibilities exist because of efforts done for educating people, government efforts for improving the lot of slum dwellers, concentration of efforts of voluntary organisation for meeting the needs of slum dwellers, imparting of vocational education, rapid socialization and increasing awareness among people towards slum dwellers and their problems.

Only 37.33 per cent of respondents have expressed about lack of existence of possibilities in working/ living conditions in slums. The reasons enumerated for this have been : prevalence of exploitation of slum dwellers by their employers, ignorance and lack of awareness among slum dwellers regarding their problems and slum improvement programmes, lack of interest on the part of Government officials and prevalence of vested interests even in providing help and support to the poor people.

11. Arrangement for minimum basic facilities such as potable drinking water, drainage, light, means of access etc.; opening of fair price shop in slum areas, launching of awareness campaigns among the slum dwellers regarding health and hygiene, arrangement for hand pumps, immunization, training of women in different trades etc. in order to make them economically effective; opening of Balwadis and schools, arrangement for pre-natal and post-natal help and care as well as nutrition and education; security to slum dwellers by arranging them clear title of the land: organisation of literacy campaign and classes; propagation as well as information about poverty; alleviation programmes; regular health checkup of slum

dwellers; drive against drug addiction and anti-social elements; regular cleanliness of the area, facilities to handicapped persons and opening of consumer stores have been offered by respondents as suggestions for improving the working/living conditions in slum areas.

SUGGESTIONS

Adolescent girls, in general and of slum aeras in particular, have been a neglected lot in the matter of reach of social agencies. Their developmental needs will require special attention in order to prepare them for adult roles. Social work is a reaching out practice where client is to be found out, not waited for. The aim of social work is to prevent or atleast to alleviate. The socially and psychologically damaging effects of crisis situation and social injustice and to remove barriers to the healthy development of individuals, groups and communites (Friedlender, 1976: p. 2). This demands that social worker should remind herself/himself that she/he is not an armchair philosopher of laboratory scientist. She/He is, or should be, an involved and commited person, and that involvement must leave aside cold, neutral objectivity and rather help the community to describe, identify and articulate its aspirations into something which is tangible and then mobilise. The community to strive to achieve them (Kulkarni, 1978: p. 11). In this way, social worker should intervene in slums for planned and induced development towards goals and objectives desired by slum dwellers. The following suggestions can be offered for improving the lot of slum dwellers in general and adolescent girls in particular.

A. Suggestions for Improvement in Overall Physical Conditions of the Slum Areas

1. Efforts should be directed to provide security to slum dwellers by managing clear titles to the land occupied by them either on lease or outright sale

with an insistance on need and systematic lay-out providing accessibility and incorporating of least minimum facilities such as play ground, balwadis, schools, clinics, etc. Government and local bodies should be approached for bearing the cost of the infrastructure such as roads, footpaths, water supply, drainage and lights.

2. Group housing on coopoerative basis should be introduced and costs can be reduced by sharing a common walls and common facilities. These societies can manage the loans for construction purpose easily.
3. The responsibility of cleanliness of the area should be taken up by these cooperative societies instead of local bodies which are not performing this responsibility in proper manner.
4. Slum dwellers should be helped in doing small tasks such as writing letters of complaints to concerned officials, arranging contracts with related functionaries etc. pertaining to their problem situations which are normally related to the cleanliness of the area, disposal of waste water and material, availability of potable drinking water, arrangement of latrines, common space for holding common functions such as marriage, etc.
5. Sanitation drives should be organised from time to time jointly by residents of the locality and concerned officials.
6. Social worker should act as a link between officials and people of slum and render needed help and support to the people to represent their views regarding non-availability of basic civic amenities in the area as well as for arranging title of land occupied by residents of slum areas.

B. Suggestion for the Organisation of Literacy, Education and Awareness Activities for Slum Dwellers Including Adolescent Girls

1. Existing infrastructure, both governmental as well as non-governmental for providing literacy should be mobilised.
2. Awareness regarding rights and responsibilities should be created among slum dwellers.
3. Slum dwellers should be made conscious towards social evils which considerably tax them both physically and economically.
4. Support of voluntary agencies, interested in literacy, education and awareness building, should be mobilised.
5. The acivities of Anganbadi Centres should be arranged for slum dwellers.
6. Evil efforts of alcoholic drinks and other bad habits should be propagated among slum dwellers through adult literacy classes.
7. Special drive should be taken up for school enrolment in slum areas.

C. Suggestions for the Organisation of Health and Nutrition Activities for Slum Dwellers Inclusive of Adolescent Girls

1. Programmes of mass and continuous immunization; Iodine Deficiency Disorders Control, Aids Awareness, Urban Base Services, etc. should be launched.
2. Anti-drug addiction drive and prohibition propaganda should be organised.
3. Health education programme should be undertaken for developing social health practices such as washing hands after defecation,

cleanliness at cooking place, cleanliness of children, etc.

4. Special attraction could be focussed on handicapped persons by arranging them artificial limbs, wheel chairs, etc.
5. Alcoholics and drug abuses should be lcoated and counselling programme should be arranged for them.
6. Pre-natal and post-natal health as well as nutrition education should be arranged for women.

D. Suggestions for the Organisation of Economic Activities in Slum Areas

1. Family centred approach should be undertaken in which every family of the area should be approached for knowing their existing economic needs, locating resources of family, deciding priority among these economic needs as for resources available and this, developing habit of doing planned expenditure.
2. Income generation programme launched by Government as Prime Minister's Rozgar Yojna for self-employment, Mahila Samridha Yojna, Employment Assurance Scheme, Swakshay Vimati Plan, Urban Base Service Programme, Mid-day Meal Programme, Maternity Benefits Programme, Social Assistance Programme, etc. should be propagated among slum dwellers and necessary assistance should be given to families for availing of facilities available under the programme.
3. Economic activities on group or cooperative basis can also be chalked out where group can be formed for common economic activity for common production and marketing.
4. Vocational guidance and counselling services for

young/adolescent boys and girls should be arranged.

5. With then help and support of Governmental and Non-Government organisations, Craft Training-cum-Production Centre can be established for rendering training in different crafts to women and girls of the area and undertaking the production of school garments, hospital uniforms, games dresses, children's clothes, napkins, etc.
6. Arrangement for fair price shops and consumer stores in slum areas should be done.

E. Establishment of Family Life Education Centre for Adolescent Girls in Slum Areas

This type of centre should be established in the area for assisting adolescent girls in their emotional, physical and social development so that they become knowledgeable and skillful in facing the challenges of adult life, conflicting of personal relationships and understand the responsibilities towards the family and society, thereby growing of into confident, caring and responsible adults.

Appendix

THE U.P. SLUM AREAS (IMPROVEMENT AND CLEARANCE) ACT, 1986 *(AS PASSED BY THE U.P. LEGISLATION)*

An Act to provide for the improvement and clearance of slum areas, rehabilitation of their residents and protection from eviction of tenants of such areas.

It is hereby enacted in the thirty eight year of the Public of India as follows :

CHAPTER I

Preliminary

1. Short title, extent and communication- (1) This Act may be called the Uttar Pradesh Slum Areas (Improvement and Clearance) Act, 1986.

(a) It extends to the whole of Uttar Pradesh.

(b) This section shall come into force at once and the remaining sections shall come into force on such date as the State Government may, by notification in the official Gazette, appoint, and different dates may be appointed for different areas of Uttar Pradesh.

Note: The Act received the assent of the President on November 24, 1986 and the English translation of the Act was published in U.P. Gazette, Extraordinary, dated December 3, 1986.

2. Definitions - In this Act, unless there is anything repugnant in the subject or context -

(a) "arbitrator" means the person appointed as such,

by notification in the official Gazette, by the State Government for the purpose of this Act.

(b) "building" includes any structure or erection or any part thereof, for whatsoever purpose, and of whatsoever material constructed, but does not include plant or machinery comprised in the building;

(c) "Clearance area" means an area which is declared as such under Section 10;

(d) "Competent Authority" means such officer or authority as the State Government may, by notification in the official Gazette, appoint for such areas as may be specified therein for the purpose of this Act;

(e) "erection" in relation to a building includes extension, alteration or re-erection;

(f) "occupier" includes the following :

(i) any person for the time being paying or liable to pay rent or any portion thereof to the owner in respect of any land or building for which rent is paid or is payable;

(ii) an owner who is in occupation of his land or building or uses the same in any other manner;

(iii) a tenant of any land or building, who is exempt from payment of rent;

(iv) a licensee who is in occupation of any land or building and

(v) any person, who is liable to pay damages to the owner in respect of use and occupation of any land or building.

(g) "owner" includes any person who is receiving or is entitled to receive the rent of any building or land whether on his own account or on behalf of himself and others or as agent or trustee or who would so receive the rent or be entitled to receive it if the building or land were let to a tenant;

(h) "prescribed" means prescribed by rules made under this Act;

(i) "slum area" means an area declared as such under Section 3;

(j) "slum clearance" means the clearance of any slum area by the total or partial demolition or removal of buildings therefrom and includes the making of works of improvement in the existing buildings or land in that area;

(k) "State Government" means the Government of Uttar Pradesh; and

(l) "Work of improvement" in relation to any building or land in a slum area includes the execution of any or more of the following works; namely -

- (i) necessary repairs;
- (ii) structural alterations;
- (iii) arrangement for light, including street lighting and arrangement for water-supply;
- (iv) construction of roads, parks and drains, open or covered;
- (v) providing latrines;
- (vi) providing additional or improved fixtures or fittings;
- (vii) opening up or paving of court-yards;
- (viii) removal of rubbish; and
- (ix) any other work including the demolition of any building or any part thereof which in the opinion of the Competent Authority is necessary for executing any of the works specified above.

CHAPTER II

3. Declaration of slum areas - (1) Where the Competent Authority upon information received or otherwise in its possession is satisfied as respects any area that a majority of the buildings in that area are -

(a) by reasons of dilapidation, over-crowding, faculty arrangement of design of such buildings, narrowness or faulty arrangement of streets, lack of ventilation light or sanitation facilities, or any combination of these factors, detrimental to safety, health or morals of the inhabitants in that area; or

(b) otherwise in any respect unfit for human habitation; it may, by notification in the official Gazette, declare such area to be a slum area.

(2) In determining whether a building is unfit for human habitation, regard shall be had to the following matters, that is to say -

(a) extent of necessary repairs;

(b) stability;

(c) extent of dampness;

(d) availability of natural light and air;

(e) water-supply;

(f) arrangements for privies, drainage and sanitation;

(g) facilities for storage, preparation and cooking of food and for the disposal of waste matter and water; and the building shall be deemed to be unfit as aforesaid if it is so far defective in one or more of the aforesaid matters that it is not reasonably suitable for occupation in that condition.

CHAPTER III

Slum Improvement

4. Power of Competent Authority to require improvement of building unfit for human habitation - (1)

where the Competent Authority upon information received or otherwise in its possession is satisfied that any building in a slum area is in any respect unfit for human habitation or any land in that area requires any work of improvement, it may, unless in its opinion the building is not capable of being rendered so fit at a reasonable expense or the required improvements in the land are not capable of being affected at a reasonable expense, serve upon the owner of the building or the land, as the case may be, a notice requiring him within such reasonable time not being less than forty five days as may be specified in the notice or as may be extended by the Competent Authority from time to time, to render the building fit for human habitation or execute on the land the works of improvement, specified therein. The notice shall also state the things which in the opinion of the Competent Authority will render the building fit for human habitation and required works of improvement on the hand together with the estimated cost of such things and works.

Explanation I. In determining whether a building can be rendered fit for human habitation at a reasonable expense, or the required improvement can be effected on the land at a reasonable expense, regard shall be had to the estimated cost of the works necessary to render the building so fit, or of the required improvement on the lend to be effected, and the estimated value of the building or the land after the works have been completed or improvement effected.

Explanation II. For the purpose of this sub-section "reasonable expense" in relation to rendering a building fit for human habitation means expenses not exceeding fifty per cent of the value of the building.

(2) In addition to serving a notice under this section on the owner, the Competent Authority may also serve a copy thereof on any other person having interest in the building or the land whether as lessee, mortgagee or otherwise.

5. Enforcement of notice requiring execution of works of improvement - (1) If a notice under Section 4 is not

complied with, the Competent Authority may, after the expiration of the time fixed therein or extended by it from time to time, by itself do, or through such agency as may be authorised by it in this behalf cause to do be done, all or any of the things required to be done by the notice.

(2) All expenses incurred by the Competent Authority under this section together with interest, at such rate as may be prescribed, from the date of demand till the date of payment shall be first charged on the building or the land, as the case may be, and may be recovered by the Competent Authority from the owner of the building or of the land, as the case may be, as arrears of land revenue in such installments as may be fixed in the prescribed manner.

Provided that the liability of the owner, on his satisfying the Competent Authority that he -

(a) is receiving the rent merely as agent or trustee for some other person; and

(b) has not in his hands on behalf of that other person sufficient money to satisfy the whole demand of the Competent Authority, shall be limited to the total amount of the money in his hands as agent or trustee.

(3) If the owner of the building is different from the person who owns the land on which the building stands and the expense incurred by the Competent Authority under this section are recoverable from both these persons, then such expenses shall be recovered from them in such proportion as may be determined by the Competent Authority, having regard to their proportionate value and such other facts as may be prescribed.

6. Expenses of maintenance of work of improvement etc., to be recoverable from the occupiers of building - Where works of improvement have been executed in any building in a slum area in pursuance of the provision of Sections 4 and 5, the expenses incurred by the Competent Authority in connection with the maintenance of such works of

improvement or the enjoyment of amenities and conveniences rendered possible by such works, may be recovered from the occupier of the building as arrears of land revenue. Where there are more occupiers than one of the Competent Authority shall determine the amount recoverable from each having regard to the benefits conferred and the services rendered to each.

7. Prohibition regarding constructions extensions and alteration of building - No person shall except with the previous permission of the Competent Authority, to be obtained in the manner prescribed construct new building or make any extension, or alteration in an existing building on any land in a slum area.

8. Power of Competent Authority to order demolition of building unfit for human habitation - (1) where the Competent Authority upon information received or otherwise in its possession, is satisfied that any building within a slum area is unfit for human habitation and is not capable at a reasonable expense of being rendered so fit, it shall serve upon the owner of the building and upon every other person having, within its knowledge, interest in the building, whether as lessee, mortgagee, or otherwise, a notice to show cause, within such time as may be specified in the notice, as to why an order of demolition of the building be not made.

(2) If the person upon whom a notice under sub-section (1) is served fails within the period specified in the notice to satisfy the Competent Authority, even after having been afforded reasonable opportunity of being heard and producing evidence, if any, that an order of demolition will not be just and proper, the Competent Authority, shall, except in cases covered by sub-section (3) or as otherwise provided by or under this Act, pass an order of demolition of the building or any part thereof, as may be considered necessary by it for carrying out the purposes of this Act.

(3) No order for the demolition of any building in

pursuance of the notice under sub-section (1) shall, except as provided in sub-section (4), be passed by the Competent Authority, if any, of the persons upon whom the said notice has been served, appears before it and either.

(a) satisfies the Competent Authority that an order of demolition will not be just and proper; or

(b) gives an undertaking to it that he shall -

(i) within a period agreed to by the Competent Authority execute such works of improvement in relation to the building as will in its opinion render it fit for human habitation; or

(ii) not use the building for human habitation until the Competent Authority on being satisfied that it has been rendered fit for that purpose cancels the undertaking.

(4) The Competent Authority may, where -

(i) no such undertaking as is mentioned in sub-section (3) is given; or

(ii) any such undertaking has been given but any work of improvement to which the undertaking relates is not carried out to the satisfaction of the Competent Authority within the specified period; or

(iii) the building is at any time used in contravention of the terms of the undertaking, make an order for the demolition of the building in respect of which a notice under sub-section (1) has been served, and call upon the occupier thereof to vacate the building within the period to be specified in the order, not being less than forty-five days from the date of the service of the order, and call upon the owner to demolish the building within six weeks after the expiration of the period allowed for its vacation.

9. Procedure to be followed where demolition order has been made - (1) Where an order for the demolition of a building under Section 8 has been made and it is not vacated or demolished within the time allowed for that purpose, the Competent Authority or any person authorised by it in this behalf, may cause to be vacated and demolished. The Competent Authority may for the purpose of vacation and demolition use such force as may be necessary.

(2) The Competent Authority may sell by public action the materials of a building demolished under sub-section (1) and the expenses incurred in demolishing the building shall be deemed to have been reimbursed in full from the sale proceeds thereof.

Provided that if the owner of the building desires to remove the materials or any portion thereof before the auction, he may remove the same after payment to the Competent Authority, within the period fixed by it, of the entire expense incurred in the demolition of the building.

CHAPTER IV

Slum Clearance and Redevelopment

10. Power to declare any slum area to be a clearance area - Where the Competent Authority upon information or otherwise in its possession is satisfied as respect any slum area, or any part thereof, that a majority of the buildings in that area cannot be rendered fit for human habitation or the required works of improvement on the land in that area cannot effected otherwise than by demolition of the buildings therein, it may, by order notified in the official Gazette, declare the area to be a clearance area.

11. Show cause notice - The Competent Authority shall, before any area is declared as a clearance area under Section 10, serve or cause to be served a notice upon every person owning or occupying any building in the area proposed to be notified as a clearance area indicating that it is proposed

to declare the area as a clearance area and calling upon him to show cause within the period mentioned in the notice, not being loss than thirty days, who the order proposed be not passed. The notice under this section shall also be published in the Official Gazette, and two of the local papers.

12. Disposal of Objections - A (1) Any objection received under Section 11 shall, after affording reasonable opportunity of being heard to the objector, be disposed of by the Competent Authority.

(2) Where the Competent Authority decides that it is necessary so to do in the public interest it shall declare the area as a clearance area, and decide which of the buildings in the area be demolished for the purpose of this Act.

(3) The Competent Authority shall forthwith transmit to the state government a copy of the order under sub-section (2), together with a statement showing:

(i) the number of persons who on the date of notice issued under Section 11 were occupying the buildings in the area proposed to be notified as a clearance area;

(ii) the names of the owners of the buildings together with necessary particulars of the building, in the area, which are to be demolished; and

(iii) the buildings and lands which it would be necessary to acquire for redevelopment of the area.

(4) The State Government may either confirm the order into or subject to such variations as may be considered just and reasonable by it or reject the order.

(5) If the State Government confirms the order, the order shall be published in the official Gazette and it shall become operative from the date of its publication.

13. Slum Clearance Order - (1) The Competent Authority shall, as soon as may be, after a slum area has been declared to be a clearance area in accordance with the

provisions of Section 10 and 12, and it has become operative under sub-section (5) of Section 12, make a slum clearance order in respect of that area ordering vacation, within a period specified therein, not being less than thirty days from the date of service of the order, of all such buildings which have to be demolished in pursuance of the decision under Section 12, by the owner or occupier as the case may be, of the building and directing the owner to demolish the same within six weeks of the date by which vacation is required by the order or before the expiry of such further period as the Competent Authority may; considering the circumstances of the case, specify in this behalf.

(2) Where the owner or the occupier of a building fails to vacate the same within the period specified in the order under sub-section (1) the Competent Authority shall cause it to be vacated and may use such force for that purpose as may be necessary.

(3) If any building is not demolished before the expiration of the period fixed therefore under sub-section (1), the Competent Authority may enter and demolish the same and sell the materials thereof by public auction and the expenses incurred in the demolishing of the building shall be deemed to have been reimbursed in full from the sale proceeds thereof. The balance, if any, of the amount of sale proceeds of the materials, after deducting the cost of demolition of the building and the expenses on the sale of the materials thereof, shall be paid to the owner of the building in the manner prescribed:

Provided that if the owner of the building desires to remove the materials or any portion thereof before the auction, he may remove the same after payment to the Competent Authority within the period fixed by it of the entire expenses incurred in the demolition of the building, within the time prescribed by it.

(4) Where any building has been demolished in pursuance of an order under this section the Competent

Authority shall, as far as may be, offer temporary alternative accommodation to the building, in such manner and to such extent or may be prescribed.

14. Power to refuse permission to redevelop the land in a clearance area : As and from the date a slum clearance order becomes operative in any area, no person shall, except as hereinafter provided, build upon any land, or made any alteration or repairs in any building, in that area, except in accordance with plane approved by the Competent Authority and with his prior approval in writing.

15. (1) The Competent Authority shall, on the application of the owner of any land or building in a clearance area which is not intended to be acquired for the purposes of this Act, permit him, subject to such conditions and regulations as may be prescribed, to make fresh construction on such land or alterations or repairs such building.

(2) Where an application under sub-section (1) is not disposed of by the Competent Authority within a period of thirty days from the date of its receipt, the owner of the land or building seeking to make construction on such land or alterations or repairs in such building may, after expiry of fifteen days from the date of service of a further notice intimating the Competent Authority of his intention so to do, make fresh construction on such land or alterations or repairs in such building subject to such conditions and regulations as may otherwise have been imposed under the plan approved by the Competent Authority and any existing law relating to the construction of buildings.

16. Power of Competent Authority to redevelop clearance area or any part thereof : (1) Where land has been cleared of buildings in accordance with a slum clearance order, the Competent Authority may, any time after the expiry of thirty days from the date of demolition of all buildings in that area in respect of which decision for demolition has been taken under Section 12 determine to

redevelop the land in the area, or in part thereof, not being land which on the date of the making of the order has been, or is in the process of being redeveloped by the owner of the land or of the building entitled to do so, in accordance with the provisions of Section 15 and in accordance with the plan prepared by it, the owner of the land or building, entitled to do so, has developed or is redeveloping in accordance with the provisions of Section 15 and plan approved by it.

(2) Where the Competent Authority has determined to redevelop the land under sub-section (1), it shall be its duty to do so, as far as may be, within a period of two years from the date of determination.

(3) Where the Competent Authority is unable or fails, to redevelop the land within the period of two years it shall report to the State Government the reasons for its inability or failure. The State Government may thereupon require the redevelopment of the land to be completed within such period as it may fix in this behalf.

CHAPTER V

Acquisition of Land

17. Power of State Government to acquire land: (1) Where the Competent Authority, on information received or otherwise in the possession, is satisfied that acquisition of any land or building or both in a slum area or in a clearance area is necessary for the purpose of executing any work of improvement in relation to any building or land or for carrying out order of demolition of building in that area or for the purpose of redevelopment of any clearance area of rehabilitation of residents of slum areas, it may, by notification in the official Gazette, declare its intention to that effect.

The Competent Authority shall also serve or cause to be served a notice on the owner of the land or building, as the case may be, and altos on every other person who is known to be interested in such land or building calling upon him to show cause why the same would not be acquired for the purpose of this Act.

(2) Any objection filed in pursuance of the notice under sub-section (1) shall, after affording reasonable opportunity of being heard to the objector, be disposed of by the Competent Authority in such manner as may be prescribed.

(3) The Competent Authority shall thereupon, submit its recommendations, as to the land or buildings which are proposed to be acquired for the purpose of this Act, to the State Government for decision thereon.

(4) Where, on receipt of the recommendation of the Competent Authority, the State Government decides that the acquisition of such land or building is necessary in public interest, for the purposes of this Act, it shall be publication in the official Gazette make a declaration to that effect. The publication of the declaration shall constitute sufficient notice to all persons concerned.

(5) Upon the publication of the notification under sub-section (4) of the land or building specified therein shall, with effect from the date of the publication, vast absolutely in the State Government free from all encumbrances.

18. Land acquired by the State Government to be made available to the Competent Authority : (1) Where any land or building has been acquired under this Act, the State Government shall make it available to the Competent Authority for the purpose of executing any work of improvement or for carrying out order of demolition or for the purpose of redevelopment or rehabilitation of inhabitants of slum areas or for any other purpose under this Act and thereupon the Competent Authority shall utilize the land or buildings so made available for the said purpose.

(2) Where any houses have been constructed on the land made available to the Competent Authority under sub-

section (1), the same shall, as far as it may be possible as to do, be first offered for allotment to the occupiers of the buildings demolished in that area in such manner and subject to such conditions as may be as prescribed.

Explanation - Where a house or part thereof, or vacant land is to be allotted to any person under this Act, the Competent Authority may lease out the same to the allottee for such period and on such rent and other conditions as may be prescribed.

19. Payment of Compensation : (1) Every person whose land or building or any interest therein has been acquired under the provision of this Act shall be entitled to, and be paid; compensation by the State Government in accordance with the provisions of this Act in the manner prescribed.

(2) The payment of compensation in accordance with the provisions of this Act shall be be full discharge of the liability of the State Government to make such payment to the person as may have rightful claim, but shall not prejudice any right in respect of such compensation which any other person may be entitled to enforce against the person to whom payment is so made.

20. Determination of Compensation : (1) The amount payable as compensation in respect of any land or building acquired under this Act shall be an amount equal to one hundred times of the net average monthly income actually derived from such land or building during the period of five consecutive years immediately proceeding the date of publication of the declaration under sub-section (4) of Section 17.

(2) The net average monthly income referred to in sub-section (1) shall be calculated in the manner and in accordance with the principles set forth in the schedule.

(3) The Competent Authority shall, after holding inquiry in such manner as may be prescribed, provisionally determine in accordance with the provisions of sub-section

(2) the net average monthly income of the land or building and serve or cause to be served upon the owner of the land or building and every person having interest therein, a notice along with a memo of the provisional net monthly average income of the land or building as determined by it, to make .paobjection thereto, if any, by the date specified in the notice.

(4) Any objection made in pursuance of the notice under sub-section (3) shall, after affording reasonable opportunity of being heard to the objector, be disposed of the Competent Authority.

(5) Where no objection is made in pursuance of the notice under sub-section (3) against the provisional determination of the notice net average monthly income of the land or building within the time fixed therefor, in the notice or where objections have been made, after the same have been disposed of under sub-section (4), the Competent Authority shall, by publication in the official Gazette declare the net monthly income of the land or the building as determined by it, to make objection thereto, if any, by the date specified in the notice.

(4) Where no objection is made in pursuance of the notice under sub-section (3) against the provisional determination of the average monthly income of the land or building within the time fixed therefor, in the notice or where objections have been made, after the same have been disposed of under sub-section (4), the Competent Authority shall, by publication in the official Gazette declare the net average monthly income of the land or the building as finally determined by it.

(5) Any person feeling aggrieved with the final determination of the net average monthly income by the Competent Authority under sub-section (6) may, within thirty days from the date of publication thereof, prefer an appeal to the Commissioner of the Division or such their authority or court as may be notified in this behalf by the

State Government.

(7) The Appellate Authority shall, after affording reasonable opportunity of being heard to the appellant, determine the net average monthly income of the land or building, whose decision in this regard shall be final and be not questioned in any court of law.

21. Appointment of Compensation : (1) Where several persons claim to be interested in the amount of compensation determined under Section 20, the Competent Authority shall determine the person who, in its opinion, are entitled to receive compensation and the amount payable to each one of them.

(2) If any dispute arises as to the apportionment of compensation or any part thereof, or as to the persons to whom the same or any part thereof is payable, the Competent Authority may refer the dispute to the Arbitrator.

(3) The Arbitrator in deciding a dispute referred to under sub-section (2) shall, as far as may be, follow the Provisions of Part III of the Land Acquisition Act, 1894.

22. Payment of Compensation or deposit of the same in Court - (1) The Competent Authority shall, after final determination of the amount of compensation, tender payment of and pay, the compensation on behalf of the State Government to the persons entitled thereto.

(2) If the persons entitled to the compensation as determined by the Competent Authority or the Arbitrator, as the case may be, do not accept the same or if theer by any dispute as to the appointment thereof, the Competent Authority shall deposit as to the apportionment thereof, the Competent Authority shall deposit it in the Court of the District Judge and that Court shall deal with the amount so deposited in the manner laid down in Sections 32 and 33 of the Land Acquisition Act, 1894.

CHAPTER VI

Protection of Tenants in Slum Areas from Eviction

23. Tenant in slum areas not to be evicted without permission of the Competent Authority : (1) No decree or order for the eviction of tenant from any building or land in a slum area shall, except as hereinafter provided and till such time the declaration under Section 3 is in the force, be capable of being executed; anything contained in any other law for the time being in force to the contrary notwithstanding.

(2) A decree or order referred to in sub-section (1) may be put into execution after obtaining the permission of the Competent Authority in accordance with the provisions of sub-section (3).

(3) An application for obtaining the permission of the Competent Authority under Sub-section (2) shall be made in such form and contain such particulars may be prescribed.

(4) On receipt of such application the Competent Authority, after affording reasonable opportunity to the applicant and the tenant of being heard and after making such inquiry into the circumstances of the case it thinks fit, may, where it is of the opinion that the execution of the decree or order shall defeat or be detrimental to the enforcement of the provisions of this Act, reject the application but in all other cases grant it.

(5) Where the Competent Authority refuses to grant the permission, it shall record in brief its reasons for such refusal and make available a copy thereof to the applicant.

24. Right of Appeal: Any person aggrieved by an order of the Competent Authority under sub-section (4) of Section 23 may, within thirty days of the date of receipt of order, prefer an appeal against it to the Commissioner of the Division, or such officer or court as may be notified in this behalf by the State Government whose, decision thereon shall be final and be not questioned in any court of law.

CHAPTER VII

Miscellaneous

25. Power of entry and inspection : (1) Upon the issue of a declaration under Section 3 in respect of an area as a slum area or under section 10 in respect of clearance area, the Competent Authority or any other person authorised by it in this behalf may-

a) enter into any building or upon any land in such area with or without assistants or workmen in order to make any inquiry, inspection, measurement, valuation or survey or for the execution of any work which is necessary and is authorised by or under this Act or the rules made thereunder.

b) inspect any drain, latrine, urinal cess-pool, pipe, sewer or channel in or on any building or land in such area, and in his discretion cause the ground to be opened for the purpose of preventing or removing any nuisance arising from the drain, latrine, urinal, cess-pool, pipe, sewer or channel, as the case maybe;

c) examine works under construction in such area, to take levels or to remove, test, examine, replace or ready any meter;

d) make any entry into any place to open or cause to be opened any door, gate or other barrier.

i) if he considers the opening thereof necessary for the purpose of entry authorised by or under this Act; and

ii) if the owner or occupier is absent, or being present refuses to open such door, gate or barrier.

e) enter on any land or without assistants or workmen within fifty yards of any work in such area, which is authorised by or under this Act, or the rules made there under for the purpose of depositing thereon any soil, gravel, stone or other materials or for obtaining access to such work or for any other purposes connected therewith.

(2) Any person authorised under sub-section (1) so to enter shall before entering on any land, state the purpose thereof, and shall, if so required by the occupier or owner, fence off so much of the land as may be required for such purpose.

(3) No entry authorised by or under this Act shall be made except between the hours of sun-rise and sun-set.

(4) Except as otherwise provided in this Act, no building or land shall ordinarily be entered into without the consent of the occupier, or if there is no occupier, of the owner thereof, and no such entry shall be made without giving the said occupier or owner as he case may be, not less than twentyfour hours written notice of the intension to make such entry;

Provided that no such notice shall be necessary if the place to be inspected is a shed for cattle or a latrine urinal or work under construction.

(5) The person authorised under sub-section (1) shall in exercising any power conferred by this section avoid causing damage as far as may be possible.

(6) Where any damage is caused to any building or land by any person while exercising any power conferred by this section, the damage shall in the first instance to be made good by restoring the building or the land, as the case may be, to its condition as it existed prior to its being damaged by the person authorised under this section.

(7) Where the Competent Authority is of the opinion that the building or the land, to which damage has been caused by a person exercising any power conferred by this section cannot in its opinion be put into the condition as it existed prior to its being damaged by the person authorised under this section, a reasonable amount of compensation shall be determined therefore by it and paid to the owner or

occupier of such building or land or to both.

Provided that any owner or occupier of such land or building get the amount of compensation determined by the Competent Authority may prefer an appeal to the Commissioner of the Division who shall after affording reasonable opportunity of being heard to the parties concerned, give his decision thereon. The decision of the Commissioner shall be final and conclusive and be no questioned in any court of law.

26. Power of eviction to be exercised only by the Competent Authority- Where the Competent Authority is satisfied upon representation by the owner of building or upon other information in its possession that the occupants of the building have not vacated it in compliance with any note, order or direction issued or given by it under this Act or the rules made thereunder, it may, by order in writing, direct the eviction of the occupants therefrom in such manner and within such times as may be specified in the order any may, for this purpose, use of cause to be used such force as may be necessary:

Provided that before making any order under this saction, the Competent Authority shall afford reasonable opportunity to the occupants of the building to show cause against the order proposed.

27. Powers to remove offensive or obnoxious trades from slum areas - (1) Where the State Government is of the opinion that any trade is offensive or obnoxious to the health, morality or safety of the persons residing in a slum area it may, by notification in the official Gazette, make a declaration to that effect.

(2) On publication of the declaration under sub-section (1) the Competent Authority shall, after affording reasonable opportunity of being heard to a person carrying on a trade, specified in the declaration, direct him in writing to remove the same from the slum area within such time as may be

specified in the direction.

(3) If any person fails to remove the trade in a slum area within the time specified in the direction undern sub-section (2) the Competent Authority shall came it to be removed and may for this purpose use or cause to be used such force as may be necessary.

29. Appeals - (1) Except as otherwise expressly provided in the Act, any person aggrieved by any order passed or direction issued by the Competent Aauthority may appeal to the Commissioner of the division, or such other officer or court as may be notified in this behalf by the State Government, within a period of thirty days from the date of receipt of such order or direction.

(2) Every appeal under this Act shall be made by petition in writing accompanied by a copy of the order or direction appealed against.

(3) Where an appeal is preferred under this Act the Appellate Authority may stay enforcement of the order passed or direction issued by the Competent Authority for such time and on such conditions, as may be deemed fit.

(4) In hearing and deciding an appeal under this Act, the Appellate Court shall have all the powers and the privileges of a Civil Court and follow the procedure for the hearing and disposal of appeals laid down in the Code of Civil Procedure, 1908.

(5) Where under the provisions of this Act, an appeal lies to the District Judge, the District Judge may either hear the appeal himself or transfer it for hearing to any Civil Judge subordinate to him.

(6) Revisional power of the State Government - The State Government may at any time either on its own motion or on application made to it in this behlaf, call for the record of any case disposed of by the Competent Authority or any other person, authority, officer of Court under the Act or

the rules made thereunder, for the purpose of satisfying itself as to the legality or propriety of any order passed or direction issued and may pass such order or issue such direction in relation thereto as it may think fit:

Provided that the State Government shall not pass an order prejudicial to any person without affording such person a reasonable opportunity of being heard.

30. Penalties - Whoever does any act in contravention of any notice, order or direction issue or given under this Act or the rules made thereunder or commences to be commenced any work, in contravention of any restriction of condition imposed under Sections 14 and 15, or of any plan for the redevelopment of a clearance area, shall be punishable with imprisonment for a term which may extend to three months, or with fine which may extend to one thousand rupees or with both, and in case of continuing contravention to a further fine not exceeding rupees fifty for each day during which the contravention continues.

31. Offences by Companies (1) If the person committing any offence under this Act is a company, every person who at the time the offence was committed was in charge of and was responsible to, the company for the conduct of its business, as well as the company shall be deemed to be guilty of the offence and shall be liable to be punished under Section 30:

Provided that nothing contained in this sub-section shall render any such person liable to any punishment if he proves that the offences was committed without his knowledge or that he exercised all due diligence to prevent the commission of such offence.

(2) Notwithstanding anything contained in sub-section (1) where an offence under this Act has been committed by a company and it is proved that the offence has been committed with the consent or connivance of, or is attributable to any neglect on the part of any director or

manager, secretary or other officer shall also be deemed to be guilty of that offence and shall be liable to be punished.

Explanation - for the purposes of this section -

(a) "Company" means any body corporate and includes a firm or other association of individuals; and

(b) "Director" in relation to a firm means a partner in the firm.

32. Order of demolition of buildings in certain cases - (1) where the erection of any building has been commenced, or is being carried out has been completed. In contravention of any restriction or condition imposed under Section 14 and 15 or a plan for the redevelopment of any clearance area or in under this Act, or the rules made thereunder the Competent Authority may, in addition to such other remedy as may be available to it under this Act or any other law, make an order directing that such erection shall be demolished by the owner thereof within such time not exceeding two months, as may be specified in the order, and on the failure of the owner to comply with the order, the Competent Authority may, through such agency as may empowered by it in this behalf, cause the erection to be demolished at the cost of the owner.

(2) The Competent Authority may in getting the erection demolished under sub-section (a), use or cause to be used such force as may be considered necessary.

(3) No order under sub-section (1) shall be made unless the owner has been afforded reasonable opportunity of being heard.

33. Jurisdiction of Courts

(1) No court interior to that of a Magistrate of the first class shall try an offence punishable under this Act.

(2) Previous sanction of the Competent Authority or officer authorised by it for prosecution - No prosecution for

any offence punishable under this Act shall be instituted except with the previous sanction of the Competent Authority or an officer authorised by it in this behalf.

34. Application of certain provisions of the Indian Limitation Act, 1903 (Act IX of 1908). The provisions of sactions 5 and 12 of the Indian Limitation Act, 1908, shall be applicable to all proceedings, including proceedings in appeals applications and objections under this Act.

35. Power to delegate - The Competent Authority may, with the previous approval of the State Government, by notification in the official Gazette, direct that any power exercisable by it under this Act may also be exercised, in such cases and subject to such conditions as may be specified in the notification, by such officer or authority as may be mentioned therein.

36. Protection of action taken in good faith - No suit, prosecution or other legal proceeding shall lie against any person for anything which is in good faith done or intended to be done under this Act or the rules made thereunder.

37. Competent Authority etc., to be public servant - The Competent Authority, and any person authorised by it under this Act shall be deemed to be a public servant within the meaning of Section 21 of the Indian Penal Code.

38. Act of Override other Laws - The provisions of this Act and the rules made thereunder shall have effect notwithstanding any thing inconsistent therewith contained in any other law for the time being in force.

39. Power to make rules - (1) The State Government may by notification in the official Gazette, make rules to carry out the purpose of this Act.

(2) In particular and without prejudice to the generally of the foregoing power, such rules may provide for all or any of the following matters, namely :

(a) the manner of authentication of notices, orders and

other instruments of the Competent Authority;

(b) the preparation of plans for the redevelopment of any slum area, and matters to be included in such plan;

(c) the principles for determining the proportion in which the expenses incurred by the Competent Authority may be recovered from owners of land and owners of buildings under sub-section (3) of Section 5;

(d) the procedure and the manner of payment of compensation;

(e) the form and matter in which applications for permission under sub-section (2) of Section 23 shall be made and the fees to be levied in respect of such applications;

(f) the manner of service of notices, order or directions issued under this Act; and

(g) any other matter which has to be, or may be prescribed.

(3) All rules made under this Act shall, as soon as may be after they are made, be laid before each House of the State Legislature while it is in session, for a total period of fourteen days extending in its one session or more than one successive sessions and shall, unless some latter date is appointed, take effect, from the date of their publication in the official Gazette, subject to such modifications or annulments as the two Houses of the Legislature may agree to make; so however, that any such modification or annulment shall be without prejudice to the validity of anything previously done thereunder.

THE SCHEDULE

Principles for Determination of the Net Average Monthly Income

1. The average monthly gross rent of any building or land in a slum or clearance area shall one-sixtieth of the total gross rent actually accrued to the owner thereof during the period of five consecutive years proceeding the date of notification under Section 17.

2. In determining the average monthly gross rent the Competent Authority or such officer as may be empowered by it in this behalf may for such determination hold local enquiry and obtain, if necessary, certified copies of such extracts from the property tax assessment books of the municipal or other local authority concerned showing the rental value of the land or building and such other information in this regard as may be deemed necessary by it or him.

3. The net average monthly income for the purposes of subsection (1) of section 20 shall be sixty percent of the average monthly gross rent, determined in the manner laid down in Para 1. The remaining forty per cent of the average money gross rent shall not be taken into consideration in determining the net average monthly income but shall be deducted in lieu of the property tax payable to a local authority, income-tax, collection charges, bad debts, repairs and maintenance of the building and other incidental charges.

4. In case any land or building, or any part thereof, has remained unoccupied or no rent in respect thereof has accrued to the owner during the whole or any part of the said five years, the gross rent of such land or building or part thereof, shall be determined on the basis of the rent actually derived from a similar land or building in the vicinity of the land or building, as the case may be, during the period it remained vacant.

The Uttar Pradesh Slum Areas (Improvement and Clearance) Rules, 1989

1. Short title - (a) These rules may be called the Uttar

Pradesh Slum Areas (Improvement and Clearance) Rules, 1965.

(b) They shall come into force with effect from the date of their publication in the official Gazette.

2. Definitions - In these rules, unless there is anythying repugnant in the subject or context -

(a) "Act" means the Uttar Pradesh Slum Areas (Improvement and Clearance) Act, 1986 (U.P. Act No. XVIII of 1986)

(b) "Form" means a form appended to these values;

(c) "Government" means the Government of Uttar Pradesh;

(d) "Section" and "Sub-section" refer to section and sub-section of the Act;

(e) "Allottee" means a person to whom; a plot of land or a building with or without land has been allotted by way of lease or in any other manner as may be decided by the Competent Authority.

(f) "Allotment letter" means a letter in such form as may be prescribed by the Competent Authority from time to time for making allotment of a particular property to an applicant.

Under Section 39(2) (a)

3. Authentication of Notices, Orders and other instruments - All notices, orders and other instruments of the Competent Authority under the Act shall be signed either by the Competent Authority or an officer authorised in this behalf by the Competent Authority.

Under Section 39 (b)

4. The notification issued under sub-section (1) of Section 3 and section 10 shall be published besides the

official Gazette, in two papers having local circulation, at least one of which shall be in Hindi paper, on three consecutive days, giving full details of the area declared as the Slum Area or Clearance Area as the case may be. The Competent Authority shall also display in his office prominently the notifications alongwith a blue-print of the area showing clearly the houses which shall come therein, and if possible their numbers.

5. The notices to be served by the Competent Authority under sub-section (1) of Section 4 shall be in Form 'A'.

Under Sections 5 (2) and 39 (2) (g)

6. (1) The rate of interests which shall be charged by the Competent Authority from the owner of the house on account of the expenses incurred by it under Section 5 shall be 6 percent per annum.

(2) The amount of such expenses with interest thereon may, subject to the provisions of sub-rule (3), be recovered in instalments in the following manner:

(a) amount exceeding rupees 50 and not exceedings Rs. 200 in two equal quarterly instalments;

(b) amount exceeding Rs. 200 but not exceeding Rs. 500 in four equal quaterly instalments; and

(c) amount exceeding Rs. 500 in eight equal quaterly instalments.

(3) Where the amount of expenses alongwith interest thereon referred to sub-rule (2) does not exceed Rs. 50 it may be recovered in a lump-sum.

Under Sections 5(3) and 39(2) (g)

7. In determining the proportion for the purposes of recovery of expenses under Section 5, the following factors, besides that mentioned in sub-section (3) of Section 5, shall be taken into consideration:

(i) the expenditure incurred on such works of improvement as have increased the value of the building such as expenditure on repairs, alterations and extensions in the building;

(ii) the expenditure incurred on such works of improvement as have increased the value of the land such as expenditure on levelling the ground, providing greater facility to approach roads and lanes, etc.; and

(iii) the expenditure incurred on such works of improvement as have increased the value of the building and land both such as expenditure on drainage, water connection, electric connection, sewer connection, etc.

Under Sections 7 and 39(2) (g)

8. (1) If any person desires to obtain permission for constructing a new building or make any extension or alteration in an existing building, on any land in a slum area he shall make an application to this effect to the Competent Authority. Such application shall be accompanied by a plan of the new building and in the case of any extension or alteration in an existing building, by a plan of the existing building showing the proposed extension or alteration, as the case may be.

(2) The plan of a new building or the extension or alteration of an existing building, as the case may be shall be in conformity with the lay out plan of the development of the slum area and in accordance with the bye-laws of the Local Authority, if any, and where the U.P. (Regulation of Building Operations) Act, 1958, is in force in the Slum Area, then also in accordance with the directions and regulations issued under that Act.

(3) (a) On receipt of an application referred to in sub-rule (1), the Competent Authority may within thirty days from the date of the receipt of the application grant permission for constructing a new building or making any

extensin or alteration in an existing building, or for reasons to be recorded, reject the application.

(b) Where the Competent Authority fails to pass any order on the said application within the period prescribed in this sub-rule the applicant may, by a notice in writing request the Competent Authority to pass order. In case the Competent Authority fails to pass order within a period of thirty days from the date of service of such notice, the permission to construct a new building or make any extension or alteration in an existing building, as the case may be, shall be deemed to have been granted.

Under Section 39(1)

9. The notice to be served by the Competent Authority under sub-section (1) of Section 8 shall be in Form 'B'.

10. The undertaking referred to in sub-section (3) of Section 8 shall be given in Form 'C' and the schedule mentioned in the said Form shall give full details, with specifications, if necessary, of the works of improvement to be carried out.

11. The notice to be served by the Competent Authority under Section 11 of the Act shall be in Form 'D'.

12. The objections under Section 11 or Section 17 shall inter alia, specify how the objector is interested in the land or building or both.

13. Alongwith the copy of the order and the statement referred to in sub-section (3) of Section 12, the Competent Authority shall also furnish Plans for re-development of the slum area proposed to be declared as Clearance Area. The Plan shall include the following:

(a) description of the properties which may fit in the redevelopment plan either in their present form or after carrying out certain additions, alterations or improvements; and

(b) roads, open spaces and sites for schools, hospitals, shopping centres, maternity and child welfare centres and similar amenities, if any.

Under Sections 13 (3) and (2) (g)

14. For the purpose of payment under sub-section (3) of Section 13, the balance, if any, of the amount of sale proceeds of the materials, after deducting the cost of the demolition of the building and the expenses on the sales of the materials thereof, the Competent Authority shall give to the owner of such building a notice specifying the date, time and place where the payment shall be made. The notice shall be accompanied by a statement showing the details of sale proceeds, cost of demolition expenses on the sale of the materials and the balance to the owner. On the date and at the time and place mentioned in the notice, the Competent Authority shall pay the amount to the owner of the building in cash or by cheque.

Under Sections 13 (4) and 39 (2) (g)

15. The occupier of a building demolished in pursuance of an order under section 13 may be offered temporary alternative accommodation in any -

(a) building with facilities of latrine, bathroom and kitchen, or

(b) temporary sheds of barrack type covered by corrugated tin or asbestos sheets or any other material, constructed for the purpose with facilities of public latrine, public bathrooms and street light.

Under Section 29 (1)

16. Where an occupier shifts to the temporary alternative accommodation offered under Rule 15, the expenses of transportation of his goods to such temporary alternative accommodation shall be borne by the Competent Authority.

Under Section 15 (1) and 32 (2) (g)

17. The permission under sub-section (1) of Section 15 shall be given by the Competent Authority subject to the following conditions and regulations -

(1) The owner of the land of building, as the case may be, shall submit alongwith his application, the plan of the fresh constructions, and in the case of alterations or repairs in any existing building, a plan of the existing building and the proposed alterations or repairs.

(2) The plan of fresh constructions or the alterations or repairs of any existing building shall be in conformity with the lay-out plan of the clearance area and in accordance with bye-laws of the local authority, if any, and where the U.P. (Regulation of Building Operations) Act, 1958, is in force in the clearance area then also in accordance with the directions and regulations and under this Act.

(3) The owner of the land or building, as the case may be, shall pay to the Competent Authority the development charges to such extent and in such manner as the Competent Authority may determine.

18. The development charges to be paid by the owner of land or building under Rule 17 shall be determined by the Competent Authority keeping in view the proportionate cost of development of the area on which such fresh constructions, alterations, or repairs are permitted.

Under Section 39 (1)

19. In the notice referred to in sub-section (1) of Section 17 a minimum period of thirty days from the date of service of the notice shall be allowed to the owner of the land or building for filing objections.

Under Sections 17(2) and 39(2) (g)

20. Any objection field in reply to the notice received under sub-section (1) of Section 17 shall be disposed by the

Competent Authority only after the Competent Authority has intimated the date and time to the objectors to appear in person or through pleader, and if necessary to adduce any oral or documentary evidence in support of their objections. The order disposing of the objections shall contain reasons.

Under Sections 17 (2) and 39 (2) (g)

21. (1) The houses constructed on the land made available to the Competent Authority under sub-section (1) of Section 18 shall be allotted in the following manner:

(a) The houses shall first be offered for allotment to those slum dwellers who occupied the building demolished under the Act in the particular clearance area and whose incomes do not exceed Rs. 175 per month;

(b) The houses shall next be offered for allotment to the slum dwellers who occupied buildings demolished under the Act in a clearance area other than that referred to in clause (a) and whose income do not exceed Rs. 175 per month.

(c) The house shall next be offered for allotment to those slum dwellers who occupied buildings which are proposed to be demolished under the Act in any clearance area of the city or town, as the case may be and whose income do not exceed Rs. 175 per month.

(d) The houses shall then be offered for allotment on economic rent to those occupiers of buildings demolished in the same area or in any other area under the Act whose income exceeds Rs. 175 per month; and

(e) The houses shall then be offered for allotment on economic rent to any other person in the city or town, as the case may be.

(2) The rent of the houses shall be fixed by the State Government with due regard to the subsidy element in the

cost of construction.

(3) If any person to whom a house has been so offered for allotment refuses to occupy the same on the ground of rent or for any other reasons, he shall not have any claim for any other alternative accommodation.

(4) Execution of Deeds - All deeds and other documents made under these rules shall be executed on behalf of the Competent Authority by an officer or Authority to whom powers have been delegated in accordance with Section 35 of the Act.

(5) Disposal of Property - Land shall be transferred on lease which may either be a lease with rent or a lease with premium together with the rent, and not on free hold basis. The structure over the land shall be transferred on ownership basis. The lease shall be subject to the conditions and rates decided by the State Government from time to time.

(6) Period of Lease - The land shall be transferred on lease for a period upto ninety years and subject to enhancement of lease rent by fifty per cent after every thirty year over the rental immediately preceding.

Under Sections 19 (1) and 39 (2) (d)

22. (1) Every person whose land or building or any interest therein has been acquired under the provisions of the Act shall be paid compensation in cash or by cheque or money order in the manner hereinafter provided.

(2) The Competent Authority, shall, as far as possible arrange to make payment in or near the slum or clearance area concerned, he will inform the payee about the date, time and place of the disbursement of the compensation.

(3) Where a payee fails to appear on the date, and at the time and place fixed under sub-rule (3), the Competent Authority may remit the amount of compensation awarded

to him by money order after deducting the money order fees.

(4) The acceptance by any person of the compensation under this rule, shall not affect him right of appeal under sub-section (6) or Section 20.

Under Section 20 (3) and 39 (2) (g)

23. (1) The Competent Authority in order to provisionally determine the net average monthly income of the land or bulding under sub-section (3) of Section 20, shall cause a public notice, indicating his intention to do so, to be fixed at a prominent place on or near such land or building, and also to be published in papers having local circulation, at least one of which shall be a Hindi paper. The notice shall specify the date by which any person interested in such land or building may produce documentary evidence on which he relies for the purpose of correct determination of the net average monthly income.

(2) The Competent Authority, before provisionally determining the net average monthly income may -

i) hold local inquiry;
ii) obtain certified copies of such extracts from the property tax assessment books of the municipal or other local authority concerned showing the rental value of the land or
iii) take into consideration such documentary evidence as may be produced under sub-rule (1) by any person interested in the land or building.

Under Sections 23 (2) and 39 (2)

24. (1) Every application for obtaining permission of the Competent Authority under sub-section (2) of Section 23 be in Form 'E' and shall

i. State the grounds on which such permission is sought for; and

ii. be accompanied by a certified copy of the degree or order, as the case may be.

(2) There shall be paid fee of Rs. 5 in cash, in respect of every application for obtaining the permission of the Competent Authority under sub-section (2) or Section 23.

Under Section 39 (l)

25. (1) On receiving the application under sub-section (2) of Section 23, the Comptent Authority shall fix a date of hearing of such application and form the application accordingly. The Competent Authority shall cause a notice of such date served on the tenant. On the date fixed for hearing or such other date to which the hearing may be adjourned or further adjourned, the Competent Authority shall hear the parties.

(2) If either of the parties is absent on any date of hearing, the Competent Authority may proceed in his absence and after hearing party present pass such order as it thinks fit.

Under Section 39 (lf)

26. (1) Every notice, order or direction under the provisions of this Act or these rules by the Competent Authority shall be deemed to be fully served upon or issued or presented to the person concerned :

a) if it has been served through a messenger who has derived it to the person concerned, after obtaining his signature; or

b) if such person is not available, delivered through a messenger to some adult member or servant of his family after obtaining his signature; and

c) if none of the means aforesaid is available, by causing the said notice, order or direction to be affixed on some conspicuous part of the building or land to which the same relates in presence of a local witness.

(2) Whenever the person on whom any notice, order or direction is to be served is a minor, service upon his guardian shall be deemed to be a service upon the minor.

(3) Whenever any notice, order or direction is required to be served on several owners or occupiers of the same land or building, service on the persons recorded as owner or occupier in the property tax assessment book of the local authority concerned shall be deemed to be served on all owners or occupiers of the land or building.

Under Section 39(1)

27. The Competent Authority shall finalise the layout plan of the development of slum clearance areas in consultation with the Chief Engineer, Town and Village Planning Department, Uttar Pradesh.

Bibliography

Alam Manzoor S. and Geeta Ram Reddy, *Process of Urbanization and Urban Systems of India,* Paper presented at the Indo-Soviet Seminar on Problems of Migration in the Process of Urbanisation, 18-23 September 1984, Hyderabad.

Aldons, J.: *Study of Parental Role Functions*. Family Life Coordinator, 1961.

Ansbacher, H.L.: Religion and Individual Psychology. McGraw Hill Book Company, New York, 1971.

Ashoka Mehta: The Future of Indian Cities, National Issues and Goals, Roy Turner (ed.), *op. cit*.

Barbar, B.: "Social Stratification", D.L. Sitls,(Ed.) *International Encyclopedia of Social Sciences,* The Macmillan Co. & The Press, Vol. 15, p. 289.

Barclay, A. and D.R. Cusumano: "Father Absence, Cross-Sex, Identity, and Field - Dependent Behaviour in Adolescents." *Child Development*, 1967.

Bienvenu, M.L.: *Measurement of Parent-Adolescent Communication, Family Coordination,* 1969.

Brookover, W.B. and D. Gottlieb: *A Sociology of Education*. 2nd Ed. New York: American Book Co., 1964.

Chowdhury, P.K.: *Changing Values Among Young Women,* Delhi: Amar Prakashan, 1988.

Cohen, B. and J.Kapnek: When the Family Meets for Meals. *Journal of Home Economics*, 40: 1948.

Cole Luella and Hall Irma Nelson: *Psychology of Adolescence*: Holt Rinehart and Winston, Inc., 1969.

Cole Luella : *Psychology of Adolescence,* 3rd ed., New York, Holt, Rinehart & Winston, 1961.

Desai, A.P. and S.D.Pillai : *World Slums: An Overview, A Profile of an Indian Slum,* University of Bombay, 1972.

Draft Master Plan for Delhi, 1959.

Employment News, New Delhi, 2-8 September 1995.

Fraser, E.: *Home Environment and the School,* London: University of London Press Ltd., 1959.

Gesell, A., F.L. Ilg and L.B. Ames: *Youth: The Years from the Ten to Sixteen.* New York: Harper and Row, 1956.

Government of India, National Commission on Urbanization, *Report of the Commission,* Vol. I, 1988.

Government of India, *Second Five Year Plan.*

Havighurst, R.J.: *Human Development and Education,* London: Longmans Green & Co. Ltd., 1953.

Health Action, Vol. 8, No. 11, November, Pragati Art Printers, Hyderabad, 1995.

Hollingworth, L.S.: *Children Above 180 IQ: Origin and Development,* New York: Harcourt, Brace and World, 1950.

Hurlock, B. Elizabeth, *Adolescent Development,* McGraw Hill Book Co., New York. 1973.

Harrocks, J.E.: *The Psychology of Adolescence.* Boston, Houghton Mifflin, 1951.

Hyman, H. Herber: "The Value Systems of Different Classes: A Social, Psychological Contribution to the Analysis of Stratification" in R. Benedin and S.M. Lipsett (Ed.), *op.cit.* New York, The Free Press, 1953.

Iffert, R.E.: *Retention and Withdrawal of College Students,* United States Department of Health, Education & Welfare Bulletin No. 1, 1958.

India: A Reference Annual, 1979.

Juhoda, N. and others: *Research Methods in Social Relations*, Holt-Rinehart and Winston, New York, 1942.

Jamison and Malm: *Adolescence*, New York and Torento and London : McGraw Hill Book Co., Inc. 1952.

Jersild, A.T. and R.J. Tasch: *Children's Interest and What They Suggest for Education*. New York: Teacher's College Bureau of Publications, 1949.

Koolinger, F.N.: *Foundations of Behavioural Research*, Holt-Rinehart and Winston, Inc., New York, 1966.

K.C. Zachariah and J.P. Ambannavar: "Population Redistribution in India, Inter-state and Rural Urban," in Ashish Bose (ed.), *Pattern of Population Change in India, 1951-61*, Allied Publishers, New Delhi, 1967.

Kingsley, Davis: Urbanisation in India, Past and Future, in Roy Turner (ed.), *India's Urban Future*, University of California Press, Berkeley, 1962.

Kumar, Ashok: *Women in Cantemporary Indian Society*, New Delhi, Anmol Publications Pvt. Ltd., 1993.

Kundu, Amitabh: Migration and Urbanisation and Inter-Regional Inequality: An Emerging Social Political Change, *Economic and Political Weekly*, No. 5, 1986.

Lahovitz, S. and R. Hangeelorn: *Introduction to Social Research*, McGraw Hill Book Co., New York, 1973.

Laxmi Devi et al.: *Encyclopaedia of Sociology* (5 Vols.), New Delhi, Anmol Publications Pvt. Ltd., 1997.

Mahavir Prasad: *Development, Regional Differentiation and the Urbanization Process*, CEGET, Bordeaux, 1985.

Mahale, N. Meera : *The Adolescents: Their Family Situations & Education*, Mittal Publications, Delhi, 1987.

Manuja Devi, K.: *Rural Women: Poverty Alleviation Programme*, New Delhi, Anmol Publications Pvt. Ltd., 1997.

Ministry of Information and Broadcasting, Govt. of India, *A Reference Annual*, 1979.

Mitra, Arup: *Urbanisation, Slums, Informal Sector Employment and Poverty—An Explorating Study,* B.R. Publishing Corporation, Delhi, 1974.

Moonis, Raza: Nature of Rural-Urban Interactions. *IASSI Quarterly,* Vol. 10, No. 1, July-September. 1991.

Nye, F.I.: Child Adjustment in Broken and in Unhappy Unbroken Homes, *Marriage and Family Living,* 1957.

Nye, Carlson and Garrett: Family Size, Interaction, Affect and Stresses, *Journal of Marriage and the Family,* 32: 1970.

Planning Department, Govt. of Uttar Pradesh, Lucknow: *Status Paper on Housing and Urban Development,* 1990-95.

Pruthi, Raj et al.: *Encyclopaedia of Women, Society & Culture* (15 Vols.), New Delhi, Anmol Publications Pvt. Ltd., 1995.

Ralhan, O.P.: *Indian Women Through Ages,* New Delhi, Anmol Publications Pvt. Ltd., 1995.

Ramachandran, R.: *Urbanization and Urban Systems in India,* Oxford University Press, Walton Street, Oxford, 1989.

Reddy, N.Y.: A Study of the Relationship between Ordinal Position of Adolescents and Their Adjustment. *Psychol. Stud.* 1967.

Sachdeva, D.R.: *Social Welfare Administration in India,* Kitab Mahal, Allahabad, 1993.

Social Welfare Housing, Vol. XXXIII, No. 11 Feb. 1948.

Stogdill, R.M.: Personal Factors Associated with Leadership: A Survey of the Literature. J. Psychol. 25, 1948.

Surgell, quoted by Jaya Singh "Slums: Where Crime is a Way of Life," *Social Welfare,* Vol. XXXI, No. 11, Feb. 1985.

T.G. McGee: The Urbanisation Process in the Third World 1971 and Clifford Geertz Peddlers and Princes — *Social Change and Economic Modernisation in Two*

Industrial Towns, 1965.

Turner, R.H.: Role: Sociological Aspects, *International Encyclopedia of Social Sciences*, Vol. 13.

Thomas, P.: *Indian Women Through the Ages*, Bombay: Asia Publishing House, 1964.

U.P. Planning Department, Draft Five Year Plan, 1978-83 and Annual Plan 1979-80, Vol. III.

Visaria, Pravin and Devendra Kothari: Data Base for the Study of Migration and Urbanisation in India: A Critical Analysis, Gujarat Institute of Area Planning, Working Paper No. 2, 1985.

Walters, J. and J. Stinnett: Parent-Child Relationships: A Decade: Review of Research. *J. Marriage & Family*, 1971.

Wallin, P.: Marital Happiness of Parents and Their Children's Attitude to Marriage. *Amer. Social Rev.*, 1954.

Wardlow, M.E. and J.E. Greene: An Exploratory Sociometric Study of Peer Status Among Adolescent Girls, *Sociometry*, 1952.

Weisingher, R.: *The Indian Adolescent Girls: A Psychological Study of Hindu Girls*, Bombay: University of Bombay, 1963.

Winch, R.F.: *The Modern Family*, Revised Edition, New York: Holt, Rinehart and Winston, 1963.

